Angels and the Afterlife

Laverne Stewart

Pottersfield Press, Lawrencetown Beach, Nova Scotia, Canada

Library and Archives Canada Cataloguing in Publication

Stewart, Laverne

    Angels and the afterlife / Laverne Stewart.

ISBN 978-1-897426-24-1

    1. Angels. 2. Future life. 3. Spirituality. I. Title.

BL477.S74 2011   202'.15   C2010-907960-4

Cover design by Gail LeBlanc
Cover photo by Judy Gaudreau
Author photo by Jodi Michalak

Pottersfield Press acknowledges the financial support of the Government of Canada through the Book Publishing Industry Development Program for our publishing activities, and the ongoing support of The Canada Council for the Arts, which last year invested $20.1 million in writing and publishing throughout Canada. We also thank the Province of Nova Scotia for its support through the Department of Communities, Culture and Heritage.

Pottersfield Press
83 Leslie Road
East Lawrencetown, Nova Scotia, Canada, B2Z 1P8
Website: www.PottersfieldPress.com
To order, phone 1-800-NIMBUS9 (1-800-646-2879) or visit www.nimbus.ns.ca

The Canada Council Le Conseil des Arts
for the Arts du Canada

MIX
Paper from
responsible sources
FSC
www.fsc.org FSC® C013916

NOVA SCOTIA
Communities, Culture and Heritage

Contents

Acknowledgements

The list of people I have to thank for helping me bring this book together is very long. It starts with my husband, Robert Burtt, for having patience and understanding over many long months as I did research, interviewed dozens of people and then wrote this book. My children, Mary Louise and Nicolas, had to give up many hours of my time too. For all of their sacrifice I thank my precious family and want to tell them I love them with all of my heart.

For everyone who helped me to understand the angelic and spiritual realm, I thank you. Thanks as well to all of those who shared the stories of their encounters with angels and spirits. Thank you to Pam McCaughey for all of the many hours she selflessly devoted to this book. Most of all, I want to thank God, the angels and those in the afterlife for reminding me of your presence in this world. Whether or not we see, hear or feel you, you love, guide and protect us.

Foreword by Pamela McCaughey

The world we live in is fraught with fear and chaos. Natural disasters, financial and economic woes, violent conflicts between religions and ideologies fill newspapers, are repeated on the evening news and available for study on the Internet. Never, at any time in history, has technological communication been able to span the globe with such speed. But for all our scientific advances and improvements in technology, humanity is still faced with the same struggles, the same concerns and the same flaws which have kept us from evolving into a better species and kept us bound to this physical world.

That is why this book is so important. As a species, we humans need to understand that not only is there something greater than ourselves, but that we can reach out and grasp the Divine, and the help sent to us by the Divine, if we just take the opportunity. And this communion with the Divine is meant for everyone, not just a select few.

Ordinary people, like you and me, are finally telling their stories of their encounters with angels, the messengers of the Divine. They are no longer afraid of the old joke, "If you talk to God, that's fine. If God talks to you, you're bipolar." They are experiencing a spiritual renaissance that must be shared – a gift that promises to bring comfort, encouragement and assurance to all those who seek out the Divine.

In these pages are incidents of miraculous intervention, lives turned around for the better, spiritual visitations by deceased loved ones, and interactions with angelic entities – all of which have enriched the storytellers and those who read their stories. Tap into the unseen world of the spirit and the Great Architect of the Universe. But remember: what you read here will impact your heart and soul. Be prepared to see yourself and your life's journey in a whole new light – the Divine light.

Introduction

"We are here. We are all around you. Do you feel our presence? When you are alone, do you feel someone with you? It is us. We watch you while you sleep.

"We come to you in your dreams. Do you remember us when you wake? We whisper your name. Do you hear us calling to you?

"While some can see us, most do not. We are light. We are love. You do not see because you either choose not to, or the work and worries of this world take all of your time and attention. Please stop. Stop for a moment and consider all of the possibilities if you open your mind and your heart to us. We are here for you. We are here to help you, to strengthen you, to heal you, to help you to love others and, most importantly, to love yourself.

"We want you to know that whoever you are, wherever you are on this planet, you are not alone. There is no need to feel lonely. We are here with you. We wish for you joy, peace, love, strength, contentment and abundance. All you need to do is to give yourself the permission to reach out for it. Give us permission to help bring these things to you. We wish to take away your pain, your sorrows and your fears.

"There is so much fear in the world. The fear of disease, the fear of economic crisis, the fear of war, the fear of the uncertainty of life, and fear for the future of the planet. Do not be afraid. Do not live with guilt or fear, for these things are not of God.

"We want to rescue you in times of danger, protect you from all harm, to comfort you in times of sorrow. All you need to do is call us. We will come. No matter where you are, no matter who you are, no matter what you believe or do not believe, please know this: we believe in you. We always have. We always will. You are loved."

1

My Angelic Experiences

The writing of this book has been a calling. I hadn't given much, if any, thought to the angelic and spiritual realms for years. Then, in June 2009, everything changed. I was at a women's retreat – a wonderful weekend, with lots of laughter, too much good food, and time to be quiet and meditate.

When you are quiet, you get to see within yourself. I think many of us avoid being still because we are afraid of what we might see, hear and feel. It can be scary to go deep within your soul. But when you open up to self-examination, sometimes it's like throwing open the curtains and windows, allowing light and fresh air into what was a musty, dark space. When you become quiet, you can be available to spend time with your inner spirit and your higher power. When you get quiet, it is possible to hear the voice of the Creator.

That's what happened to me in the early morning hours of June 12, 2009. I was alone in my room at the bed and breakfast where the retreat was being held. I tried to read a book I'd borrowed from a friend, but could not concentrate enough to read the words on the pages. So I put it down, closed my eyes, inhaled and exhaled deeply several times. Then I did something I hadn't done in a very long time. I prayed.

I am a wife, a mother, a journalist and a very frustrated fiction writer. For most of my life I have penned poems, short stories and the beginnings of what has eluded me for more than twenty years. There are bits and pieces of many manuscripts that sit in the drawers, desks, dressers and side tables of my home. Some are very close to completion while others are only plotlines.

Ideas will come. I feel compelled to write them and then, for some inexplicable reason, I become blocked.

So, on this early morning in June, I had a conversation with God. I expected it to be a monologue. I told God I wanted to live the life I am meant to live. I asked to be shown my life's purpose and pleaded that my life be used in whatever way would serve the greatest good in this world. Then I brought up the frustration I felt about my works of fiction and asked, "Why, God, have you given me the ability to write, and yet what I want to write will not come?"

I felt a presence so powerful I cannot describe it. Overwhelming, overflowing joy, peace, love and contentment are the only words that come to mind and yet they are not sufficient. This was when I knew I heard God's voice. It was internal, yet it was so loud and clear it was as if someone was there with me. It was, to say the least, a bit of a shock. I actually looked around the room. There was no one with me and the door was locked, so no one had come into the room while I'd been sleeping.

When I asked why I couldn't complete the works I had started over and over again with no conclusion, I heard: "I have not called you to write fiction. I have called you to write the truth."

And, as surely as I'd heard the voice, I also had a clear sense of knowing what that truth was. I knew I had to write about the angels and the spirits of our deceased loved ones that are all around us. The truth I was being called to write is that people of all faiths, and those who don't believe in anything other than the power within themselves, have encounters with angels and the spiritual realm.

Have you ever asked a question and gotten a completely unexpected response? Well, that was what I felt in that moment. To be quite honest, I was a little annoyed.

"Write a book about angels and how they are manifesting in people's lives?"

Except for the angel that brought news of the birth of Jesus Christ in my Sunday school Christmas pageants, I knew nothing about angels. They were not discussed in my home when I was a child. They were not readily apparent in my life or in the lives of anyone I knew.

So I was supposed to write a book about angels? How was I supposed to do this? I didn't know the first thing about angels. Anyone who knows me will tell you I am a redhead with a big mouth and a short fuse. I tend to get fired up and explode quickly, and sometimes I regret the words I say shortly after I have said them. So, in my frustration, I challenged God to get involved in this assignment.

"Okay, God. I don't know anything about angels. I don't know anyone who knows anything about angels either. If you want this book to be written, and if it's me you want to write it, then you are going to have to send people to me to interview because I don't have the time, energy or interest in this stuff to start digging for it on my own. You want it done? You make it happen!"

God did.

A couple of days later I was reminded about a woman I had interviewed for *The Daily Gleaner*. In 2008, I met Suzanne Riley, a very gifted intuitive who immediately impressed me with her abilities when I went to her home in Oromocto to interview her for the Fredericton, New Brunswick, newspaper.

Have you ever met someone and sensed *déjà vu*, like you'd met them before? That's what I sensed when I first met Suzanne. As we sat in her living room, she admitted to being nervous since she had never shared her intuitive abilities in such a public way before.

As a child she could see the spirits of the deceased. A parish priest and a nun helped her to understand she had been given a gift from God. She didn't want it. For years she fought against it because she didn't want others to judge her.

Over time, Suzanne learned she needed to pay attention to her abilities and to use them to help others. She's a full-time intuitive. People find her when they need her. Even the RCMP and other police agencies contact her when they need help with missing person cases or homicide investigations. There is nothing pretentious about this woman. What you see is what you get. She is earthy and honest.

Almost one year after that interview, I wrote her an e-mail, telling her I had a strong feeling I was supposed to write a book about people's encounters with angels and the spiritual realm. Within a couple of hours there was a reply. Suzanne told me she was very excited about the book and she had been wondering when I was going to get around to contacting her about it.

I immediately answered, "Wait a minute, Suzanne. Until just a few days ago *I* didn't know about this. How do *you* know?"

She replied, "Darlin', I've known for six months you were going to be doing this. I am so excited for you! I will help you in any way I can."

She invited me to her home to talk about angels and spirits of the deceased, who, she tells me, come to earth with us when we are born to act as our guides throughout our lives. She told me my spirit guide's name is Elleise, who was with us in that moment.

"She is showing me the front of the book. It's got stories of people who believe they've encountered angels, of angels who've intervened. It's also got people who talk of earth angels or God's intervention through other persons as earth angels." Suzanne told me she saw six stories in my head but that I hadn't been able to do anything with them.

"You have to do this book, first because deep down you don't think you can write. Elleise is showing me a balaclava. You think you've been pulling the wool over people's eyes. You still don't think you have this genuine talent. You think you have made do this whole time," Suzanne said as she stared off into a corner of the room. It was true. My self-confidence in my writing has been lacking since I was in middle school.

"You're scared. You think, 'What if they don't like it? What if they don't like me?'"

She said she saw this going back to grade eight, the first time I shared some of my writing with kids in school.

"They laughed at you. Elleise is here to tell you this is why this book comes first. It's just going to flow right out of you. And what she is showing me is a series of books after this. Because you are a compassionate and sensitive woman, you are scared for people to think, 'Oh, who does she think she is?' This is your journey. This book says, 'I'm Laverne. I believe in what I've written and so do others.'"

When I told Suzanne I was still not sure why I am supposed to do this book, she explained it's because people are searching for answers, looking for something that will help confirm what they have experienced, but are too afraid to talk about. They worry about the reaction they will get from others.

"It will be well received, and will implement your faith in the Divine and your faith in you. That's why it's got to be you. You lost your faith for a long time. This is just part of your journey."

It's always been my belief that God created angels to act as intermediaries between humans and heaven. She said I've been inspired by God to write this book.

"This is why your faith is coming back."

Elleise is the spirit guide Suzanne told me I chose before I was born, and I chose her because of my struggles with self-confidence from the time I was very young. Elleise showed her that I feel things very deeply and yet try to hide those feelings.

"You put a good mask on for most people but anything that's going on hits you right here," Suzanne said, pointing to my heart. "That's why you chose her. She says you felt you didn't fit in right from day one. Most people will have that feeling but you truly felt it. You felt you couldn't achieve enough or do enough, and she was there to help with that."

Suzanne went on to say the biggest influence on my life so far has been my husband.

"Elleise says she literally pushed you into him. Remember the second time you went out? She's showing me a door jamb. When you stepped over it you tripped and fell onto him and he put his arm around you right away; he didn't laugh at you. She literally pushed you into him because she knew you needed him."

It's true. I do need Robert. He is a kind, caring, stable, funny, wonderful man who likes me in spite of my weird ways.

"Spirit guides don't take over your life or live your life for you, but they help steer you to the supports and the positives you need to do that," Suzanne explained. Elleise has always been my protector too, saving me from serious injury and death five times.

In 1974 I was nine years old, living with my family in Sheet Harbour, Nova Scotia. It happened on a day that I ran out of my house and into the street without looking. A neighbour was driving a wood-panelled station wagon. He was speeding. I remember that man and that car. Suzanne is right. It was a very close call.

"Elleise stopped you from getting hit by whoever it was that lived four doors down from you. Was there a swimming accident? She is showing me water up over your head. She is showing me water going into your nose and mouth."

When I was twelve, my family moved from Sheet Harbour to Bridgewater. I asked my parents if I could go for a swim in the hotel's indoor pool. The signs warned there was no lifeguard on duty and to swim alone was at your own risk. There was no one around and I was stupid enough to swim by myself. I dove into the water, which was too shallow, and struck my head on the bottom of the concrete pool. I don't remember what happened. I think

I'd been knocked unconscious. I remember the feeling of being lifted from the water and being placed on the pool deck. There was no one else in the pool. Still, I remember the feeling that I was not alone, that someone was there with me. I lay on the pool deck for a long time, and all the while it was as if someone was there with me holding my hand.

Suzanne told me it was Elleise.

In 1986 I was a passenger in a single-engine Cessna on a sightseeing trip in Nova Scotia's Annapolis Valley. The pilot was buzzing over farms and a photographer was taking aerial photographs they hoped to sell to the farmers. We were flying too low and too slow. The engine stalled and the plane started to go down. I was in the back with no seatbelt. I can remember thinking we were getting too close to the treeline. The pilot turned and screamed at me to get buckled up. That was the last thing I remember before I lost consciousness. When I woke up I was lying on the ceiling of the plane.

We were all fine, with nothing but a few cuts and scratches. The plane was a twisted pile of metal and broken glass. We walked out of the woods on our own and into a farmer's field just as the RCMP were heading up a search party to look for us.

Did Elleise intervene on my behalf that time? "No," said Suzanne. "She was there but that was somebody watching over the pilot. She shows me he felt complete warmth around him and a reassurance that all would be fine, where he should have been in an absolute panic," she went on.

I believe I have had many encounters with angels. One happened in 1988 while I lived in Saint John, New Brunswick. I was twenty-three, sharing an apartment with two roommates. After midnight, I was alone in my darkened bedroom reciting The Lord's Prayer. In the middle of that prayer the room filled with a bright shining light and I had an overwhelming sense of peace, contentment and love. I couldn't contain the emotion or the tears and couldn't sleep the rest of the night. It was a taste of what I can only imagine to be the sweetness that is the heavenly realm. I was so overcome by the experience I was unable to go to work the next day.

In 1999, while driving home from work one November evening I came around a bend in the road, into the path of a moose and her calf. Don't ask me how, but somehow I managed to avoid striking the mother. The calf was killed when it landed on the hood and rolled off the windshield into the ditch.

The only cut I received was from a splinter of glass on the floor of the car as I reached for my cell phone to call 911. Six months pregnant, I was worried about my baby. But I was reassured at the Emergency Department that the baby was just fine too.

The police told me how lucky I was not to have hit the larger animal. That massive wall of bone and muscle surely would have been my end, and the end of the life I was carrying, said the officers.

I know I prayed in the seconds before impact. Was it luck or divine intervention? I think the latter.

Suzanne mentioned Elleise also intervened to prevent my premature death in 2000, when I had just given birth to my daughter.

"She's showing medical forms. Did you have a severe allergic reaction? You should have been dead then."

She was right. I have a fatal allergy to ASA. Following the birth of my daughter I was given Indocid, an anti-inflammatory drug with an ASA base. My husband and I had told the doctors and nurses about my drug allergy. It was supposed to have been documented on my medical chart, but it was overlooked. Minutes after my daughter was born they gave me the drug. I went into convulsions. Apparently Elleise intervened that night too.

There are so many times I have been protected from accidents. In 2000 I was at my parent's home near St. Stephen, New Brunswick, preparing to celebrate an uncle's birthday. A cousin wanted to attend the party but didn't have a car so I offered to pick her up. I had an overwhelming sense that I should not take my infant daughter with me. So I asked my parents to watch the baby while I drove to St. Andrews, about thirty minutes from their home.

About halfway there I heard a voice say in a clear, loud voice, "Slow down, slow down, slow down."

I listened and put my foot on the brake pedal, slowing down just in time. A car came barrelling through a stop sign located on a side road and nearly broadsided my car. Was that an angel or Elleise?

"That was an intervention. It could have been either."

Elleise was there again after my son Nicolas was born in 2002. He had to be taken to the neonatal intensive care unit because too much amniotic fluid remained in his lungs. He was struggling to breathe. For three days I lay in my hospital bed thinking that my son was dying. The first day and night I was unable to get up because I was hooked to an intravenous and catheter. Early the second morning a petite blond nurse woke me at about five a.m. to say she was worried about Nicolas as he wasn't doing well. The next morning, about the same time, the same petite blond nurse in a white uniform stood at the door of my room and said I needed to insist that the IV and catheter be removed so I could go to the unit to hold my son, because he was gravely ill and needed me.

Later that morning another nurse helped me into a wheelchair and took me to the unit where I saw my sweet, tiny baby boy in an incubator with tubes and wires attached to him. He looked very frail. I held him to my chest and prayed to God that he would survive. The next morning the petite blond nurse in the old-fashioned uniform came to my room. She smiled and told me not to worry about Nicolas, saying he was going to be fine and would grow up to be a healthy man.

That was the last time I saw her. When I asked another nurse where the little blond-haired nurse in the old-fashioned uniform was the next morning the woman looked at me as though she didn't know what I was talking about.

"What nurse?" she asked.

"The one who comes to see me every morning to tell me about Nicolas," I replied.

She shook her head and told me she had been my duty nurse since I delivered the baby and no other nurse had cared for me each morning except for herself. I found it odd when she said there was no one on the maternity floor like the person I'd described. Suzanne said this was Elleise.

It's difficult for many, including me, to understand why bad things such as disease, horrific accidents and murder happen to some very good people if there are guardian angels and spirit guides to help protect us.

Suzanne explained, "Some things have to happen. We do not all have wonderful, perfect lives where we are completely coddled. There is disease, death, murder, rape, assault, fires. I don't know why and I don't pretend to know why. But I do know that out of every negative or bad thing that happens, something positive will happen too or there will be a life lesson for the family, friends and even strangers who might hear about it. It doesn't mean you deserve bad things. It means things will happen.

"Angels and spirit guides will steer you away from making choices that will lead you into bad situations. As humans we are all born with free will. We can choose to go one way or another. Sometimes we don't listen to that small, quiet voice directing us out of harm's way. The worst, most degenerate people on the earth all have angels and spirit guides around them who are trying to help show them the best path to take. They do bad things because they aren't listening and choose to go another way. There are such things as fallen angels who do things for selfish reasons. They are those angels who decided not to follow God. Angels are directly from God. They do not have the human emotions of fear, sadness, or anger. They have all of the positive emotions such as joy and compassion, but they don't have any of our human frailties."

One of the best ways to distinguish between a true angel or fallen angel is that a true angel will never guide you to cause irreparable harm to yourself or others. Determining between angels and ego can be difficult because the "right path" can many times be uncomfortable or seem unrewarding.

Suzanne has seen many spirit guides but never an angel. What's the difference between a spirit guide and an angel? I asked.

"An angel is directly from God. Guides are human souls who have lived before. They have learned their lessons and have gone home. We choose them as a heightened soul to walk with us."

Everybody has different beliefs and opinions. A lot of people think angels and spirit guides are the same thing. Not Suzanne.

"My personal belief is there's God, our Holy Mother Mary, her Son our Lord Jesus Christ. Among the direct angels, we have the Archangels, the lower angels – there are levels – and we have our guides, people who have lived before who have chosen not to be born again, but who will walk with us humans."

I asked who Elleise was when she was alive. A teacher and writer who'd been married with children and grandchildren, she was a Christian who went to a Presbyterian church.

"What she's showing me," said Suzanne, "is that she was from lower Manitoba, south of Winnipeg. Early in the 1900s is when she passed. She taught in a small community school. Writing was her passion. This is why you are careful with your hand script. She would teach that so it would look pleasing to the eye. She learned her lessons. She felt she had experienced the human life as much as she needed. She ascended to Heaven and you chose her."

If Elleise is my spirit guide, then who are the angels around me?

"Angels are everywhere and they are around everybody. We don't have angels that are specific to us. We have angels we relate to. One of the gifts from God is our guides."

The terms guardian angel and spirit guide, Suzanne explained, are one and the same. It's the difference between the two terms rain and drizzle – two different words but the meaning is the same.

While Suzanne has never seen an angel, she has met people who say they've had earthly encounters with these heavenly beings.

"I pray to the angels," Suzanne told me, "and ask Raphael and Gabriel to protect our home and our family. We can pray to the angels. They are there to intercede. Praying is talking."

"But don't mistake angels for God, because they are not," she said.

Everybody, I believe, has an assigned time and place to die. Why have I had so many close calls with death and lived to tell about them? Do angels and spirit guides intervene to keep us from dying before our time?

Suzanne agreed this happens. "I don't know how to explain that. I just accept it as it is."

I believe God wants to use me and this book to get people thinking outside the confinements of their religious views, and to understand that angels and spirit guides are here to help us on our life's path.

Some people believe they can see, feel and hear angels. Others believe that you can't be that close to an angel or you will melt. Some people believe that angels intervene but don't make physical contact with humans.

This book will feature those who believe they have had direct contact with angels, those who believe they hear, see and feel angelic presence and that of the dead who are with them in spirit. Some people will discuss how their lives have been saved by what they refer to as earth angels. Others believe they have pictures of angels and the spirits of loved ones who watch over them. Others don't believe angels directly intervene in our lives, but they do believe the spirits of loved ones and spirit guides take the place of angels in our daily lives.

I know one thing for sure: this book has been a spiritual journey for me, and God has directed every step I have taken along the way. The creator has put people on my path to make me think, to expand my spiritual horizons and to help me grow as a human being. It has been a very exciting expedition so far and I am open to anything that's in store as this journey continues. I have spoken to experts on angels to better my understanding of them. I have met ordinary people who have had encounters that have brought me to tears and made me realize this earthly existence is but a fraction of who we truly are.

I left myself open to the message and resigned myself to the fact I have simply been the ears that listened to the stories of angelic encounters and the hands that helped to put those stories into the written word. I also left it entirely up to God how this would be written. To do this, I had to write from the heart, rather than the head. The writing of this book has been a wonderful experience that has blessed me more than words can say. It has taught me that when I choose to listen to the voice of God I am never sorry. When I ignore that voice I always regret it.

I am not responsible for anyone's soul except my own. I am not trying to change anyone's belief system or their faith. I can't tell anyone where to go on their spiritual journey, or give them directions as they make their way along their own pathway to God. These are my experiences with the Divine as well as the experiences of others as they have been told to me. The pages that follow are the stories of people who say they too have had encounters with angels and spirit guides. I hope they fill your heart with joy and give you the same knowledge that I have. Truly, we are not alone.

2

The Intuitives and the Angels

Suzanne Riley – A Gifted Spiritual Intuitive

I first met Suzanne Riley in 2008 when I interviewed her for an article on dream interpretation. She impressed me so much I asked if I could write a special article for *The Daily Gleaner*'s weekend feature section about her. She had never consented to an interview that looked into her personal life before. She agreed, she said, because she knew it would somehow help someone who would be coming to her in the future, who needed to understand that intuitive gifts are nothing to fear or to be ashamed of. This is what appeared in *The Daily Gleaner* of March 1, 2008, after I interviewed her:

As Suzanne Riley opens her front door to a stranger, it's as though the person on her doorstep is a dear old friend.

"Come in," she says. "Where would you like to sit, at the kitchen table or in the living room?"

Then she serves freshly brewed coffee. As she reclines on a black leather chair, she admits to being nervous about being interviewed. This is the first time she has ever shared her life story.

Growing up in the Northwest Territories, she says, was idyllic. She spent her summers hunting, fishing and swimming. Her family attended a Roman Catholic church which was the centre of the community's social life with lots of music, dances, picnics and games. Riley and her younger brother were educated at a Catholic school.

From the time she was born, her family knew there is something very special about her. She was speaking in full sentences by the time she was nine months old and reading before she started kindergarten.

By third grade, she realized she had another rare ability. She recalls one morning in class when she saw an elderly woman standing behind one of her classmates. The woman spoke to Riley and asked her to tell the girl she was OK and not to worry about her.

The girl explained her grandmother was very ill. By noon that day, the girl's parents came to pick her up because her grandmother had died that morning.

Her classmates taunted Riley after this incident.

"They called me a freak, a witch, a liar."

But thanks to the reassurance of her parish priest and a kindly nun, she came to understand this was a gift from God. Some gifts are unwanted. For the first 30 years of her life, she says, she fought against it.

"I was reluctant to be judged."

Then, she says, she learned a difficult lesson about what can happen when she withholds information. A woman was visiting her at home.

"I looked over her shoulder and her spirit guide was there and said, 'Don't let her go home.' I didn't say anything. When she went home, her boyfriend beat her almost to death."

Having this ability comes with many burdens and responsibilities, she explains.

"I've known when my family members were going to die before they did. That is hard. So I am very cautious about what I say because I don't want to influence them or change their path. When you die is between you and God."

This ability runs in her family. Her maternal great-grandmother was also very intuitive, she's been told. When she thinks back to her childhood, she smiles and says she couldn't imagine more loving, supportive parents who've always accepted her no matter what.

Also supportive are her husband and children.

She met Patrick Riley on a blind date. Instantly they made an emotional connection. Within a week they were engaged and they married a year later.

"He is the most loving and compassionate man I know besides my dad."

Together they are raising a son and daughter. Devon-Lynne is eighteen and Jacob is ten. They moved here last summer from Alberta.

From the time she was a youngster, she had dreamed of becoming a reporter. Eventually she was hired as a photographer at a weekly newspaper in Medicine Hat, Alberta. But it wasn't long before her psychic abilities started to collide with her day job, she says.

In 2003 she was assigned to cover a Terry Fox run at CFB Suffield. She was told she should travel in a car with Cpl. Stephen Gibson.

"I had a bad feeling; a heaviness in my stomach. My (spirit) guides were telling me 'No!'"

She never misplaces her keys but this morning she couldn't find them. So she called ahead and said she would meet him at a checkpoint along the route.

She arrived there and waited. Before Cpl. Gibson's car crested a hill, she and others saw a huge black smoke plume. Cpl. Gibson's car had been hit by a tractor trailer and he was killed instantly.

She had a job to do and she went to the accident scene.

"I took a photo for the newspaper. It made the front page."

But the tragedy shook her to the core. She knew she wasn't doing what she was meant to do so she quit.

It was then that she decided to do full-time psychic work. She doesn't promote herself in any way or seek out clients. People find her when they need her, she says.

"What I do for a person is to bring them confirmation of what they're doing and I bring closure for unsettled issues or the loss of loved ones."

Police sometimes contact her when they need help with missing person cases or homicide investigations. Sometimes people come to her looking for help with missing loved ones or unsolved deaths but Riley always asks them to seek help through law enforcement agencies first.

She will not tell people when or how they will die. She refuses to tell people whether a spouse is faithful and she will never disclose information that is none of someone's business.

She may be able to see into the past, present and future of others but she is unable to see her future.

"Because I am human and I would use it to my advantage."

Even though she is unable to see into her own future, she is looking forward to a long, healthy life surrounded by family.

"I don't care where we live as long as we're together."

Can she see what's coming for her husband and children? Yes, she says, but only in what she calls "flashes."

"I see for them when I need to but they never ask."

Riley says she has come to terms with this ability. She is content.

"I am happy with who I am and what I am doing."

Experience has taught her the importance of putting family first in a loving, nurturing, supportive home. When they are together, the Rileys enjoy barbecues, camping and card games.

Riley's time could be constantly in demand if she didn't set strict work hours.

"When our son was seven he said, 'Mom, can I book an appointment?' I had to learn to say no. I'm just like everyone else. I am a wife, a mother, a friend, but I have been blessed with this."

* * * * *

Angels have always existed in Suzanne's life. Everybody, she explained, has an intuition, a link or a connection to the angels. But as we get older, we learn to shut that part of ourselves off, because we're told by adults that it isn't real or that it's silly.

"I believe we all have this in childhood. I can sit and visit with any two-year-old and I can feel it. They are wide open. I had the best mom and dad. I give complete credit to my mom and dad."

While she has never seen an angel, she has always felt them around her. "I just know they are there. Because you know it to be true, it is, and that is what we, as adults, can get back to, if we choose to." She has felt angels around her often and they come in the form of warmth and a tingling in her spine. Nothing else in this world or in the spirit realm makes her feel that way.

"If I go into a home that people think is haunted, I'll feel warmth. I'll feel it or I just know or sense they are there. When I'm talking to somebody's guides I just get tingly." But when she feels an angelic presence, it is like somebody is running a lint roller over her back producing a mild electrical current.

"I feel that at weddings. It doesn't matter what church. I feel it often at funerals. I feel it when someone is having a baby. I can really feel it in a maternity ward all the time."

She also feels it when doing guided meditations that she calls the Circle of Angels, and when she's dealing with somebody in a heartbreaking situation. She feels it is now more socially acceptable for people to talk about their connection to angels and the spirit realm. What used to be considered a mental health issue fifty years ago is now accepted by many. And she believes more people are encountering angelic manifestations – whether they are seen, heard or felt – because of the times we live in.

"People are reaching out more. They need that confirmation. They need that feeling of solace and serenity. People are feeling more of a connection, especially with the angels."

Suzanne also noted, "People now are on a quest for the spiritual because they have discovered that all of the material things in life haven't brought them any real sense of fulfillment. We are a society that has more than any other generation has ever had, and our expectations are higher than any other generation, but we are still not happy. People are walking away from what I consider to be the organized religions because it doesn't hold anything for them; what's missing is that basic faith. I don't care what church you go to: if you have that basic faith you will receive fulfillment. The angels want us to remember the basics of who we are. We are on this human journey to learn and at no time are we alone in doing this."

Rampant consumerism has caused many people to feel empty. We might have instant communication with others through e-mail, but we are not connecting in any way that fulfills us. "You talk to many people and they will tell you they have more lonely days than good days. There are less of what I consider to be concrete friendships. You know when you had that best girlfriend? Lots of women today haven't got that. They might have lots of friends and acquaintances, but they don't have that intimate connection of sharing oneself with someone special. I think we are having more encounters with angels today because they want to remind us that we are not alone."

We live in a time where we instantly know what is happening around the world the moment it happens. This has made us feel the threat of global devastation more than ever before. We also do not have the sense of community and family as people did decades before. "The less of a community we have, the less of that connection to church, family, community, the more there is angelic intervention."

Suzanne makes the point that the state of fear that exists today really started on September 11, 2001. "Predictions about the end of the world have always existed, and always will, but I don't believe the world is going to end."

Suzanne says she has seen the evolution of the world into a global community where there will be no wars over religion. People will be able to accept that people are on their own journeys and all are valid.

"What I see for the future is an end of the world as we know it, and the beginning of a world that evolves into something better. There is not going to be a physical, tangible end of the world, as in boom, the earth is gone. It is the end of what we perceive as our world; the end of the struggle, of anger, of persecution. That is coming. When? I have no idea. Way beyond this generation. Looking at it, I would say ten to twelve generations from now.

"When I have meditated about this, when I have asked about it, what I have been shown is a state of calm, a peace, and a global community. What I have been shown, however, is that over the next twenty-five years, we are going to have a real difficulty reconciling Christianity and Islam. There are small core groups on each side that propagate hate and negative energy.

"Organized religion is the cause of so much of this strife. We have walked away from what truly the appreciation of a higher power is. Every religion and culture has a belief in angels. They are here to provide comfort, peace and sometimes direct intervention. My work with them involves comfort and releasing things from one's life."

Suzanne started the Circle of Angels guided meditations in 2004 because she felt people were holding on to too much negativity, self-blame, self-hate, past hurts, and what they perceived to be past failures. All of these feelings hold people back. She called it the Circle of Angels because when she was a girl, her mother used to tell her to call in her circle of angels whenever she needed to release something from her life.

She has always been able to talk to her angels and ask them to take things from her that were holding her back or making her unhappy. She wanted to help others learn how to do this too. Many people who attend these guided meditations will have a sense of angels literally and physically encircling them. For others it isn't as real.

"When I am doing the circle, I see all your energies and what people are releasing – either a little bit or a lot. It's like a shimmer above them. I see different types of colours and shimmers and energy. It's hard to explain.

You know the shimmer you see when heat is coming off of pavement in the summer? That's what it's like but with colour."

Some people believe in God and some don't. Some believe in prayer and some don't. Some accept the word faith and some don't. But the one thing people believe in, she says, is angels. "To me that is part of our humanity."

Each Circle of Angels guided meditation is different, based on what she feels coming from the people who are there. "I can sense what's going to be the theme or which is the strongest of the energies we are dealing with that night. Do I know what I am going to say? No. Is it ever the same way twice? No."

On a very hot July night in 2009 I attended one of the sessions. There were forty women in an elementary school gym where padded mats had been placed in a circle. Everyone was asked to bring a pillow and blanket with them. Then we were instructed to find a spot on the floor and lie down, with our heads facing the centre of the gym. Suzanne played very soft, soothing music. She told everyone to find a comfortable position, and to close our eyes so we could concentrate on her voice and the sound of our own breathing. With each inhalation we were asked to say silently to ourselves "Let." And with each exhalation we were asked to say "Go." "Let." "Go." "Let." "Go."

When people were in a very relaxed state, Suzanne called in the first of nine angels we should envision as standing over us, then kneeling and taking away from us things such as money issues, grief, self-loathing over body image, or anything that could be holding us back, weighing us down or causing us fear and anxiety, preventing us from living in the light of our true and authentic selves. In the more than five years she's been doing this, thousands of people have experienced these guided meditations. The main thing people have received from these events has been a real sense of calm and a feeling of relief.

In my mind's eye, I could see massive, faceless, genderless, soft, gentle beings wearing white flowing gowns appear. (This is what eighty percent of the people who attend these guided meditations tell Riley they see. The other twenty percent say the angels are symbolic.) As the meditation continued, I could hear every word and yet I was very relaxed. When the session was over several people, including Suzanne, told me I was snoring.

I felt calm, relaxed, and had a deep sense of comfort, support and energy. This sense of comfort and the knowledge that we are not alone is what the angels want for us. Suzanne believes everybody in the world has the ability to connect with angels and the other realm, but most people have closed themselves off to it as they left childhood behind.

When I asked her about angels in her life and the Circle of Angels, she said, "Developing the Circle of Angels was a lifetime process, even though at first I had no clue how my life would progress spiritually. As a child, my parents said I would sit in the tree in our backyard and talk and sing. When they asked who I was talking to, I would always say, 'My Angels.' Do I remember that? Not really. But I remember how uplifting and comforting it was. I remember the tree and how much I still love to sit and reflect with trees around me and just breathe. As a young adult I would always pray to the angels, partially due to my Catholic upbringing, but again, because I always felt such warmth and comfort. It is still so much a part of my daily life.

"Very young, I realized I had a gift, that I could see and talk to people's guides and deliver messages. After a few years of doing readings, I held my first women's retreat, a three-day camping weekend where we discussed spiritual topics and the benefits of faith and prayer. I found the one subject everyone was in agreement with was the universally held belief that angels do exist and do watch over us.

"I know I believe this with all my heart and being. It was on this belief that I first began writing a meditation that incorporated the warmth and comfort I felt when I would speak to my own angels as a child. The ultimate goal of meditation is to know ourselves. Self-knowledge brings peace and joy to your everyday life, helping you to live thoroughly, focus on mundane tasks and feel a stronger connection to the spirituality that is within. Meditation helps you to discover you, your inner self and to become aware of who you really are.

"Living in a world with so much external input, so many responsibilities, and so much going on in your life, it can be hard to quiet your mind and teach it to focus. When you relax and truly go within yourself, you learn a true and deep knowledge of your motivations, emotions, thinking patterns – how and why you do the things you do. You become aware of yourself on all levels – physical, mental and spiritual – and learn to love and accept many things about yourself.

"When you are physically self-aware, you know not only your limitations, but your capabilities and your potential as well. The same is true for your mental and spiritual self. And once you know yourself, you can come to like and accept yourself, realize and accept your past mistakes, enabling you to let them go and move forward in your growth. Emotional meditation focuses on opening and expanding the emotions to be able to better relate to others and the universe. Its goal is to learn to love God, to love others and to love self.

"Who better to open yourself emotionally to than your angels? The Circle of Angels is a guided meditation that allows you to relax, focus on yourself and release any feelings of negativity. Each of the angels within the circle visits you and asks you to hand over the many feelings we all harbour. Personal feelings of inferiority, anxiety, anger, grief and fear are given over to the angels. Many clients physically feel a change in the energy and space around them as we do the session. So many people experience immediate feelings of comfort and support.

One of my clients said that she was happily amazed. The peacefulness she experienced was new to her. The woman told me, 'I didn't want to move, it was such a wonderful feeling. The Circle of Angels was the first time I have ever felt that way. I was totally relaxed, almost paralyzed, but it was so calming and soothing.' For her, peacefulness is most times hard to attain. Her role in the mental health field is demanding, at times overwhelming, and at all times, she must maintain a sense of calm and professionalism. So letting go is often difficult."

Did she in fact feel that angels were beside her? The woman had this to say about her experience with Suzanne's Circle of Angels: "As much as it is unnerving for me to say this, I know that I felt a presence. Years of study and degrees have educated me to the fact that we create our own realities at times, but at the circle evening I know I felt a presence. This was so new and different for me, and I didn't quite understand where it was coming from, but I do know that after the circle I felt totally relaxed and at ease. I almost had this tingling feeling. It's hard to describe, but it was very serene."

An integral part of the meditation is to have an angel arrive to take from you anything that you do not want to carry anymore. You are asked to let go of those particular feelings or hurts and give them over to the angels, and when you do, a feeling of lightening will occur. Clients tell her they feel relieved and peaceful. This is a natural part of meditation; however, when asking the angels to lift your burdens while in the meditative state, the effect is even stronger and more long-term.

Angel Channeller Pam Nadeau

I first met Pam Nadeau in November 2007 when I wrote a feature article about this woman who says she is a conduit between this world and the heavenly realm. She is a channeller of angels, spirit guides, saints and the ascended masters that exist in many religious faiths. On Christmas Eve, 2007, I wrote a feature article for *The Daily Gleaner* about angels, focusing on Pam Nadeau:

Pamela Nadeau speaks to angels and listens for their voices. This sounds crazy, she admits. For a woman who holds a degree in psychology and spent a career as a government researcher and policy planner, she too questioned the sanity of this at first.

It started in the late 1980s when she was studying astrology. She read a how-to book on discovering one's higher self. "It's basically your soul. It's your spirit. It's that aspect of you that always lives in the heavenly light."

She followed the book's instructions, putting herself into a meditative trance-like state. What happened next was so overwhelming she says she dismissed the experience. "When you channel for yourself you think you're insane, you're making it up, and you're listening to voices in your head."

But she tried again. And again, she was overwhelmed by a sense of pure love. Over time, she has connected with many spirit guides. These are beings who've lived before and who've passed on.

"They are spirits who volunteer to be with you through your life to make sure you have a joyful life experience. Your main spirit guide is someone you've known in your eternal journey."

Nadeau's main spirit guide is someone she calls Grace.

"My maiden name was Easterbrook and there was a Grace Easterbrook born exactly on my birthday in 1752. I'm pretty sure that's who she is."

When she channels for herself or others, Nadeau sees winged angels who are surrounded by light and who are filled with pure love. "They are really aspects of God. They have never incarnated. We can have so many angels around us."

After she started channeling for her sister and close friends, she came to believe this was more than a figment of her imagination.

When she does a reading for herself or others, she says about one hundred entities arrive, including angels, the spirits of those who've passed over to the other side, as well as the saints and apostles.

"Because I'm a woman and most of my clients are women, Mary (the Virgin Mary) comes a lot."

Those who come to her don't question any of this except, how deeply they are loved by God.

Why are we loved so deeply?

"Why not? We are all aspects of God. The way the spirit guides describe it is we have a spark of God in our hearts. That's our spirit. We are all one. We are all of God."

Young children sometimes talk about seeing angels or having invisible friends. When children talk about it and are discouraged, they learn to shut this part of themselves down, eventually forgetting their angels and spirit guides. The reason the spirit guides come is to help people fulfill their life purpose in a way that's joyful, explains Nadeau.

She isn't a psychic. Rather, she says, she acts as a conduit through which people can learn to connect with their spirit, their guides and the heavenly realm.

Nadeau has published three books on this subject and has recently recorded a series of CDs to reach a greater number of people.

Nadeau did so at the insistence of another of her spirit guides. The ancient Egyptian Princess Hatshupset, who lived five thousand years ago, told her to record these CDs so she could help many in need of spiritual healing. She and the princess are good friends now, but when this entity first started speaking to her, once again she questioned her grip on reality. "I'd really thought I'd lost my mind." But over time she has become quite comfortable with the princess, who has taught her a lot about the ancient art of healing wounded souls.

"When people come for a reading most of them have on their hearts a relationship that is hurting them. We all have something in our lives or in our past that has really hurt us."

Before she channels spirits, angels and saints, she prays first, asking for protection from any entities that are not of God. Often, she says, Archangel Michael stands guard over her home, while other angels, saints and spirits advise. They will advise, but they will never intervene on someone's life circumstance.

"The number one law of the universe is freedom of will. The guides say this over and over again. They will never tell you what to do. They only advise. Even if you ask for a healing they will check in, find out what needs to be done, tell you about it and then ask your permission. You have to wish it. You have to desire it. They do not intervene without you desiring it."

* * * * *

I contacted Pam again in June 2009 and, like Suzanne Riley, she too said she knew I would be writing this book. She agreed to meet me to share her experiences with the angelic realm and to share more about spirit guides. We met at a restaurant, where, over a meal, she shared all of her personal encounters with angels.

I asked her if she could see any angels around us in the restaurant where we and about fifty other people were eating lunch. She said they were standing behind people and on the roof of the building. They were here to hold in the light. She told me to look around, to take note of all the people who looked worried, depressed or sad. "The angels are here to watch over them and to keep out the darkness."

In 1974 Pam had taught herself to drive. Inexperienced behind the wheel, she got into an accident one winter's day on the highway near Bay Ste. Anne, New Brunswick, as she turned a corner too fast and went into a skid.

"I flew off the road and hit the only rock in the ditch. It was a huge, huge rock. I went flying and landed on the ice of a lake, and the car was still going. I was in an altered state already and thinking, 'When you go under water are you supposed to have your car windows up or down?' My car was heading towards open water because the lake was not fully frozen. I thought I was going to die. Then I had this thought that maybe I should turn the car around. When I think of it, given the state I was in, someone seeded that thought in my mind. So I did. The car turned around. I got it back to the shore. But it was quite a deep ditch and I couldn't drive back up to the road. I got out of the car. I was a wreck, I was shaking so badly. I climbed up to the road. Then this guy came along in a Lounsbury's tow truck."

Pam recalled that the man said he could help. He and a couple of other men pulled her car out of the deep ditch and on to the road. He then test drove the car for her. There was nothing wrong with it. He asked if she was going to be all right to drive the car to Newcastle, where she was staying. She assured him she was fine and offered to pay him for his time and effort. He wouldn't accept any compensation. Then he offered to escort her to Newcastle, which has an hour and a half out of his day.

"When we got to Newcastle he vanished. He just vanished. I really wanted to thank him."

Over the next year, every time she was in the area she looked for the man who had come to her rescue. Finally, she went to the company where he said he worked and was told there was no one there to match the man's description and no truck to match the one he was driving.

"I didn't know it was an angel. I just knew my life had been saved. I just knew I was going to die that day."

In 2002 she went on a pilgrimage held every August by the Roman Catholic church just outside Canterbury, New Brunswick. There were hundreds of people standing there on a very wet day. That afternoon many priests did hands-on healings. Pam, who suffers from migraine headaches, decided to go to one of the priests for a healing prayer.

"I'm watching the priest and his pupils are really wide. Obviously he's in an altered state. He'd probably blessed thirty or forty people by the time he got to us. I was watching him as my friend Maggie stepped forward and I saw an angel behind him. I usually don't see angels unless I go into a trance. There was a huge angel behind him and two angels standing on either side of the priest's shoulders and then Maggie stepped forward with her big belly. They said, 'There's a baby!' and they went shooting right through him so they could embrace the baby and the mother."

In May 2003 she was visiting her son in Dawson City, Yukon. The snow was still in the hills and the bears were just coming out of hibernation. Her son had a dog who loved to run and he'd often take the dog out. Pam went with her son and the dog that day. They drove deeper and deeper into the wilderness. They were on their way back to Dawson City and her son was driving his truck hard and fast.

"I was freaking out. The roads were wet and slippery. There was snow everywhere. There was nobody around. You can't use cell phones there and we had no satellite phone. We came to a point where we met another truck ahead of us. I have no idea where he came from. There was no way my son could get by. I was watching this guy and praying, 'Please God, stay with me.' The man stayed with us until we got right down to the bottom of the hill where it was solid flat ground and he just pulled off to the side and waited and we went forward. We were half a kilometre away when we saw a mother bear with her cubs. Meanwhile, I was watching this guy. I thought why would he pull over? There's nobody here. The next thing I know he pulls the car around and goes back the way we came. He saved my hide. I was terrified. I didn't know where he'd gone. There was nowhere to go. I thought 'Well, that's weird.' There was no where for him to disappear to in the twenty-second interval."

Pam likes to explain that some people hear angels, see them, or feel their presence. The first time she channeled angels, she was at work on her lunch break with no one around. "I wanted to cry so much because it was like a feeling of aching love. That's how they appear in your heart. You know that kind of aching feeling you get in your heart when you see a puppy or a baby? You'd have to multiply that by hundreds."

Angels see humans in terms of light. Some people, like light bulbs, burn brighter, others are dimmer. Angelic beings are pure white or golden light. Spirit guides are light with a lot of colour, because they have lived as human beings before, so they are bringing in light that is not as pure (that is, non-angelic) but it's still light, and it's all from Heaven.

"We are all one. Everything has a light."

If you have ever had a profound emotional experience such as being brought to tears while praying, you may very well have had an emotional encounter with God, your angels, your spirit guide or your own soul. So when you are praying or meditating you are opening up that floodgate. At that time you are opening into your divinity and your soul experiences much happiness.

Many people think God is angry with them for something they have or haven't done. They feel that upon coming into God's presence they will be lectured or punished in some way.

A lot of people fear the end of the world is near and worry about what will happen to them when they die. Many think they are bound for hell. Many have been told, and believe, they have no chance of redemption no matter what they do, because of the bad things they have done in their lifetime. Pam recalled one colleague who told her she believed she was going to hell because she'd had an extramarital affair. "I said, 'Well, don't you know about forgiveness?' The woman refused to believe there was any possible way she would be absolved from the sin of adultery. She was saying 'I won't forgive myself, therefore, I'm going to go to hell and I'm going to hang on to this life as long as I can because I don't like the alternative.'"

Some people feel they have no angels around them. But it isn't long before people start to feel the love and energy of God and the angels when Pam channels their angels for them.

"I don't have to say a word. They feel it. The room becomes overfilled with all of these loving entities, whether they are angels or spirit guides or your own spirit. They are over the moon happy because we become open to the possibility that they exist and that we have guides and angels. They want to make a connection because that's the path, the beginning of your awakening and you're coming back to the light that Jesus and all of the other prophets have been talking about."

As humans, our souls have free will. We have the choice to accept or reject the idea of God, angels, spirit guides. We can choose to seek after spiritual things and to go deep into the spiritual journey or even to deny the experience. Once people accept the idea that they have angels, these beings are ready and willing to help when asked to intervene in people's lives. More than ever, Pam says, people are hungry to learn about angels because they are worried and live in fear about so many things.

"That's why the angels are getting us to write books and go out and talk to people. The absence of fear is love. That's why you have to go from doubt to knowing and not to faith, because faith still allows the element of doubt and fear."

What many people fail to see is the love God has for all of us, no matter who we are, what our faith is, or even if we don't believe in God at all.

When Pam was employed with the federal government, she was sent to work in Jordan in December 1995. As she would have to go before Christmas and wouldn't return to Canada until the New Year, she was adamant she didn't want to be away from home and family over the holiday season. When her boss reminded her she would be near the Holy Land over the holidays, she finally agreed to go.

"I flew over there and I said to God, 'A woman travelling alone in those countries isn't a really good idea. I don't know how you are going to do it, but I'd love to be near Bethlehem.' We only had one day off a week, which was Friday, the holy day of Muslims. On Friday, December 22, we were going to go on a trip to Petra."

She and a co-worker boarded a bus, but when they discovered they were on the wrong vehicle and not going to Petra, her colleague started to make a scene and swear.

"We were at the border between Jordan and Israel, one of the most volatile border crossings in the world. He was dressed all in his Tilley-best, prepared to go on this expedition to Petra. Well, I said, 'I'm going to Bethlehem.'

He was making a total ass of himself. This was a fifty-three-year-old having a little boy's tantrum. Then a man sidled up to him and said, 'I know you. You live around the corner from me. I do your laundry. What is your problem?' Then he looked at me and I said, 'We thought we were going to Petra but we took the wrong bus. I'm going to Bethlehem.'"

The man then turned to her colleague and said, "It is God's will that you go to Bethlehem today."

"This man was going to the Al-Aqsa mosque in Jerusalem, which is one of the most holy mosques in the Muslim world. He was going there because it was his holy day and it's a very big deal for them to be able to get out of the country. So he said, 'I will help you.' He took us to a place on the Israeli border where we could change our Jordanian money to the Israeli currency and he said, 'You will take the same taxi as us to Jerusalem and I will find you transportation and you will go to Bethlehem today.'"

Even at the best of times Jerusalem is a very crowded city. It would have been almost impossible for two English-speaking Canadians to get to Bethlehem without the man's help. Pam believes this man was an earth angel that day.

"The next thing we know a big white limousine pulled up. He said for a hundred dollars American we could get back to the border by noontime. A Palestinian taxi driver took us in the beautiful stretch limo to Bethlehem. The night before [it had been ceded to] the Palestinians. The Palestinians were celebrating. There was a huge party going on. We could never have gotten there at Christmas. The traffic was jammed. The buses were stuck in it. There were big parades and parties and the new Palestinian police were all in their uniforms and the Palestinian army with their trucks and their guns in the air. Everybody was happy and it was a big celebration. This guy took us around the back way. We drove in a white limousine up to the Church of the Nativity. We went in and there may have been four or five other tourists in this immense place."

They say Christ was born in a grotto in the basement of this church. Pam took her time and prayed on December 22, 1995. "I was in total awe. Afterwards, I was praying in the little chapel and I felt hushed grace every-where. It was profound and it was deep and I knew I was in a holy place."

She felt a great amount of hope while she was there. She was too excited about being in the place of Christ's birth to tune into angels, but she does believe there are people in the world who God uses as earth angels. This

Muslim man from Jordan had no reason to take himself out of his way to help get these Canadians to Bethlehem. But he understood her need to get to this holy place and wanted to help her and did what he could to make it happen.

"When he looked into my colleague's eyes and he said, 'It is God's will that you go (to Bethlehem),' I was pretty sure he was channeling the voice of an angel."

Pam returned to Jordan in March and again went to Jerusalem. In a mosque, she tuned into her ability to see and feel angels. "I was overwhelmed with how many angels there were there. I was overwhelmed – it was just so beautiful. I felt them and saw them. It felt like such a holy place. The place was crowded with angels. Some people say angels don't have wings, but to me I see the presence of wings. I see tall beings always dressed in white, bringing grace and love. The beauty comes from within them because I don't really see their faces."

Michelle Russell's Experiences With Spirit

From her earliest memories, intuitive medium Michelle Russell of Oromocto, New Brunswick, has been able to see, hear and feel the presence of those in spirit.

Her earliest recollection: when she was three, she woke up to see two men standing at the foot of her bed. One was tall with blond hair, dressed in jeans, a white T-shirt and leather jacket. The other was shorter, with dark hair and wore a military uniform with medals on the jacket.

"When I was four months old my biological father passed away. He was in the military and stationed in Germany." Her mother brought her back to Canada and eventually remarried. While there were pictures of her biological father available, she had never seen them as a child. Because she didn't know who the men were, she was frightened and called for her parents. Her mother tried to reassure her there was no one in the room with her, but she couldn't be convinced because she could see them standing there. "I described the men to a T." That man in the uniform, she now knows, was her father. The second man was her mother's brother, who'd died in a car accident. "He was calling my mom Maggie. Her name is Marguerite, but he was the only one who ever called her Maggie. She knew there was no way I would have known that."

Once Michelle described the visitors her mother was frightened. Her step-dad tried to diffuse the situation by humouring her, telling the men it was time to leave. She now understands that the spirits of her biological father and uncle would come to her to watch over her while she slept.

In elementary school Michelle saw angels in the playground, sitting on the swing sets, beside children – their guardian angels. She remembered telling one boy not to sit on a certain swing, because the guardian angel of another student was already there. What she said was relayed to her teacher, who called her mother. In an effort to protect her from ridicule, her mother told her not to talk about seeing angels and spirits ever again.

The visitations did not stop even as Michelle was being told not to speak of them. Spirits came to her from time to time as she was growing up, to check in on her. She refused to communicate with any of the spirits, because she was afraid. Afraid of what was happening, afraid to speak of it and encounter ridicule from others.

Even though she shut her intuitive abilities down until she was an adult, she can remember having the feeling she was never alone. "I would always feel someone behind me, especially if I was in a frightening situation. If I was walking somewhere by myself, I would always feel that presence behind me. Like there was someone watching over me."

Michelle was unable to completely tune out her intuitive abilities. She would have very vivid premonition dreams and knew when someone was ill or going to die. In grade eight she could see cancerous tumors in her uncle's stomach. She could sense his death was near. When he was very sick, he asked her mother for a photo of Michelle as he wanted her to be near him. He understood that his niece could see angels surrounding him as his time of death drew near to help him to pass from this world to the spiritual realm. A week later her uncle died.

Her intuitive abilities came back to her full force after her father-in-law died on December 2, 1998. They received a call from Ontario to let them know he'd passed away. When her husband hung up the phone she received messages from his father, telling her things he wanted them to know before they arrived for his wake and funeral.

"I saw his dad in physical form. He had the most beautiful golden light around him. He started listing off things. I wrote them down on the back of a Visa bill. He said: 'When you go to my house there's going to be a cross that I laid out for you on my bed. When you go into my closet there's going to be a wooden crate. Open it up and there's a gift from me to you in there. I've written you a letter and you will find it on my desk. Know that I love your mom.'"

When they arrived at her father-in-law's house they found two guitars that he'd placed on his bed: they formed a cross. They opened the closet and found the wooden crate. Inside, packed between old woolen blankets, were Christmas presents he had bought and wrapped for them. On his desk was a letter for her husband.

Her father-in-law's body was to be flown back to Mirimachi, New Brunswick, for burial. He told her that because there was no gravesite for him, his brother was there digging one for him in the family's plot.

Her father-in-law died from a sudden heart attack. She believes he knew his death was near and he prepared for it by cleaning his home and leaving signs for them to see, such as the guitars in the shape of a cross, the Christmas presents and the letters he wrote. All of this was tremendously healing for her husband.

Michelle had no idea what to do with the intuitive information she was now being bombarded with; it varied as information for her, for family members and even for strangers. Once in Moncton on a shopping trip, she saw a little boy sitting in a shopping cart, smiling and waving to her. An older woman was walking beside the cart and a younger woman, who was pushing it, looked as though she was in emotional distress. Michelle mentioned to her husband that the boy kept trying to get his mother's attention but she wasn't looking or listening to him.

"My husband said, 'Michelle, there's no one in the cart.' It struck me that the boy was with his grandmother. The little boy was trying so hard to say to his mother that he was okay. He said to her, 'You sit in my room at night and you play the Winnie the Pooh song.' He said to me, 'Can you tell my mom that she can't be in my room any more, and that she has to change the room and that it's time to let go. She has to let me go.'"

Michelle had no idea what to do. She didn't want to walk up to a complete stranger and share this information with her. It greatly upset her. She went to a psychologist to try and make sense out of it all. At the time, she was a civilian employee of the Fredericton police force. She had access to information about many crimes, and she was also seeing, hearing and feeling things about these crimes. She had no idea what to do about the things she saw, heard and felt. Eventually she came to accept that she was gifted.

In 2003, Russell was involved in a serious car accident when she collided with a truck. The result was a serious brain injury, which erased her short-term memory and left her unable to remember how to read or write. It took her two and a half years to relearn the things she had forgotten how to do. Even today, she still struggles with her memory and her speech to find the right words. She carries a BlackBerry with her to remind her of things such as schedules and appointments. She was unable to return to her job with the police force, but her intuitive abilities became much more intense and she came to know she is meant to use the gift she has been given to help others.

Michelle's husband is a soldier. While he served in Afghanistan in 2006, she would see images of huge angels guarding the armoured personnel carriers which drove on the dangerous roads every day in the war zone, assisting supply convoys. She wasn't the only one who knew the angels were there. Her husband and other soldiers said they could feel angels around them giving protection. Others would see angels that would come in the form of balls of light. "Pictures they took overseas would have angel orbs. There would be a ball of light around them. They would be huge."

There were several cases in which soldiers were killed in roadside bombings. And there was always a light over that soldier in photos taken of them shortly before their deaths.

In 2007, while expecting her second son, she was doing readings for people part time, but the demand increased dramatically and she couldn't continue.

"I was getting messages that I needed to stop when I was pregnant with my second son, Cooper. I slipped on the ice in December 2007 and couldn't feel any movement for twenty-four hours. We went to the hospital and he was fine. I slowed down and I still did some sessions, but in January or February I very clearly got a message that I needed to stop or it would cause harm to Cooper, that he would feel the stress. So in February I stopped doing any sessions with people."

From that time until February 2010 she devoted herself to being at home with her sons. Then she decided it was the right time to return to her calling.

"I know my boundaries now – before I just wanted to help everyone who called. I know I have to take care of myself and my family first and then I will have more energy to help others. I know I am a better intuitive now because my mind is focused. It is very clear and concise where my limits are."

Her husband is very supportive of what she does and her gift. For years, he has witnessed her ability to connect with the spiritual realm, and has no doubt she is connected to the other side and to the spirits of those who have died.

Michelle maintains every human being signs a contract before they are born that details the experiences they will have and the lessons they will learn when they are here in their physical bodies. In her understanding of what she has seen, heard and felt from the spirits of those who have crossed over, we all have a time and a place to die and we actually know this before we come to earth.

"They [the spirits of the dead] say there is a life contract on the other side. It's almost as if there is a checklist of the things they want to do and experience."

Some babies who only survive a few hours after birth, she says, are only meant to be here for this amount of time and for a specific reason, while other people are born and live to be over a hundred. In some cases people die suddenly before their contracted time is over.

"I have seen the spirits of soldiers who have died in Afghanistan come through and pass messages on that they knew they were going to die."

Those soldiers had premonitions of their own deaths. They would try to prepare others for their passing in advance in the e-mails sent home to loved ones, in conversations they had with other soldiers, in the way they prepared their bunk and their belongings before their death. From her conversations with those who have crossed over, she thinks that most people misunderstand the purpose of life and the Divine plan for the human experience.

Everyone, no matter who we are, or what we believe, is meant to come to earth to have many experiences and to learn many lessons. It doesn't matter what religion we follow or even if we choose not to believe in anything beyond this world. In the end we all go home to the Creator.

"I always see there is a higher being, whether it's called God, the Source, the Universe, the Creator, or Allah. That higher power wants us to know we are all connected; that our souls are all connected, that through love we are all connected. That connection continues throughout our interactions with one another, whether they are physical or spiritual interactions with angels and people who have crossed over. On earth we have one mindset. For some people it is very black and white – they see God with blinders on when they are here."

The Divine is pure, loving and willing to take us as we are. This much she has learned from her experiences with the spirits of those who once lived on earth. God, the angels and those we have loved who have crossed over are always with us and want us to live in love and joy. We are never alone.

Michelle recalls one case in which a man was killed in a motorcycle accident. As his body was dying, he didn't understand that his soul had left his physical body. "He was being resuscitated and he was coming in and out of consciousness. His spirit was standing over his body watching what was happening and he was confused. He was saying, 'I don't understand what is happening.' It took him a long time to understand that the angels, God, the universal energy was around him. He was very confused at why he passed because he was a good motorcycle driver."

Once the man's spirit realized he was no longer with his body, he accepted that it was time to move on and he was able to go home. What she has seen is that once someone has died and accepts their death, their spirit crosses from this world and goes to be with the Creator. Sometimes they become stuck here, because their loved ones hang on to them and are not willing to accept their death.

When we die, we are surrounded by angels and our loved ones who have passed before us. "We are never alone when we die."

If one is present at someone's death, it is an honour. While we humans view death with great sadness, it is not viewed the same way on the other side. It is considered a time of celebration, because it is a homecoming.

We grieve because our loved ones are not physically with us, but Michelle explains that those we love who have crossed over are always with us when we think of them. She thinks of them and she will hear them as internal voices or see images in her mind's eye or smell scents that will remind her of them.

"I believe the more we acknowledge our connection to the other side, whether it is our loved ones or the angels, the more it will come."

Our loved ones who are in spirit, and the angels, will come to us in a variety of ways: through songs we hear on the radio that remind us of them, through lights that flicker, through computer monitors and TV screens that turn off and on, through scents of perfume, tiny feathers you will see on the ground, or birds or butterflies in flight.

"Sometimes I have heard in recorded sessions the sound of a resounding heartbeat."

Michelle is hopeful for the future. She says there is a universal shift happening and when she thinks of it, she feels lightness. We are also coming into a time of strength.

"There is no need to fear what's coming. We are loved and we are connected. We are connected with each other and we are connected with the other side and with the Divine."

Michelle sees a time when the separation between earth and the spiritual realm will be no more. She already sees it happening. Children being born today are more open to spirit. "I think they are seeing far beyond what I saw as a child. They see angels and loved ones that have passed. It is very matter-of-fact. The more we become open to it, the more we will realize that they are right here with us. We are not separated. God's right here with us."

Angels Save Michelle Arbeau and Open Her Intuitive Abilities

Michelle Arbeau is a wife and mother of two who lives near Fredericton. Her experience with angels started very early in life, when she was about three years old.

She and a couple of her distant cousins, who were a few years older, were playing in a bedroom. They offered her a Gobstopper that she swallowed but the large candy blocked her airway so she started to choke. The boys thought she was pretending, refused to let her out of the room and locked the door.

"I was getting really panicky. Then all of a sudden I started to slip backward, as if the room was separating from me and I was in a sort of a bubble. I felt a lot of people around me. I started to feel really warm and calm and the feeling of panic left me. The boys opened the door and I made it as far as the hallway and then I collapsed. I could see everything going on around me. My mom was cradling my head in her lap and she was trying to dig the Gobstopper out of my throat. She did. But the whole time this blinding white light was all around me."

Michelle was surrounded by beings that were like pillars of light, reassuring her that everything was going to be okay. Recently she learned from her mother that shortly after this incident she started to talk to what her mother thought was an imaginary friend she called Michael.

"I would have long conversations with him. I guess I talked to him quite a bit and quite often. I definitely think it was Archangel Michael because I really feel strongly his presence around me. It was after this near-death event that I began to experience psychic phenomenon and my psychic skills began to emerge. I hear it is common among psychics to have such an experience prior to their spiritual opening. I always said it was a gift from the angels for being such a brave little girl. To this day I have an affiliation with Archangel Michael. There's a real connection with him. Out of all of the Archangels, he is probably the one I share the biggest connection with. He is a lot like me. I am a very strong person. He has a lot of masculine qualities. I know angels usually aren't male or female but he's very strong, protective. He's bold. More like the warrior. That's a lot like me, I guess."

Michelle has no religious affiliation. She was never taken to church or any place of worship as a child. Religion was not discussed in her home and it wasn't part of her upbringing in any way. She's always been able to sum people up and know who and what they were all about.

"When I was a kid I used to refer to people as either good or bad. Michelle Russell, a very gifted psychic, told me I had a huge angelic presence around me and that my own soul had almost angelic qualities to it. She said, 'You must have felt this presence your whole life.'"

She's had a sense that angels are all around her and always have been. As a child, because she didn't understand what the feeling of this presence was, she would hide her head beneath her bedcovers. Everything changed in her life after a psychic reading five years ago, when she was assured that the presence she felt were angels that were always around her to make sure she was safe. Michelle is an intuitive consultant and numerologist. She is claircognizant, which means she knows things about others even if they are complete strangers. As a numerologist, she reads what's happening in people's lives through the numbers that surround them, such as their birthdate.

"Numerology is kind of like astrology. It's similar but it's a different way to see things. The numbers represent energy and we are all energy patterns. The numbers are just a way to represent that. I've had people say, 'Wow, you are so good at what you do.' I haven't done it that long and I think the angels gave me this."

While she's never seen the physical manifestation of angels in adulthood, she says she hears them call her name if they want her to pay attention to something.

She says with wars, natural disasters, economic instability, and disease, people are in search of reassurance. Many want to know more about angels and the Divine. In her opinion, it's because many are afraid.

"We're living at this time when it's so scary. We're shifting. We're at this moment in time when we're going to do this complete 360-degree turn in our level of consciousness. We're scared and we need this reassuring, protective energy. People are seeking that out. They want to find that rock again because everything's been shaken. The world is going crazy. It's going to hell in a handbasket. We are coming to this point where we're ready to drop the ego and to live to our true self."

What does she think about the talk of a doomsday scenario where the world will come to an end through some cataclysmic event or Armageddon? "We're heading towards this and maybe it will happen around this time, and maybe it won't, but it's getting close."

Michelle grew up in a home where open displays of affection through hugs and kisses weren't expressed. After she came to realize the presence she'd always felt since childhood was actually angelic, she understood they were with her to try and provide her with unconditional love, affection and protection.

"I think that's their message. The angels want us to know that they're here; we're protected. That love and protection is always there. It will never leave. You are always supported. Whether you call it God or source energy, it's all around us. Source energy is pure love. There's no negativity whatsoever. What I understand from the angels is they are so calming and come from a place of peace and love. The angels are trying to awaken us. This is the time of our awakening. We're waking from a deep sleep because we've been in this ego-driven world full of negativity, and it needs to be cleansed so we can breathe again and be our true spiritual selves. We've polluted ourselves with such negativity we can't even find ourselves any more. What we really are is this source energy."

When she tunes in to do numerology readings for people, she asks the angels to be with her. "When I call in the angels that's when the channel bursts wide open. I can feel a tingling all over me and it's like pure love." During these readings she can feel four or five angels with her.

"The angels don't really give messages. They will give reassuring words or a yes or a no and in that confirmation you will get shivers. Their presence is protective, it's reassuring, but other than that they're not the ones that give you the information."

Michelle believes very much in the notion of earth angels. While angels have never been human, she says, they can work through people by influencing what they do. People who have a pure connection with angels tend to be what she calls earth angels.

"They say the angels come in times of crisis, like the near-death experience that I had. The angels that came at that time were really tall. It was a really strong and powerful energy. They're not the same kind of energy that I call in when I do a reading." Spirit guides, those who've lived as human beings and are now in spirit form, come to her when she does psychic readings. "I do know the angels and our guides are there at our time of death."

She knows this because she saw an angel after there had been a murder in the apartment building she lived in as a child. A man shot his wife in the head and killed her. After the police finished with the crime scene, the building's landlord asked her mother to clean it up. Her mother was really shaken by the gruesome scene and the fact the murder had taken place in their own building. "Years later my mother said I told her it was okay, because an angel came to get the woman's spirit."

Michelle also hears what she calls angel music. It is very much like classical or orchestral music, which she hears randomly. Her seven-year-old daughter recently started to hear it too. The little girl has also seen what she describes as "fairy balls" in her bedroom in the evening, as the light is waning. Michelle doesn't go into detail with her daughter about what she is seeing, but she believes these are the type of angelic orbs which can often appear in photos.

To better understand what she does, and the concept of how numbers relate to angels, Michelle invited me to her home. She showed me into her living room where she offered me a cup of tea and a comfortable seat on her sofa. For the past five years she has dreamed in numbers. "I dream about numbers all the time – every dream. Even when I was falling asleep or waking up with the black nothingness, no dream, there would be numbers there all of the time. Then, anywhere I would go, I would see numbers, and they always meant something significant in my life. They weren't random."

When she dreams of numbers, she is receiving messages from angels. Angels will often try to communicate with us through numbers at night, when the separation between this realm and the other, where angels exist, is thinnest. For example, if you wake up at a certain time of night, the angels are likely there with you, trying to get your attention.

"I think it's somewhere between 2:30 and 3:30 a.m. when communication between the two realms is most ideal. They are always trying to get through to us, but it just so happens at that time the veil is thinnest and they are able to break through enough to get us to notice them a little bit."

Angels try to get our attention and communicate with us whichever way they think they can. One way is through numbers. How are you supposed to interpret these numbers? There are many books on this subject and lots of information available on the Internet that will help us to understand what the angels are trying to say through number sequences.

In 2009 Michelle felt as though she was at the peak of some huge event in her life. She saw the number sequence 1111 everywhere. "The number 1 in numerology means new beginnings, and it is also the gateway number to the physical plane which is a high doing number, meaning you have to get out there and do it." Seeing 1111 reaffirmed she was on the brink of something huge in her life. It started while she was visiting her friend in Calgary in June 2009. The women saw the number sequence on digital clocks, addresses, license plates. She believed this was a message from the angels that it was now time to start making her goals and dreams a reality.

Michelle has done a significant amount of research on numerology. The numeric sequence 1111 is an energetic gateway or portal of sorts. It is also an angelic message to watch your thoughts closely because you are manifesting very quickly.

"The more I began seeing 1111, the more I would feel as though something big was about to happen, and I felt on top of the world instead of my usual doubtful outlook. I have felt for a long time now, probably the better part of a year, that I was on the verge of something big, a major breakthrough not only in my spiritual work but in all aspects of my life. Lately, I have found that my whole outlook on things has been shifting. No doubt I am in the midst of rapid and radical change. I have been given many opportunities to connect with all the right people at the right time, as if they were magical coincidences, a sure sign I am on the right path."

She asserts it isn't a random occurrence, that many people are experiencing 1111 everywhere. Many intuitive people around the world are seeing this numeric sequence with increasing frequency. In Michelle's opinion, it is a call to them to embrace who they are and what they need to do during this time of great shift. "There are people who talk about Armageddon and the end of the world, but really all it is, is a shift in consciousness. Symbolically it is the end of the world as we know it."

Lately she has experienced a great deal of highs and lows. She believes this is something common to many people at this time as the world's energy continues to shift.

In the next generation, people will no longer be ego-driven, desperate for money and power. The end of war, power, and greed will mean the beginning of global oneness, social consciousness and the desire of everyone on the planet to live in peace. When people see 1111, it's a sign from the angels that we are meant to embrace the challenges and the work that will come with the shift happening on this planet. We are headed towards a time of global peace. The children of today will be the ones to usher in this time of tranquility.

"If you look at everyone's birthday in the 1900s, they had at least one nine in their birthday. Nine is the ego number. It's thinking big, a high change number. Everyone was really driven. But now we see these children who are being born in the twenty-first century, where the number nine has been replaced by the number two. Two is the number of intuition and sensitivity, a peaceful, inner, self-reflective number. They are not driven at all."

Because this generation of children is so sensitive, they are unable to deal with the negativity. Michelle says angels will become a more important part of everyone's lives as we enter this more peaceful, spiritual time. "We're just getting in touch with the other part of our selves that we've blocked out for so long."

She compares what's happening with the shift from the material to the spiritual as similar to a person craving healthy meals after living on a steady diet of junk food. We are spiritually starving and are craving something that will fill us. "We are not complete unless we have both the physical and the spiritual, and we have blocked the spiritual out for so long. There are a lot of people who are not in touch with the spiritual part of themselves at all."

Angels will often come to her in her dreams. She described one encounter where she saw the number four. According to her, the number four is the angel number. She dreamed she was biking with her family to school, a dangerous ride on busy streets and lots of close calls with vehicles. When she arrived at the school the bell was ringing. She ran down a narrow crowded hallway, unsuccessfully searching for a classroom with the number four. In her dream she felt ashamed she had to ask for help to find it. Michelle says a bicycle in a dream represents "hard work" in reaching a goal. The shame she felt came from the fact that she had to deal with her emotions about her work and what others might think of her because of it. She believes the angels were reminding her that she needs to call on them to work through these emotions and to follow her life path.

She recalls another numeric dream. "I dreamed I was in the hospital being prepared for an operation, a transformational operation. I was afraid I wouldn't recognize myself afterward. I had a hospital gown and hospital bracelet on and I was lying in a bed. The bracelet had the numbers 777 on one side and 10-10-10 on the other side. Multiple sevens mean someone is on the right path. The number 10 is the number of claircognizance (clear knowing), which is my strongest psychic sense. In the *Angel Numbers* book by Doreen Virtue, the number 10 means you are receiving divine guidance through claircognizance and to stay positive about the messages you receive."

A client recently contacted her to book a numerology reading. When Michelle e-mailed the client to confirm the date and time, she felt it was important to share some information with her. The spirit of a man who had died was coming through to Michelle. He wanted his daughter to know he was near. He told Michelle he had died unexpectedly and that the cause of his death was related to some kind of "pressure" or the blood. Michelle told the woman his death was either a heart attack or a stroke.

Soon after, the man's daughter replied, "Holy cow, Michelle, you caused some major goose bumps on my arms, let me tell you! My Dad passed away unexpectedly in May, so I'm pretty sure that's him. He went very quickly and we didn't get to say a lot of the things that we would have, had we had more time together." Later the same day the woman e-mailed Michelle once more to tell her that her father had died of a massive heart attack, even though he didn't have a history of heart trouble.

As Michelle has delved further into her spiritual self, and embraced her intuitive abilities, she has been experiencing more of these events. Take for example a client she read for, whose brother had been killed in Afghanistan. During the reading, the client's brother came through and was making a joke about someone whom Michelle named specifically, a very good friend of his and another solider. The information truly meant a lot to the loved ones of this soldier, who said they were comforted to know he has lived on in spirit and continues to watch over them.

Like many others, Michelle is beginning to see more of the spiritual realm. Increasingly, she is encountering the souls of the departed who want to make a connection with their loved ones in this world. "Our vibrations are speeding up and it seems, like Nostradamus predicted, the dead will rise up!"

And, as we continue along our spiritual evolution, many more of us, open to these experiences, will also encounter angels, spirit guides and the spirits of loved ones. The veil between this world and the other side continues to thin. Eventually there will be no separation between Heaven and earth.

Karen Forrest – From the Military to Medium

When Karen Forrest was a child she was aware of angels because she was raised in the Roman Catholic faith, but she never called upon them to help her in her life until 1994. She was a member of the Canadian Armed Forces on a training exercise when she first encountered what she now understands was her guardian angel. It happened while she was on a thirteen-kilometre march, carrying fifty pounds of gear as well as her rifle. "For me it was a lot of weight because I'm only five-foot-two. I knew I had to finish the march because it was part of my officers' training, so I could graduate – that was part of what I needed to do to become a nurse."

Struggling with the heavy load, she was falling behind and in a lot of pain. She started to pray. "I remember saying, 'Dear God, angels, you must help me – I can't take another step on my own. This is so tough and this weight is very heavy on my back. I can't do this on my own any more.' Within a few seconds I felt a slight pressure on my back. It was like someone was urging me forward. Whoever was behind me wasn't talking to me, and I appreciated that because I really needed to just focus on literally taking one step at a time. So I finished that last kilometre, and at the very end of the march I turned around to thank the person for helping me and there was nobody there. Then I realized it was my guardian angel that put the pressure on my back to gently move me forward. I really thought it had been a person behind me, because I felt a hand on my back."

Karen Forrest was a psychiatric nurse who served seventeen years in the military. Most people in the mental health profession would say if someone is hearing voices or having visions, they are likely experiencing a psychotic episode. But Karen says there is a real difference between a psychotic episode and an angelic or spiritual encounter.

Angels present themselves with love. The person who experiences this kind of encounter will feel safe, secure and have a feeling of protection, warmth and joy. An angelic encounter is one that is peaceful, but a psychotic episode is very negative and the person who is having this kind of experience will be frightened by all of the negativity and darkness.

God's energy is filled with light. It feels good, and the awareness of angels feel good, because angels are from the light. Karen has encountered demonic energies through other people and this, she says, is a completely different thing. This low, dark, negative energy can be very frightening and nothing to be fooled with. "They are not nice and nothing I call upon, but because of my work, when I am releasing them from other people, of course I have encountered them and it's just nasty. There are very specific skills I have to work on getting rid of that negative entity. You have to make sure you call upon God's energy to help you. That's how you get rid of that, with Divine light."

So how does a psychiatric nurse become a spiritual medium and an Angel Therapy Practitioner®? Karen says it happened because she was divinely guided to take a course that taught her how to connect with the angels.

In 2004 she was exercising at a gym when she saw a poster advertising a course in communicating with angels and how to have a daily relationship with them. She was fascinated by it. Something compelled her to register for the course. "I was a little leery. I was wondering and hoping it would be legitimate and that it wouldn't be some weird religious cult trying to suck me in, because I would have walked out. Something told me I had to go. I didn't know it was Divine guidance at the time, but I now know that it was."

In this three-hour course she learned to connect with her angels, how to communicate with them and receive messages from them. In that moment, she knew this is what she had to do with the rest of her life. "I remember being surprised by that. I was a psychiatric nurse. Why would I want to talk to angels and give messages to people? That's not who I was, that's not what I did, and that wasn't what I was trained to do. I had no idea I would do that one day. I just knew it was something I wanted to do."

Now she is a spiritual counselor, motivational speaker, Angel Therapy Practitioner® and medium who advises and teaches others how to connect with their angels and deceased loved ones. She took an Angel Therapy Practitioner® course in 2004 taught by Dr. Doreen Virtue, who is known around the world as one of the preeminent experts on angels. She also took the intensive Medium Mentorship Program in 2005, the Professional Spiritual Teachers' Program the next year, and the Advanced Angel Therapy Practitioner Course in 2008, receiving certification from Doreen Virtue. She has also studied mediumship under the instruction of James Van Praagh and has attended many workshops and lectures by Wayne Dyer, Deepak Chopra, Jack Canfield, Dr. Phil and other world-famous instructors.

Angels come to her though messages she will hear. She will also feel the angels. Most people will feel things and will call it their "gut instinct'" but Karen says this is really a feeling that comes from one's angels. She is also able to see these Divine beings. They come to her in various ways, depending on which angel comes through to her. "I sometimes see them as coloured circles of lights. Sometimes I will see them as you expect to see an angel. Michael comes to me as a tall being with dark hair and a muscular body. When I see guardian angels I always see them dressed in long white gowns with wings, as you would think an angel would look like. There is no right or wrong way to see angels but this is how I tend to see them."

Everyone can communicate with their angels, provided they are open to it and are willing to take the time to have a relationship with them. But don't expect that you will encounter your angels the same way other people do. There are four ways you can receive angelic messages, Karen explains. You might hear them, have a sense of knowing that angels are near, you might feel them, or you might see them.

Over the past several years, through one-on-one angel and spiritual medium readings and spiritual workshops she holds throughout Atlantic Canada, she has met thousands of people who are eager to connect with their angels and the spirits of their deceased loved ones. She believes her life's purpose is to connect people with them through angel readings and spiritual counseling. Everyone has the ability to receive messages from angels. It's simply a matter of recognizing them. Most people acknowledge that we all have some sort of intuition, but Forrest says this is really the angels speaking to you. Anyone can communicate with their angels. It's simply a matter of learning how to do so. "What people don't realize is that you don't have to be special or gifted to receive messages from angels. We all have the capability."

God and the angels want us to communicate with them daily, but most people think they don't have the right to do so, or they shouldn't bother the Almighty or angels except in times of emergencies. Not so, says Karen. "You can call upon them for everything and in all ways." She speaks to angels and asks for their advice on everything from relationship issues to finding a parking spot. "It makes my life so much easier. Since I started working with angels directly and constantly, my life is smoother, more peaceful and there is more joy."

Karen has also written two books on the subject: *Canadian Angels By Your Side* and *Angels of the Maritimes By Your Side*. Both bring together heart-warming stories of angel accounts from people, which range from everyday encounters to life-changing moments.

What Karen has come to know, beyond a doubt, is that everyone has angels around them throughout their lives and their angels are with them when it is time to cross over to the other side. "Yes, everyone does, but it is our choice to reach out to the angels or not. We all have a minimum of two guardian angels. One will minister to us and the other will teach us – they are with us from the day we are born until the day we die. Our guardian angels are with us constantly."

In her communication with the angels, Karen knows they desire to have a close and loving relationship with us in our everyday lives. If you want this kind of relationship with them, they will willingly connect with you. However, if you do not want to have a relationship with them, they will take several steps back. Angels cannot interfere in people's lives, so unless we ask for a relationship with them, they must respect our will. If you do want to have a relationship with your angels, all you have to do is to invite them into your life. You can do this by asking to feel your angel's presence during a time of meditation. Hold the thought and intent in your mind of connecting with your guardian angels. "Just sit quietly in their presence so you can become familiar with their energy and be able to feel their presence."

No request is too big or too small, and Karen says it is definitely not selfish to ask them for even little things. As she explains, angels do not distinguish between large or small requests, as people do. Rather, they treat everything we ask for in the same devoted manner, whether we are asking them to help get us through heavy traffic or to help us recover from a serious illness. The only thing we need to do is ask for their help and it will be given.

Many people wonder how they are supposed to ask their angels for help. This is very easy. The most important aspect is holding the intent. This can be done by saying what you want, praying about it, thinking about what you want or writing a letter of request to your angels. "There is no wrong way to communicate with them," says Karen. "As soon as you begin to ask, your angels are instantly by your side, lovingly guiding you."

Angel communication can be done in many ways. Some might wish to be able to see an angel standing right in front of them, but this isn't always possible. Some people are able to see angels through visions, dreams, or seeing images in their minds' eye because they are clairvoyant. Even if you can't see angels in the obvious way, they will make themselves appear to you in other ways, such as through angel statues, paintings, or coloured and white lights. Some may be able to hear the whispers of the angels because they are clairaudient. When you are clairaudient, your will hear words inside your head, as though you are talking to yourself. Those with claircognizance have a clear sense of knowing. You know something to be true, but you cannot explain how you have this information. Others feel the presence of their angels because they are clairsentient. This is feeling in your body, or having a gut instinct. Karen says most people are clairsentient, so it is important to pay attention to what your body is telling you.

You might wonder whether you are actually communicating with your angels. Karen explains the easiest way to tell whether you are indeed connected with your angels is to keep holding the intent that you are. When we connect with our angels, we will feel peaceful, calm, relaxed and protected. You will know you have received a message from your angels if it feels right, but when you connect with your ego, or lower self, you will feel negative, down or "off." A thought won't feel right or won't ring true to you.

If you are worried about the people in your life who you think could use some Divine intervention from the angels, you can send angels to them. When you ask angels to go to someone you love, they will go to the higher being or that true part of these people connected to the Divine, and ask if they are willing to receive their angelic help. The highest being will either accept or decline. In Karen's experience, most people accept the angels' help gladly.

People have been encountering angels forever. They simply are becoming more comfortable telling others about their experiences because now it is more socially acceptable. "I think it's because we are a little more open-minded in our society. People are a little more respectful of the opinions of others."

Karen agrees this is an all-encompassing, world-wide phenomenon. It doesn't matter where one is in the world, what religion one practises, or if someone doesn't believe in anything other than the power within themselves – people are having these experiences. "I tell people to trust their own experience to tell whether it is real. You have to experience it for yourself and believe that it is real. I am not here to convince anyone of anything."

Forrest says her religious views have changed over time. She hasn't been a practicing Roman Catholic since she was in her twenties. Now, she focuses on being spiritual rather than being religious. "My definition of being spiritual is coming from a place of love, and there are a million different ways you can do that … there is no fear when it comes to what I call God."

In preparation for this interview, Karen says she called upon God, the angels, her spirit guides and mine, Jesus Christ, and Archangel Gabriel to speak through her to get the message across that they want people to hear.

"What they are saying is this book will help spread love to others. It will cause people to open their minds to Divine beings that are loving, so they will not fear working with Divine beings. When I say the term Divine beings, it could be what people might call God, the Creator, Allah, Jesus, angels or Archangels, whoever they work with. That's okay, but it is important to work with a Divine being of some sort. They are saying that this book will bring truth and light to this world, and it will inspire people to work on themselves on a personal level."

In Karen's experience, and now mine, through the writing of this book, life is so much smoother when you give the angels permission to act on your behalf and to allow them to make your life as joyful and abundant as it is meant to be. "That's why I encourage people to invite the Divine beings into their lives every day," says Karen.

Donna Somerville and Her Connection to Angels

Donna Somerville doesn't remember any angelic encounters from her childhood but she has had many since she tapped into her intuitive abilities. She is a deeply spiritual woman who has always had a close relationship with God. "I was raised in a Roman Catholic family; we went to church even on our camping trips. If we went camping on the weekend we still went to church on Sunday morning, and our father used to get us there by saying every time you go to church you get to make a wish. My life as a teenager was very connected to the church. God had a huge impact on my life."

When her father was alive he taught her that God was always with her and cared about everything in her life, so she was always able to talk freely to her Creator. Donna didn't have a connection to angels until much later.

Her father died at age forty-eight and her mother was gone at fifty-six. When Donna was twenty-four she was offered a government job then spent fourteen years with the federal government in Ottawa', determined to become a deputy minister.

She moved from the Department of Regional Economic Development to the National Parole Board and then to the Aviation Safety Board. When she had blood pressure problems, her doctor wanted to put her on medication but she refused. Her doctor told her she had two choices. "She said either change jobs or take pills, and I said there's got to be some other way to lower my blood pressure. I dropped forty pounds and that didn't touch it. I weighed a hundred and thirty-five pounds and I still had a blood pressure problem. So I opted to try a meditation class taught by a psychic who was also a trance medium. After two weeks I quit the meditation classes – it just seemed too weird. But then I went back, and within three months my blood pressure was normal."

Her doctor told her whatever she was doing was working and she should continue doing it. At the time, if someone had told her she would one day be a spiritual medium and would experience everything she has, she would have told them they needed psychiatric medication.

Donna always wanted to be a teacher. She realized how powerful the meditation class was and how much she wanted to teach others so she apprenticed under psychic Barbara Eagles. "She taught me tarot cards. I also took psychometry, which is the reading of objects and jewelry. All the other courses I took were in healing. I call myself a medium, but really I'm a facilitator."

Through meditation, she started to see the shallowness of her life. "I was everything on the outside. Barbara taught us to look at ourselves on the inside." Donna was very frightened that if she looked inside herself she would find nothing. At the time, she was a model civil servant working her way up the federal government ladder. She looked and dressed the part. She acted the way she thought she should behave.

"I carried a briefcase. I carried *The Globe and Mail*. I did everything right on the outside. I had perfect hair, perfect makeup. I was always well dressed. But as I started to go inside of myself I realized I didn't like what I was doing anymore. There was something missing. I had a real breach from God when my father died, because he was my best friend and my mother wasn't very mentally balanced. So I was very mad at God that He would take Dad and leave me Mom – like what was He thinking? It took me about three years to get back to God. When you realize you are mad at God then what do you do? The meditation helped me find my way back. I do remember in one of my meditations Jesus coming to me, and I opened my eyes at once because it terrified me."

As she continued to develop her spirituality, one of her teachers told her she needed to "burn the church but to keep God because the church was in her way." But despite her concerns about her vision of Christ she kept going to meditation class every Tuesday night for several years with the same teacher.

She had met David Somerville in the class. He worked in a convenience store, lived with his parents and she realized he had more quality of life than she did.

Donna decided it was time to leave her government job because she was only in it for the money. She told her bosses in November that she would leave in January. "Everybody said to me, 'You can't do this!' I said, 'If one person can give me a reason that isn't $59,000 a year, then I'll stay, but don't be telling me I can't leave this kind of money. There has to be more to this than money.'"

Her boss increased the pressure at work because of her decision to leave. She decided not to give the department any more of her time. She cleaned out her desk, left notice that she quit immediately and walked away. "My director called me on Monday and said, 'You can't do this.' And I said, 'I've just done it.' I think that was my first stance of power, which is one of the things the meditation gave me because I was finding me."

For a while she used her government pension to support herself while she continued to study and become more connected to her inner self. She and David have been married for over nineteen years.

As a medium she sees, hears and feels the presence of loved ones who've passed, as well as angels. When she started this new life, she read tarot cards. Although she was good at it, she didn't like the responsibility it entailed because people wanted her to map out their lives, so she stopped.

In 1987 she started to read angelic messenger cards. She intuitively felt the messages that came from them, and she allowed the angels to speak to her through them. "I called them angel readings, messages from your angels. My prayer before I stared each reading was, 'God, whatever message is not getting through to these people from you, use me.'"

Donna says, "I could read the same cards for two different people and get two different stories. Each story unfolded and I completely understood." The cards would speak to her. Either it would be from the number on the cards or the picture. She believes she is clairsentient, clairvoyant and clairaudient. "Sometimes I see, sometimes I know, sometimes I feel as though I am translating. Sometimes I am feeling what is happening within someone's body. Sometimes I'm observing and I tell people what I see, what I'm hearing."

From all of her experiences as a medium, Donna says she knows angels are around us at all times. Everything has energy. Inanimate objects such as chairs have a denser energy than living beings such as humans. People's energy vibrates faster than inanimate objects. Angels, which are also made of energy, vibrate at a faster speed than humans. And they exist on a different plane. "The only difference between you and angels is how fast your energy vibrates."

For angel readings she would create what she calls sacred space and called in Guardians who would monitor the gates. "When I first started, I would get too many messages all at the same time. Like ten people trying to talk to me all at once. So I would always use Archangels Michael, Gabriel, Raphael and Germain. I would see them in a circle. I would actually see them. They would hold the space sacred and would let the energies and messages come in one at a time. If I was afraid, I would call on Michael. I never turned anyone away, but if I was uncomfortable with who was sitting in the chair I would call on Michael's protection. I always saw Gabriel as an angel that could take what was negative and turn it into positive. He could screen things. I was very ceremonial in the beginning. I have much more of a communion relationship with it now. This is going to sound arrogant but I evolved to it. Sometimes I feel like I am the angels and the angels are me now, whereas before they were outside of me and they were my guardians. I still call them when I do a healing, a Reiki session. I will put them around the table. I seek to bring the highest vibrations to come through."

When she does a reading now she connects with an essence. She believes this is the essence of all of the possibilities, all the power, all the potential of everything you can be. She stopped using the Archangels as her guardians about seven years ago. "Because I felt like I was asking for something I already was. I was already there."

Donna believes more people are open to the idea of angel encounters in their lives and are experiencing them for a couple of reasons. "I think the angels are a 'stepped down' version of God. A lot of us, with our histories and what we have been taught and how we've been punished, can't imagine that we can talk to God. So I think the angels are our way of being able to talk to God without feeling arrogant and also we don't feel worthy enough to talk to God in person. So the angels are our go-betweens, our translators. It's like many people feel they can work with the angels but we can never quite get to God. It is very much like the way many people see priests as the ones they go to who will intercede on their behalf with God."

Also, Donna believes many people are having encounters with angels because our world is changing. As spiritual beings, we are evolving. She has great hope for the next generation.

"My teacher explained that when we are in the womb, we still have a connection to God. But as we come through the birth canal we lose this God connection. Children being born today haven't lost their God connection. They are much more spiritual beings than the generation before them. That's why they are more adventuresome, they seem to take more risks. They know their rights because they come in with their power. I think that's the evolution of our civilization."

For adults the spiritual evolution will be more difficult. How do we catch up? How do we get rid of the stuff that blocks our "God connection"? Donna says we have to have some way to bring the divinity into the body, and she believes angels are an acceptable way for those who have traditional belief systems. It is acceptable for many to connect with angels and to believe angels are here to help us, and we can allow ourselves to use them to make our lives better. It is more palatable for many people to talk about angels, than it is to have a personal communication with a God some view as a distant, angry being. With wars, disease, natural disasters, global warming, the economic crisis, and talk of a doomsday scenario, many people are living in fear, uncertain of the future and their place in the world, or even whether the world has a future.

If people can't count on their money, health, and material possessions because they can't afford to live a lifestyle they've built on credit, they quickly see they really have nothing, and they feel great emptiness and fear. So what's left? "We are not our houses. We are not our jobs. We have lost touch with who we are," Donna explains.

If we are willing to let everything go, we will not have to let anything go. But if we hold on to everything with a closed fist, then the Creator is going to have to rip it out of our hands to show us who we are. "You have to hold on to your life with open hands like Abraham, and be willing to let everything go and find out you don't have to let anything go. I think that God looks at us and shakes His head and says 'What are you doing?'"

Donna doesn't believe we are supposed to suffer. She doesn't think life is supposed to be difficult. But it has become so at our own hands. "I believe we have gotten so in control of ourselves and so arrogant in that control, we thought we could control Mother Earth. We thought we could control one another. We thought we could control the poor. We thought we could control the helpless. We thought we could control disease. We thought we could control our bodies. We can't control anything. That's the biggest cosmic joke going. The ego loves to want more. More land, more money, more technology, bigger houses, more furniture, more cars. We have drained the resources. And Mother Earth has said 'That's it. You're done.'"

We create our own reality. The first rule of the universe is free will in every religion. The angels and God can only come so close if we will not allow them into our lives. If you say no, the Almighty and the angels never abandon you, but they take a step back and give you space. The angels cannot stop you from walking off a cliff unless you say, "Please guide me today." You have to give them permission to get involved in your life, she explains. We all have angels around us all of the time. If you don't recognize that and don't ask for their help they can't get involved in your life. They will try to do what they can to make your life as easy as possible provided you acknowledge them and ask for their assistance. Otherwise you will eventually fall off the cliff.

"I think angels are versions of God that vibrate slower than God does," says Donna. "God, the Creator, is infinite and I really believe if you say no to an experience or lesson there are an infinite number of choices. The ego mind thinks there is only one right way. Until certain things happen in the world, most people won't believe that one plus one can equal three.

"In the 'I' world, one plus one equals two. In the 'We' world, one plus one can equal three and the "we world" is your divine relationship, whether that's with an angel, God, the Creator, the Universe, Mother Earth. When we recognize the divine force that results when the Creator partners with the individual, then anything is possible."

Donna's prayer is that some day people will evolve enough so they will have a shift in mindset, and will search for something greater, something deeper. We may get to the point where it won't matter what one's religion is and there will be an end to wars fought over spiritual beliefs. She believes that what we are seeing now in these shifts, in these collapses is the rebirth of Eden. "I really believe with my whole heart and soul that I will see Eden."

Today, many people have the attitude that they have to look after themselves first and if it's convenient to help others on the way, they will. Before Donna asks God for anything in her life, she wants to make sure it will not interfere with highest good of all.

Donna believes there is a rhythm to life and the way to find the right rhythm for your life is through your intuition. When you find that rhythm you are in the right place at the right time and life is easy. God uses the angels to help reassure people in these difficult times and to help us to know that we deserve a Divine connection. "They believe in you because of God and if they didn't believe in you, they wouldn't bother trying to help."

Donna says she turns to the angels to help her feel more sacred; when she didn't believe she was good enough, they could help her to feel safer, stronger and be clearer.

She thinks angels are here to protect us from ourselves, because we create harm to ourselves as a result of our selfish behaviour. We are like children who want our own way and we fail to consider the consequences of our actions. The angels are also here to watch how we treat one another. Do we look them in the eye and see that panhandler as a person? He is somebody's son. She is somebody's daughter. The person on the street could very well be an angel who is there to help you see beyond yourself and to look to help others. She adds, "I actually think we do have the angelic within us and we use angels outside of us until we see an angel inside of us. I think every single person is an angel. The angelic is just an expression of your divinity and the angel makes it an acceptable expression of your divinity."

Imagine the possibilities if we all stepped out of our self-centered lives and thought of others before ourselves? What would our lives be like if we didn't live in fear and doubt? What if we lived in strength, with the certainty that we are loved, protected and strengthened by God because we are His creations? Donna understands the beauty and peace that comes from a life lived this way. She rejects fear because fear is the thing that claimed her mother. "Fear killed my mother. I was very fortunate to have her as my mother. I didn't know that until I was forty-five but I did come to that. She showed me what fear will take. I will not let anyone make me afraid of my world. My God didn't create a frightening world. People make the world frightening. But I still believe in the core of everyone is a Divine spark. This is how the Creator has made us. So when you ask me if I have angels, if I have guides, if I have guardians I say I have all. I really work at not excluding anything. I have whatever I need. When I need Archangel Michael he is there."

When we know that God is in our lives and the angels are here to protect us and keep us from harm, or from harming ourselves, then the fear drops away. If there is no fear then the possibilities are endless. Imagine what would happen if people didn't fear death. Our whole world would be different. How do we learn to be intuitive and self-aware if we are protected at every moment? Don't we have to fall down to know what it feels like to scrape our knees? No matter how much protection we receive from the angels, God still wants us to be aware of what's happening around us.

While many angels have names and appearances, Donna says they are not individualized in her encounters with them. When she connects to angelic forces there's no individuality. They come to us as individual beings so we can identify with them because as humans we are individualized. So it is easier for us to identify with Archangel Michael than an angelic force.

"From my experience in all of the years I have been doing readings, which is over ten years now, depending on the evolution of the person I am working with, the angels will decide how much individualization they need to take. What you need will come when you need it and God knows what you need before you do."

When Donna was about ten years old she was approached by a man in a department store. Alarm bells went off in her head and she ran. She wasn't a street-smart kid but something inside her, her divine instinct for protection, said "Move!" Some people would say that was an angel whispering in her ear. "All I know is that I looked at him and I got scared and I ran all the way home. We need to develop that instinct in ourselves. That is our inner authority. Our divine spark is our inner authority. We are living in a world where everything is the outside authority. The trainer tells you how much to exercise, the doctor tells you how much to eat, the designer tells you what colour to wear. Where is the inner authority? We have given all of our power over to all these outside authorities and we have nothing left inside. We are not puppets whose strings can be pulled by others. When you come from the inner authority people cannot manipulate you." The angels can serve to remind us of our inner authority and of the strength we have as a result of the spark of divinity within each of us.

Donna sees the world as we know it coming to an end but not with a big bang. Instead, she says, visionaries such as Nostradamus saw a change in civilization and she believes it has already begun. "If someone in the 1960s heard there was going to be a black U.S. president in 2008 they would have said it was impossible. To me the black president is part of what Nostradamus saw. I think that all of these changes are radical for us. I am sure there are Americans who are beside themselves that they are represented by a black president so for them, this is Armageddon. For them the devil is taking over the universe. Barack Obama, a highly educated, articulate man with a sense of unification and justice for all, is for some almost too good to be true." She also recalls some of her contemporaries described George W. Bush as the antichrist because he pushed the country into a war with Iraq.

Our world is yin and yang, good and bad. Donna's teachers said that every soul wants to experience what it is like to come to earth and live as a human being. However, when we are born and live in the incarnate form it is not easy. It's tough stuff because there are so many choices, so many complications with emotion. We can lose ourselves so easily, but we can gain so much wisdom in one lifetime because earth has so many complications.

Donna doesn't believe in good and evil anymore, and she doesn't believe in Satan either. "I believe there are negative energies. People do things for selfish reasons. That's negativity. I think we have demons within us and I think those demons are our selfishness and our fear and our belief that we are separated from God – that God doesn't care about us – that's our demons. My God, the one that I was raised with, creates everything and everything is created by light. No one is born a murderer; no one is born a rapist. Our environment, our choices, our reaction to those choices, makes us who we are. When I couldn't forgive God for taking my father, I turned my back on Him. He never left me. I turned my back on Him and I put all of my effort into becoming successful. I had money, a career, I was successful. I was determined that I would never be abandoned again and I was empty inside."

The shift happening in society is that people have made the realization that all of their money and material possessions have not filled the emptiness they feel inside. Only a fulfilled spiritual life can fill one's soul. They might have a big home, luxury car, powerful job and money in the bank, or they have accumulated immeasurable amounts of debt to project an image of wealth and power, but they are living a life that is nothing more than an empty shell, a façade with nothing inside.

A changing world and a world of uncertainty is a very frightening place for many. But when we choose not to live in fear but to live in the light and the knowledge that we are loved and protected by our angels, we can rise above those negative emotions that weigh us down and keep us from living our true, authentic lives. While the world isn't coming to an end, Donna has been shown there will be pockets of chaos in the world as well as pockets of Eden.

Pockets of chaos, she explains, occur when people lose everything and experience trauma in their lives – war, murder, mayhem, job loss, ending up out on the street with neither home nor money – whereas Eden is perhaps not owning a house, but still having shelter, food, clothing. We might not be eating steak every Thursday but we're not going hungry. We might not have designer clothing but we have something to wear.

"I think there is a huge difference between our needs and our wants and the ego has made our world all about wants. Our ego is never satisfied. I am so wealthy because I have simple desires. I think everyone eventually gets to the point like I did, where they have the house, the car, the money, the position and something is still missing. Eventually people stop and say, 'Well, maybe it's not outside of me. Maybe it's inside.' But sometimes it takes a while. I really think what changed my whole journey was my father's death."

When we are spiritually full we don't need to try and fill our lives up with material things. "I think the simpler your needs are, the easier it is to go through this time. Those who are tied to their money and lose it all in these times of uncertainty might have to turn to loved ones for help and that might be an extremely difficult thing for them to bear. We are tribal beings, we are not meant to be individualized. We are supposed to care about each other and this crisis is going to force us to care about each other."

The chaos will happen in people's lives if they try to hang on to what becomes necessary to let go of. Donna says God and the angels want us to live comfortably and happily, but it is also vital that we understand what is truly important. We are not what we wear. We are not what we drive. We are not expensive homes. Rather, we are spiritual beings meant to experience joy and love and in community with others on this planet. If we can understand all of this, she thinks it will be far easier to get through the coming years of change.

Donna is sure the world will continue, but it will not be recognizable as the world we know today. When she has looked ahead to the future she has seen a world where humanity is recreating. The world will carry on.

Donna used to believe that when she died she would ascend to
Heaven. Now she says she believes ascension is finding her angelic self and
being an angel on earth. She thinks we are meant to live as though we are in
Heaven here on earth, and she believes Jesus was here not to be adored but to
show us what was possible. He was here to say, "This is what you are capable
of."

"I think we need to want to make a difference in other people's lives.
That's what the angels do. But you see we make it this heavenly unattainable
thing. Religion makes it unattainable. We say only Jesus can do it. Only the
angels can do it. That's not true. The angels, I think, are a safe way to consider who else you could be. When I started meditating and my instructor wanted
me to look inside myself, I was terrified. Underneath the jewelry and the best
clothes with the designer labels, I didn't think there was anything there. There
was a hole because I was missing my connection to the Divine. I had it as a
little girl because I knew God really well. And the reason I can do what I do
now, is because I'm back to knowing God really well. Our souls are not here
to do harm. We're here to have an experience. The angels are within us and if
we can't believe that, then the angels will come outside of you until you can
believe they'll come inside."

The crises in the world are showing us that we have no more excuses.
Our things aren't going to do it any more. As human beings we create our
own realities through our thoughts, our choices, our language and our expectations. "We don't realize that we are the Creators. We have the Creator's spark
within us. We are a beam of God so we have creative potential. We keep blaming God. God is the chef in the restaurant and we send in our orders. God fulfills these statements because He wants to give us what we want, that's how I
look at it. He's a Father who will spoil you rotten, so whatever you ask for you
get. Unfortunately, we are much more open to receiving the negatives than the
positives. We get what we really think we can have. We really believe we are allowed a bitchy mother and the loss of our house. It breaks my heart to witness
people hurting themselves."

Resignation is different than acceptance because resignation is a part of
the self that says it doesn't matter what I do, things are never going to change.
We have to accept this because it is hopeless and we're stuck – that's ego.
Sometimes we think that's acceptance. It's not. Acceptance is always hopeful.
God never, ever gives up hope.

Donna doesn't believe God or the angels want to be adored. Instead, the relationship we have with God and the angels is meant to be one of communion. "Do you want your children to adore you? Do you want your children to put you on a pedestal and think they can't be near you or tell you anything?" God wants a relationship with us. He sends His angels to us to make our lives better. If for some reason people feel they cannot get close enough to have a personal relationship with the Creator, it is the angels who will minister to us on His behalf.

Paleki Phaphapeuneua Has Seen Heaven

On a cold and rainy night in October of 2009, a Unitarian Church in Fredericton, New Brunswick, is filled to capacity. People are here to listen to fifth-generation spiritual medium Paleki Phaphapeuneua, who recently changed his name from Brett MacFarlane. Paleki's done a lot of research on the subject of angels, but his most profound understanding of them comes from his personal experience with them. This man explains he has crossed over to the "other side" many times, has seen the beauty of Heaven and can see and hear angels and spirit guides. What do they look like?

"Whatever you need them to look like. They will manifest themselves in exactly the form they need to. They can come across looking like they have big wings and white robes. Some of them will come across looking more like people."

Angels have a higher vibration frequency than spirit guides. Because angels have never been human, they have the highest form of energy. Spirit guides have a higher energy vibration than those who have died but who do not serve as guides. The spirits of our loved ones exist on a higher energy level than most people in the world. Some people, like Paleki, have learned to raise their energy levels to the point where they are able to connect to angels, spirit guides and spirits of the deceased.

Like angels, spirit guides can manifest themselves in many forms. Sometimes they will appear as humans, other times they can appear in animal form. "One of my spirit guides is a horse. It gives me strength and gentleness. A lot of people will get a butterfly or a dragonfly because they are very gentle. In Native tradition the eagle is the connection between the two worlds, and in Celtic tradition the crow is the messenger between the doors of the two realms."

Angels and spirit guides want to play a role in our lives but they must wait until we ask for their help. Many times they play a role in protecting people who have been in car accidents or other situations where their lives are in jeopardy. If it is not one's time to die, they can intervene without being asked to do so.

"That's why you hear of people who walk away unharmed from serious accidents," says Paleki. "Or then you will get people who fall, receive what appears to be a non-threatening injury, but they'll die because it was their time to go home. When it's not somebody's time to die, the angels will surround them with protection to get them through the accident unharmed."

Earth angels, he says, are those spirits who come to earth in human form to help out in times of crisis. On any given day, you may encounter an earth angel on the street or in a coffee shop and never know you were speaking to an angel. Angels do not seek attention because they don't have an ego. So if you encounter someone who comes into your life just when you need someone's help, you might have encountered an earth angel.

One of the most frequent issues Paleki deals with is the misunderstanding some people have that spiritual mediums are dabbling in evil things. This just isn't so. He compares himself to a big radio able to tune into the spirit realm when people's spirit guides and deceased loved ones want to come through with a message. "I help people connect with one another. Spirit communication is a very sacred, specialized thing."

When he was a boy his grandmother died, but she would still come to him at night and read bedtime stories to him. When he was in grade seven, he knew he was meant to follow the path of a spiritual medium. He trained for thirteen years with his mother, also a spiritual medium, who helped him to learn to connect with the other side.

Everybody has one primary guide that comes with them to earth when they are born, and remains with them throughout their lives, and then crosses back over to Heaven at the time of their deaths.

The number of angels we have around us depends upon our life journey. Some people have more angels and guides than others. For example, those in the healing professions might have more than people in less stressful occupations because they need that support and guidance. Most people have more than one spirit guide in their lifetime, depending on what's happening in their lives, and throughout one's life, spirit guides can change.

Fears about the economy, war and disease are all things people mani-fest. Paleki maintains that as soon as you start worrying about these things, messages are sent to the angels and guides that there is a lack of trust in them to be able to protect from harm. Dwelling on worries over money sends out the message that a person wants to experience poverty. When you think constantly about sickness, you're sending a message that you want to experience sickness. He says it is important to dwell on the positives in life for more positive things such as health and abundance to come your way.

Sometimes angels and guides will physically appear to him, but only if they really want his attention about something specific. At other times, they will come to him in his mind's eye and will speak to him as if having a face-to-face conversation with him. When he hears them, messages come in the form of an internal voice. He doesn't see spirits of the deceased all of the time, because he learned to shut himself off from the other realm when necessary. Otherwise he would be bombarded with spirits who want to make contact with the living. It's simply a matter of adjusting his energy vibration. Once he low-ers it, spirits of the deceased cannot contact him.

In his communication with angels and spirit guides he has come to understand that every single living being on the earth goes to Heaven.

"Think of all of the people you know who don't think they deserve to go home. We don't understand the concept of an all-loving Creator so we don't think we deserve to go to Heaven. When you work on surrounding yourself with love, picturing love, understanding that you are surrounded by love all of the time, then it is easy to understand that if God looked after you the whole time you were alive, then why wouldn't we go home to Heaven when we die? We are all welcome to go back home. Every single person goes home when they are meant to. Loved ones are waiting to welcome you back home. Angels and spirit guides will welcome you home too."

There is no such place as hell, he says, but sometimes a person can get stuck in a place of lower energy vibration, either because they feel they don't deserve to go home, or because there is someone they know in the world of the living who is hanging on to them, so they cannot go.

"As soon as we acknowledge the light when we die, we go home, and we will get there with the help of our angels, spirit guides and loved ones who have already crossed over. At the time of death, we must go through a life review. We will experience all of the emotions of everyone we have encountered in our lives to know and appreciate how our behaviour towards them made them feel.

"People who commit suicide get to go home. Their life review will show them everything they missed out on by taking their life. Then they will have to take responsibility and they will have an opportunity to be born again quickly to continue on a life journey. To take your life is a very selfish action. Most people who commit suicide volunteer to come back in another body to continue their life journey. Murderers go home and they have to go through their life review too. We all have to take responsibility for our actions but there is no judgment on the other side."

When people are in severe car accidents they often describe the moment as if it happened in slow motion and that they saw their whole life flash before their eyes. Paleki says time actually does slow down. Literally this is what happens when you have a near-death experience: when you die your spirit downloads everything you experienced in life so you can take it back with you to review once you go home to Heaven.

Most people wonder why bad things keep happening to them over and over again in their lives. He explains it is because we are supposed to learn a lesson from these experiences, and if we do not learn the lesson, then it will keep being repeated until we finally understand.

Paleki encourages people to ask their angels, spirit guides and deceased loved ones for help in small ways, and to believe this help will be given. Ask for their help, believe they can help, but we don't have to tell them exactly how to bring us that help. For example, he asks his deceased grandmother to help him pay his bills each month. The money always comes to him just when he needs it. They don't mind helping, but they aren't going to hand it to you. You will get the money to pay the bills but don't tell them how to do it. Leave it up to them how they will give it to you. They are not worried about helping out with things such as money. If they can help you, they will."

Every spiritual path and religion is recognized in Heaven, he says. If we are spiritual, it makes it easier to cross over because we are anticipating life after death, he explains. Even those who don't believe in anything still go there after they die, he has discovered.

Anyone is capable of connecting with the other side but it takes a long time to learn how to do this and how to protect you from lower energy vibrations that might be very frightening. The easiest way to communicate with deceased loved ones is through your spirit guide. They will help to protect you from anyone or anything that shouldn't come across to this realm. No spirit is allowed to come if it is unwanted. If you feel anything near that makes you uncomfortable, you can command it to leave and it will. It is important to take the time to acknowledge them daily. You can light a candle and say a prayer. You can take a walk outside and have a conversation with them. One can even pray a small mantra such as: "Please bless the space and make it holy and lower level spirits won't be able to come through."

It's important to acknowledge deceased loved ones. They may not be here physically but they are always connected to us spiritually. Many people no longer talk to their loved ones after they die but Paleki explains, "When we speak their names, or think about them, they can hear you."

All pathways lead to God, no matter what life journey you are on, and no matter what religion you choose to practice, or even if you are an atheist. Many people are turning away from traditional religions that make people feel fear and guilt over their lifestyle choices that they have been told will damn them eternally. Many homosexuals turn away from traditional religions because they have been told their lifestyle is evil and they will go to hell when they die. What Paleki knows from his communications with the dead and angels is that homosexuality is not evil, that gay people are not damned and there is a place for everyone in Heaven, no matter what their sexual orientation, religion or lifestyle when they die.

Paleki doesn't spend any time worrying about the future. He pays no attention to talk of Armageddon or the end of the Mayan calendar in 2012, which some say is a signal that the world will be coming to an end.

"You are not supposed to live your entire existence waiting for the end. You are supposed to live each day like it might be your end. And whether it does end in 2012 or it doesn't, it shouldn't be of any consequence. The amount of effort it would take to end a planet of fourteen billion people would be too much. They [those in heaven including the Creator, the saints and the angels] are very skilled at what they do, but there is no way they could have fourteen billion people return home at the exact some moment because there would be way too much chaos and there would be too many lessons unfinished. It would overwhelm things and there would be really no point."

Everyone, even in their dreams, is connected to the other side. Have you ever had the sensation that you are falling in your dreams? According to Paleki, this happens when your spirit returns to your body after it has gone back to Heaven for a while in your sleeping hours. Every day when he wakes, he has a conversation with angels and spirit guides. Knowing angels, spirit guides and the spirits of loved ones are around reminds him that he is never alone, so he never feels lonely. When you come to accept the presence of angels, spirit guides and the spirits of loved ones in your life, there is no need to feel lonely or alone.

"I feel mine around me 24-7. I never feel alone," he says.

Everyone has the ability to communicate with their angels, spirit guides and deceased loved ones, but it takes time and effort to learn. If you take the time to be quiet and to raise your energy levels through meditation and prayer, you possibly will be able to hear, see and feel them. "They are not going to waste their time if you are not listening or if you are not going to pay attention to what they have to say."

Paleki advises the best way to connect to your angels and spirit guides is to learn to become very still and silent, to quiet all of your other thoughts. One of the best places to connect with them is in nature. Find a quiet spot where you can be alone with your angels and spirit guides and wait for them to come to you as a whisper, a feeling or a vision. It doesn't have to be a big undertaking or production. Just learn to be still and spend time with them.

"People make it so complicated, but it is really very simple."

After communicating with angels and guides, it is important to thank them for their time and the effort they make to come through to you.

Connecting with angels, spirit guides and loved ones is not to be done through using alcohol or drugs, as these substances can alter your energy vibrations and make it very difficult for them to communicate.

Paleki answers one of the big questions: Where is God?

"God is everywhere. When we die, we will not go to Heaven and meet an old man with a long white beard. This is an image many people have of God. Nobody knows what God looks like."

He says there are no words in any language that can truly describe the Creator. Those who have crossed over and have raised themselves up to fully understand God don't come back to earth to describe the Almighty. They have no reason to come back, because they know they are home and don't want to return here.

Heaven is more spectacular than we can possibly imagine. Paleki has had glimpses of it when he has raised his energy vibrations high enough to see it. "The gardens in heaven are probably the best place. It is absolute perfection. The gardens here on earth are a representation of what they are like there. That's why we have flowers on this side, so we will remember where we came from."

In Christianity, the Bible tells the story of how Adam and Eve fell from the Garden of Eden and were then cast out from it to suffer. Christianity has the right representation, he comments, in that we came from the Garden and we enter into this life where sadness and suffering exist. When we come to earth we aren't cast out of Heaven. Instead, as spirits, we choose to come to earth to experience life lessons in a human body.

Life on earth is supposed to be a wonderful, happy experience, one where we smell the flowers, eat delicious foods, love with all of our hearts and feel limitless joy. Coming to earth is supposed to be a wonderful experience, yet for many people it is anything but, because we find ways to expose the worst.

"Human beings are not nice to one another. If everybody lived in love and had the understanding of where they came from, nobody would be mean to anybody else. Wars and murder wouldn't exist, because you would have an understanding that to kill another human being or to hurt somebody is to damage your spirit of divinity. But we do these things because we lack the understanding. When we come to earth we forget where we came from and we forget what's waiting for us when we go home."

In Paleki's understanding, we come to earth to learn lessons and can come back many times and for as long as it takes to learn all of the lessons we want to learn. Have you ever wondered why there are some people in your life who you simply cannot get along with or who make you angry? Perhaps they are here to teach you something about yourself. Many of us do not see this.

When we come to earth our life story has already been written. We choose every experience that we have on this planet. Those who experience rape or murder, for example, have chosen this path before their souls came to earth to either learn a lesson from it or to help the rapist or the murderer learn a lesson in their human experience, he says.

"Every negative experience can be turned around to something that is positive to make the world a better place. But if you get into a place where you simply focus on anger and negativity and pain, you will always remain the victim, in which case you are choosing not to learn the lesson you chose to learn before you came to earth."

The angels and spirit guides are here to help turn the negative experiences into something positive, if they are asked to. It is easier to be a victim and to blame others for the negative things that happen to us, rather than to

obviously they don't learn anything as they are often repeat offenders.

accept what has happened to us and try to learn from those experiences. When we are satisfied that we have learned all we want to learn about the human experience, we will go home and remain there because we will have no desire to come back to earth.

What is the heavenly experience like? Paleki says he has been shown that when we die, we exist in a place where there are homes and occupations. Some are teachers, some are artists and some make beautiful music. Ever wonder why some children are naturally gifted in art and music? These truly are God-given talents that these little souls learned in Heaven before they were born and they brought these gifts with them when they came to earth.

He learns more about life as it exists on the other side every day. He will learn new things when he channels for people who want to connect with their spirit guides, angels and deceased loved ones or when he spends time in meditation.

What he knows for sure is that angels love us more than we can possibly comprehend and that they are always trying to reach us. Whether or not this connection happens depends on us. We have to make an effort to seek them and spend time with them.

Dan Valkos – From Skeptic to Believer

Dan Valkos's belief in the presence of an afterlife, another realm, spirit guides and angels started in 1969. He was a nineteen-year-old student at the University of Michigan. Back then he was a skeptic.

"I thought everything was a bunch of garbage."

He went through an evolutionary process. First he believed that absolutely nothing in the psychic world existed. Then he conceded that perhaps the psychic world might exist. Later he came to understand that some people are psychic. The more he learned, he realized that everybody in the world has psychic abilities they might not have tapped into, including himself. Over time, he met people who helped him develop his intuitive abilities.

"I just know things and I am right eight, nine, ten times out of ten."

In his opinion, we all have within us intuitive potential. People, he says, can learn to enhance their intuition through meditation. "You could also say it's your own higher self, but the higher self could have information sent to them by a guardian angel or a spirit guide if you will. Fortunately, I had some very patient teachers. I wound up as the chief investigator for the Association of Psychic Investigative Researchers and was the director of the Paranormal Enlightenment Center for about seven years before I moved to Canada."

In 1985 he and his wife moved to Thunder Bay, Ontario. He knew they were meant to make the move and since he'd already been granted a work visa to do psychic readings in this country, it seemed like the right thing to do. He recalls it as the best decision he ever made. Two days after he arrived he was offered a daily radio show.

Dan senses the presence of guardian angels and believes spirit guides and angels are one and the same. Over the years, he has had hundreds of encounters with angels through readings he's done for people. Many spirit guides are the souls of people who loved us in this life, and they carry that love with them when they die and where they are in spirit, he says. The bonds of love remain attached to those who remain in this realm.

"Most people's spirit guides are people they knew when they were alive in this lifetime or in one of their prior lifetimes. They want to help us to grow and evolve. Sometimes if we're dead we might take over the role of guardian angel to help someone we love to grow and to evolve a little bit."

The reason increasing numbers of people say they have experienced encounters with guardian angels is because people are becoming more in tune with their spiritual selves and are starting to listen more. "We are an evolving species and it's just part of our own evolution as humans."

What message does he think angels are trying to send to us with the barrage of negative messages in the media about war, disease, economic crisis and more?

"That there's nothing to fear. It's all self-induced. If the world blows up it's no big deal. It might be the end of this world but it is not the end of our world. Maybe we will just reincarnate some place else, in another star system."

The most important message angels or spirit guides have for us is love. They hope we accept love and give love in return. If everyone did that, then there would be no such thing as war, greed or any of the negative things in this world that generate misery in people's lives.

"It would be a really cool place to live and we would be in a pretty good spot."

Are we going to get there? Dan says he is sure of it. "Oh yeah, I have faith in the human race."

So what happens when Dan encounters angels or spirit guides? He has a sense of knowing there's protection there. Often at his readings, deceased loved ones will show up because they want to let the living know they are near and are watching over them.

What he does is not so special, he says. We all have the ability to listen to that still small voice that exists in each one of us. And what is that still small voice? Some say it's the voice of God. Others say it's your own soul. Many believe it is the whisper of an angel or a spirit guide. It is important to pay attention.

Dan says angels or spirit guides can manifest physically but sometimes in the most innocuous of ways. Perhaps it will be a bird fluttering nearby or an old man sitting on a park bench smiling at you. What is important to remember is that the angels and guides can take on any form, so it is important not to ever discount any possibility, he explains.

"Everybody has the right to believe or not believe. If somebody thinks it's a bunch of hooey, good for them. If people want to listen, they will listen. If they don't, that's okay. The important thing is not to put your faith in someone else. Put your faith in yourself."

Annette Young Has Seen Angels Since Childhood

Reverend Annette Young is a minister and a hypnotherapist in Chicago. In her experience, people's interest in angels is growing because they are very discouraged with religion or the religion they were raised with.

"They grew up fearing God. People are saying, 'Wait a minute. That's not the God I want to worship.' So they start turning to other things. God has put the angels here to help us. People are hungry for something real and meaningful. People are always e-mailing me, asking whether it's okay to pray to God and ask for things that their whole life they were told were trivial, and that they shouldn't bother God with. I don't think anything is trivial enough not to ask for God's help. He put angels here to help people out in those situations."

Annette was baptized Catholic and was raised in a Methodist church, but now she's non-denominational. When she went to school to be ordained she studied all religions.

"All religions have a supreme being, whatever you call him. God, Allah, they still believe in one supreme God. I think it is the same God for everybody and angels exist in every religion."

The first of Annette's many encounters with angels occurred when she was three. An angel would appear just before someone in her family was about to die. She would see an angel carry them away. "I would get up in the morning and I would tell my mom, 'I saw an angel take Uncle Carl away.' Later that day, we would find out that he had died."

As a child, she would see gold spots when she was really upset. She would then get a metallic, sweet taste and smell in her mouth and nose. She knew it was her angels trying to make her feel better. When she saw them in physical form as they were taking loved ones' souls from the earth, they looked very much like what most people think of when they think of angels with flowing gowns and wings.

"But what I've come to realize is they will come to you in a manner that is most comfortable for you. Other people might see them a different way. That doesn't mean they are not seeing angels; it's just that is what is most comfortable to them."

In her adult life, Annette says angels come to her often. The first time she felt very strongly that angels were around her was when her husband was in the hospital. She believes she had an encounter with her guardian angel when she was walking home from the hospital late at night in a rough neighbourhood.

"All of a sudden, I could feel this big figure behind me and I could feel huge wings come up and wrap themselves around me. After I realized what was happening, I looked around at where I was. I was by a dark alley that wasn't a very good place for me to be in the middle of the night. I often wonder what was down that alley that I was being protected from."

How many angels do we have? Annette says it depends. Some people have more angels than others, but everyone is born with two. "The more advanced a person is, the more angels they have and you get more as you get older. I've known people to have up to nine."

She says she sees six angels around me, which tells her that I am doing what I am supposed to be doing in writing this book. "You are supposed to be enlightening people."

Are there also dark angels or evil angels? Yes, but Annette doesn't believe we can be affected by them unless we invite them into our lives. "You can welcome them in by playing with Ouija boards. Yes, there are negative entities out there. There is evil out there."

If everyone has angels around them, why do bad things such as painful deaths, murder, plane crashes and car accidents happen to some people? She explains everything, even trauma, happens for a reason. Angels don't view death as we do. The only time they intervene without being asked is to prevent someone from dying before their time. Angels will not do anything without being asked. God has given all of us free will and angels are not permitted to interfere with that unless specifically asked, such as in an emergency and the possibility of our dying before our time.

Angels do not want to be worshipped or have us pray to them, as we pray to our God. Annette doesn't pray to them, but she is in constant communication with them. "I don't say amen, like I do when I pray to God. I think you need to have something to show respect to God. Angels are intermediaries between Heaven and earth."

You can call out to any angel for assistance and one will come, but everybody has their own specific angels assigned to them. It's through communication and contact that you may discover what your angels are really skilled at.

There are many ways to communicate with your angels and no one way is better than the other. "It is very simple to contact your angels," Annette says. "All you need to do is call them. It doesn't have to be in words. All it needs to be is a thought, such as 'Angel, I need your help.' They always come. If you open yourself up to their energy, you will feel their presence."

Once you feel your angels, ask them questions. Let your mind go blank and allow your thoughts to flow, but don't try to make it happen.

With practice, she says, it won't take long for you to be able to know who your angels are by the way they feel. Each angel has a specific, unique energy, just like humans do.

"You may be able to feel their size or colour; you may be able to tell how they smell, or how they sound. Again, no one way is better than the other, it's how the angels choose to communicate with you and what's easiest for you to comprehend."

Angels are present in our lives at all times, with the exception of when we want and need our privacy. As we learn more about our angels and become more sensitive to their presence, we will be able to feel that presence.

If you take the time to think about your angels, their names will come to you. With time, you'll know which one is helping you and from there you'll know what your individual angels specialize in. This was the way Annette understood that her angel, named Magda, is very good at finding lost objects. "Every time I turned to my angels for assistance to help me find things, I came to realize it was Magda who always helped. Now, if I'm looking for something, I simply say 'Magda, can you help me find ...' It's not necessary, but it makes the communication a little more personal."

"Angels will often come to us in our dreams" says Annette, "because this is the easiest way to communicate with us. This is a time we are not dealing with everything else. If you keep a journal by your bed, try to write your dreams down before you get out of bed. Before you go to bed at night, it's a good idea to ask your angels to come to you in your dreams and then remind them to help you remember the dream so you'll be able to write it down. If you don't ask for this reminder, you may forget what they have said to you while you're asleep."

When you want to communicate with your angels during the day, go to a place where you feel most comfortable and where you will be able to relax, meditate and speak to them.

Annette says some people have turned angels into a commercialized gimmick, but that isn't what God or the angels want. The angels are here to guide us and to help us fulfill our mission and to do as we are supposed to do while we are on the earth. "They are here to point you in the right direction. They are not going to tell you how to get there but when you are on the right path, they will let you know. If we listen to them maybe we will do things differently and better."

"The angels want what God wants, and that is for everybody to just love one another. I pray every night. I know the wars aren't going to end but I pray that we can just agree to disagree with the different religions and everything. I believe in the Golden Rule. Do unto others as you would have them do unto you. Now, if you try to help somebody, they sue you. So what do you do?"

Members of Annette's family have been protected by angels. For example, after drinking at a bar her brother left and then returned to get his car keys. Before he could re-enter the bar, a man he'd never seen before asked him where he was going.

"Jimmy said, 'I'm going to get my keys.' And the man said 'No you're not.' Jimmy said 'Stop me.' And the guy punched him and knocked him down. He lost consciousness. When he got up the guy was gone. When he went into the bar to get his keys, he was told somebody already came into the bar and got them. He assumed this guy stole his keys. Somebody took Jimmy home. When he got home the keys were in his pocket. Nobody saw Jimmy get punched. They couldn't tell him who came in to get the keys. I think it was an angel stopping him because who knows what would have happened on his way home? He was drunk. There are some people who get drunk and forget, but he's not like that."

Angels are all around us. Because most of us are not sensitized to their presence we don't think about them or we dismiss them as not being real. But Annette says angels are all around us in our daily lives.

Medium Claire McGee Has Seen Spirits and Angels

Claire McGee's earliest memory of being able to see the spirits of the departed and occasionally angels was when she was nine years old. It happened when she was near a man who meant her harm.

"When I was nine years old I ended up, unbeknownst to me, in the presence of a pedophile. I heard a woman's voice say, 'Get out of here, dear. Get away.' So I did. I didn't hesitate. It was a very calm, very gentle voice. I now know it was Sarah, my spirit guide. It wasn't until much later in my life that I finally had the guts to ask my dad if there was a Sarah in the family. I used to get visitors that would wake me up at night and I'd talk to them in my room."

Claire asked her mother who the visitors might be and discovered they were her deceased ancestors. Her mother would show her old photographs and she was able to recognize each one.

Often she would be visited by someone she calls Grandpa Joe. She didn't know who he was but felt he was familiar and kind. He came at a time in her life when she questioned why she could see things others could not. She questioned everything that was happening and felt miserable. "He said, 'Hi Claire. You are going to be okay. It's a little hard right now but it's only temporary.'"

When she accepted her intuitive abilities, she was better able to cope with the spirits who came to her. She recalls the spirit of a woman appeared at her door, came across the bedroom and sat beside her on the bed. "I looked at my Grandpa Joe and said, 'Who's this?' He explained, 'That's your aunt.' I looked at her and looked back at Grandpa Joe and said, 'No, it's not, I know who my aunts are.' He replied, 'No dear, this is your Great-Aunt Mary.' I greeted her with, 'Hi Mary,' and she said, 'Hi Claire, it's nice to meet you.'"

Then another woman came out from the closet. She hovered off the floor and was wearing an old-fashioned royal blue dress, with one of her hands folded over the other on her stomach. She appeared to be very stern but Claire was unable to see her face because it appeared to be clouded. She didn't ask who the woman was. As the spirit of Grandpa Joe held his hand out she tried to touch it, but he pulled his hands away. "He said, 'Oh no, no dear. It's not your time yet. You have much to do.'"

She remembers thanking the woman in the blue dress before falling asleep on her bedroom floor. When her mother found her there in the morning, she asked what she was doing out of her bed. Claire recounted she'd been visited by the spirit of Aunt Mary. With that, her mother brought out some old photo albums and Claire pointed to a woman who looked like the spirit she'd spoken to in the night. Her mother told her it was indeed her Great-Aunt Mary.

"That was my mom's Aunt Mary, who died at the age of twenty-nine from a hole in her heart; she was gone well before my birth." Her mother had no idea who Grandpa Joe was, so Claire asked her father. He said it was his great-grandfather and everyone in the family used to call him Grandpa Joe.

Claire was also having out-of-body experiences with Grandpa Joe. She would travel with him to other realms when she was eighteen. She was being forced to make a very important decision at that point in her life, but no matter what decision she made, she felt she was in a no-win situation and very alone.

Grandpa Joe told her to close her eyes. "When I opened my eyes I was in a totally different place. We were walking down a sort of a street. I could see gardens and flowers that were more brilliant than you could possibly imagine. The flowers here pale in comparison. They had brilliant, beautiful colours. And the sky was extremely bright. Everything around me was extremely bright, almost like it glowed with florescent light, but it didn't hurt my eyes. I didn't see a sun but everything was bright; the sky was blue and there were no clouds. It was very tranquil. On my left there was a building. It reminded me of the ones you see in Rome with the big pillars – white stone with long steps. My Grandpa Joe looked at me and said, 'That's the library. We're not going in there today, dear.' We walked past it and came upon a pond around which people were sitting.

"Then Grandpa Joe pointed and said, 'Claire, look over there, dear.' He was pointing to my left. I looked and saw this magnificent, absolutely breathtaking waterfall. I couldn't hear the water landing but I could see it flowing down, and all these different flecks of lights were coming out of it. 'That's beautiful. I've never seen anything like it.'

"Grandpa Joe gestured for me to look to my right – it just got dark, very dark. It was cold and very damp. I felt this overwhelming sadness, overwhelming grief. It was awful. Then he said, 'Claire, the difference between Heaven and Hell is all in your mind. Which do you choose to see? Make your choice. You can accept and allow yourself and be okay with who you are or you can choose to punish yourself, but either way it's your choice. Close your eyes.' So I did. And when I woke up I was in my room."

Grandpa Joe would often take her on out-of-body experiences to what she has termed 'The Other Side.' "You don't go up. You don't go down. You just transform into a different form of energy. That's how I see it."

When Claire was twenty-five, the spirit whose face she couldn't see in earlier visions finally revealed her identity. She called herself Sarah and then allowed Claire to see her face. The spirit of Sarah said she was her guide. Claire discovered there was a Sarah on her father's side of the family who was her great-great grandmother and Grandpa Joe's wife. These are the spirits of people who were once alive, died and are now in another dimension watching over her.

"But I don't see them as angels. I see them as people like you and me."

Claire has had a couple of encounters with angels. In her opinion, the only difference between an angel and a human is a feeling that comes over her when she is in the presence of an angel. "It's almost like they are royalty but they're not – their composure, their status, their presence. It's a totally different feeling than when you are with a person."

The first time she saw an angel, she was twenty-one and involved in an out-of-body experience.

"I remember looking at my body. I was floating. It was very gentle. Then I heard a voice, a female, say, 'Close your eyes, dear' and I felt myself land as though on a bed of feathers. When I opened my eyes, I looked to my right and there were these people wearing royal blue robes. This woman said, 'Come with me,' and motioned that I should follow her. We were in some kind of building. The walls were massive, very tall. There was a marble floor. I don't think it was a castle but the extravagance of a building like that reminded me of one. As we were walking down the hallway, we went into an open area – there were three beings standing there. They weren't all the same height. The one in the centre was much larger than the other two. If I were to give them heights in our terms they would have been seven-feet-six to eight feet tall. They were all very tall, very large. I looked at this woman and asked, 'Are those angels?' 'Yes dear, they are angels. They are different than you and me,' she confirmed."

The woman told Claire she was to use her ability to see, hear and feel spiritual energy to help others. She would be taken to those who could teach her to utilize these skills. "Then I felt a surge of energy and I woke up."

Another incident occurred while she was taking an energy healing course called Reiki. Reiki.org explains it as a Japanese technique for stress reduction and relaxation administered by a laying on of hands that also promotes healing. It's based on the theory that a life force energy flows through us. The term is composed of two Japanese words – Rei which means "God's wisdom or the Higher Power" and Ki which is "life force energy. So Reiki is actually "spiritually guided life force energy."

Claire and the students were meditating. While they were coming out of the meditation, she looked to her left and saw a figure crouched on a wooden chair.

"He was balancing on the edge of the top of the chair. It was huge. So it was weightless, I guess. I had a difficult time determining whether it was male or female. It definitely had the form and shape of a person. I want to say 'he' because his energy was so strong and I know when I am talking to a female or a male in spirit. Men tend to have a bit of a stronger presence and I can sense that they are male versus female. Females tend to be softer. This particular presence was so strong and so powerful that I felt it was male, but I couldn't really tell because the face of this being was very soft. I will never forget that moment. It's just burned in my brain. It probably only lasted a second but it was such an impact and so strong and surreal it felt like time stopped for me. I didn't see wings or anything but I knew it wasn't human. I didn't feel threatened. I didn't feel anything other than awe. I was just in awe and asked 'Did anybody else see that?' And everyone said, 'See what?' So I was the only one who experienced this vision."

What was the angel doing there? She believes it was simply observing what was happening in the room.

Claire frequently encounters spirit guides whenever she does readings for clients who come to her to connect with their deceased loved ones. They're very different than angels. "There are guides and angels. We do go somewhere else [after we die]. We can still communicate with our loved ones after they have passed. There is still life after death."

In her experience, many people are searching for something beyond the material things in life. Spiritually starved souls want something that will fill a deep need within them. She isn't certain what the angels want us to know, because she's never asked that question. Over the past ten years, she has been able to tune into a higher energy that allows her to see, hear and feel those who have departed, but it's usually only when someone comes to her and wants to connect with loved ones who've passed.

"I have absolutely no control over what I get, or what happens or what information comes through. I have no idea. I don't use any tools – I don't read tarot cards or palms or tea leaves. I just sit here and I wait for whatever the message is."

Claire also has an opinion on darker or negative energies – they aren't necessarily evil, but may be spirits of the deceased who are angry about something that happened to them during their lives. "Sometimes they are misunderstood and perceived as negative, when in fact they are only trying to tell you their story. People in spirit communicate telepathically and through the same form of energy. When they are trying to tell somebody they are sad or angry, the best way for them to do that is to make you feel their sadness or anger. But because you feel their emotions internally, it may feel as though they are forcing their negative energy on you. They are just trying to get it across that they are [sad or angry] and looking for help." She has worked to help these spirits resolve issues so that they can cross over to the other side.

"The ones that I deal with more often than not are the ones that have already crossed."

Her clients come to her because one of their loved ones wants to talk to them. When she prepares for a reading she goes into a semi-meditative state so she is completely relaxed. "We work on different vibration frequencies. Everything is made of energy. I basically communicate with energy. Most people vibrate at a low energy. Somebody who's a medium or a psychic or who has a tendency to be more sensitive is vibrating on a little higher level. When someone has died their vibration frequencies are much higher than ours. It's denser here than it is there. To get yourself into a state where you can raise your vibrations enough to match theirs, is actually when you're sleeping, going to sleep, just waking up, or in a meditative state. When you watch people sleep, they are breathing from their stomachs, not from their chests. Their circulation calms down, their blood flows more slowly, their heart rates decrease. It's very rhythmic and allows your vibrations to naturally start rising – at that point it's easier for them [angels, spirit guides and deceased loved ones] to communicate with you."

Claire has the ability to tune into people who have passed over while other people have the ability to see, hear and feel angels. Why is this? It is something she wonders about. Recently, she spoke about this with a woman who sees both people who have passed on and the spirit guides of the living.

"She told me, 'Claire, how many doctors are there in the world? Are they all doing the same type of work?' You will find the majority of people who can do this are very sensitive people from an energetic standpoint but also from a personal standpoint. They are naturally very sensitive people."

Claire, who now lives in Halifax, Nova Scotia, has taught more than 150 people how to improve their sensitive abilities. "We all have clairsentient, clairvoyant and clairaudient abilities." She has proven to others they can do it through her five-week program. "Getting the understanding of what it's all about and the way it works with you and identifying your intuitive abilities takes five weeks. Learning to develop it and utilize it takes a lifetime."

Many people she has taught have told her they have developed communication with spirits who have passed, and angels too. "That, to me, is the most gratifying feeling in the world. I have a really hard time when I hear people say I am special and I have a gift and they try to put me on a pedestal. I say to them, 'Don't put me on a pedestal, honey, because I'll fall right off it if you do.' I am no different than anybody else. The only difference between me and anybody else is that I have taken the time to understand it. I have taken the time to research symbols and the way angels, spirit guides and the deceased communicate with us."

When someone has passed and they want to tell her how they passed, she feels it in her body. For example, if someone has died as the result of a heart attack, she will feel a crushing pain in her chest for a second. If a spirit is trying to express love for someone who is still living, she will feel that emotion. Claire is a clairvoyant, Reiki master and an ordained Spiritual Minister of Metaphysics. She can perform marriages and other ceremonies such as baptisms and funerals, depending on provincial and state regulations.

Claire isn't the only member of her family to have experienced an angel encounter. Her mother believes a guardian angel protected her from a head-on car crash while she was driving from St. Stephen, New Brunswick, to Saint John on Highway 1. She was driving with the car's cruise control on at a speed of 120 kilometres per hour. When she crested a hill there was a car attempting to move out into traffic.

"The car was blocking my mom's lane. As she came over the hill the car was right there, so she didn't have time to brake or to react. The first thing she thought was, 'Oh my God. I'm going to die!' and she closed her eyes and took her hands off the wheel. When she opened her eyes, she was on the other side of the car. Cars were still going past and she was still in cruise control. Highway 1 has only two lanes. On the right, there was a marsh, on the left she would have had a head-on collision because there was traffic coming from the opposite direction, but for some reason when she looked in the rear view mirror the car was still there. So she got on the other side of the vehicle, still in cruise control, without hitting or veering off the road, with everything still in its place, and she had no idea how she got there. The only thing she can think of is that something lifted the car up. She is sure it was her guardian angel."

3

People Who Have Seen,
Heard and Felt Angels and Spirits

Patty Donovan's Guardian Angel
Helped Carry Her Daughter to Heaven

Angels have always been a part of Patty Donovan's life but she had no idea how important they would become. As a young child she recognized them and never felt alone. Now, there is an added dimension.

"I see them now. Yes, absolutely. I am a Reiki master and a holistic health care practitioner; I use spirit guides and angels in healing others. In meditation, I see them very clearly. They come in all variety of forms, some even as old women. Some, very clearly, are winged. They change forms sometimes. I am open to all forms, so they come as they are. Sometimes I sense them, but I know they are there. I know they are here with me now."

Patty hears angels very clearly in her times of meditation. This was especially helpful after her fifteen-year-old daughter, Mary, died in November 2006. Mary had developed a rare disease called severe aplastic anemia, so she was sent to the Sick Kids Hospital in Toronto for a bone marrow transplant. She died thirty days later as a result of acute respiratory distress. Patty takes comfort in knowing her daughter is still with her in spirit. She says Mary wasn't afraid to die.

"Mary was so calm and so peaceful through this whole process. Even when she was having trouble breathing, she was not scared. She was absolutely peaceful. When she had to be put on a respirator she was awake and we were talking with the doctor. She said, 'I don't want to feel this anymore, so you can do whatever you need to do, but I want to be asleep through it.' She shook the doctor's hand and he made that promise to her, that she wouldn't feel pain anymore. He kept her in a drug-induced coma for the next three weeks until she died."

Patty, a drummer who sings in Mi'kmaq and Maliseet, has performed healing work with crystals and sweet grass in smudging ceremonies for many years. Her guides taught her how to help souls cross over. When her daughter's time of death was very near, she asked everyone to give them time together. For the next two hours she listened to her spirit guides, who told her what she needed to do to help her daughter make the transition from this world to the next.

"I made sweet grass water. I closed my eyes and spirit told me what I had to do, what crystals I had to use, what I had to say, what songs I had to sing. I smudged Mary with sweet grass and put the crystals around her. I had my eagle feather with me and used the wooden box I keep it in as a drum while I sang. I sang the eagle song, which is one of my favourites; it is a series of prayers going off to the Creator. I watched the room fill up. It absolutely filled up with spirit energy. I could see little vortexes everywhere, little spirals. The room brightened. What happened was out of her centre, almost from her belly button, a little purple spiral came out and it got bigger and bigger. I drummed and the harder I drummed and chanted the bigger it got, until it filled the room. I could barely move and I couldn't breathe, the room was so compressed. Then at the last minute, just as I thought my lungs would break, her body arched and the cord let go. Her body arched up and the room seemed for one second like I was floating in Heaven – then it left. That was her leaving. Then I was at peace. Everything was at peace. They kept her on life support for a few more days so her siblings could say goodbye."

Patty called her sister and asked her to tell their family Mary was on life support and soon the machines would be turned off.

"She said, 'Patty, the strangest thing happened Tuesday evening. I swear to God I saw Mary and I heard her. I came out into the hall and I saw her.'" She told Patty that Mary smiled at her before she walked into all three of her cousins' bedrooms to say goodbye. Friends of Mary's saw her too. She made herself seen so she could say goodbye to people she loved.

Now, whenever Patty works with clients in holistic treatments, they tell her they see a teenage girl in the room. She doesn't tell them her daughter died. The fact that others see her is soothing.

She has a very special photo Mary took through the window of the airplane on her way to Toronto. It appeared to be an angelic form to Patty when she looked at it. She was even more convinced when she saw the photo after it was digitally enhanced. The angel form was cut out of the picture then it was enlarged. All of the dark areas were made even darker and the image was returned to its original size. It looks very much like an angel. Patty believes the angel in the photo was the one who went with her on that trip to Toronto and remained at the Sick Kids Hospital until it was time to take Mary's soul to Heaven.

The photo, she says, supports her belief that we all have angels and guides. Mary may no longer be here in body but the family knows she is with them in spirit.

Since Mary has passed, Patty says she communicates with her. It didn't happen right away. For the first six months, she was too angry and heartbroken about her daughter's death, and she was rather scared too. Then she went to Toronto to study holistic health practices. Part of her training involved spending time with a psychotherapist who specializes in visualization, imagery and guided meditations. In one of those guided meditations Patty saw a cave and her daughter was there.

"Mary was floating in this beautiful pool in a crystal cave and I got down into the water with her and we had this wonderful conversation. She was saying she was happy where she was, and I had to let her go and I couldn't hang on to her. She said, 'You can come to the crystal cave any time you want. The energy is always here. There will be a time when we will all be back together again, but not in this form.'"

Angels, Patty says, want us to know there is something bigger and better beyond life's suffering, and that we can rise above everything, even in the human form, to walk in joy. If we are open to it, the angels will guide us to that joy so we can live happily in this life. She has every reason to be an angry, bitter, heartbroken mother, but she isn't. She was able to move forward and to overcome fear. She came to understand that her grief, sadness and anger were attempts to hang on to Mary. "I realized it was an illusion and I knew if I could let go of that illusion, I would have her even more."

She has learned that Mary never really belonged to her. Instead she has come to understand that Mary was a precious gift, given to her for a brief time to teach her many life lessons. "When I look back on her life, she was so amazing and a work of joy always. She'd be coughing and saying to the nurse 'How are your children this week?' She was so empathetic and kind always. She came here, and I acknowledge her sacrifice, to teach me. I think we do make spiritual contacts with one another before we come here. From Mary, I learned about sacrifice, I learned about joy, how to be a really good person and how to care about others."

Patty knows part of her life's path is to help other grieving parents. So many people live in fear and anxiety, but this woman is absolutely fearless and most of all she isn't afraid of death. "The only thing I ever feared was the safety of my children and now that I have gone through this experience I don't even have that fear."

She admits she can get anxious over things, such as making sure her bills are paid, but it isn't long before she is reminded she is not in charge of anything in her life and that she will be looked after in all things. The moment she starts to worry about anything she will receive a message from the angels to let go. "The more I let go, the more control I have over everything."

She gets messages from angels in a variety of ways. Sometimes she will overhear a conversation between two strangers and there will be a message for her in what they are saying. Angels, she says, will speak to us through other people, through animals, through nature, if we are open to hear them. When she treats people holistically, her clients tell her they feel more than just her hands on them. They feel the healing hands of the angels. Reiki practitioners are open to this for a reason.

"It's because we have chosen to open that channel and invited God, the universe, the angels and spirit guides to dance with us and through us. The one downside of it is that I become a target for darkness, negative energetic blocks. I don't believe for one minute that we have bad spirits going around hurting people. What I do see and feel and know is that negative energy creates energy blocks. What I see from incarcerated women coming out of jail is that they have a dark energy about them, and they just suck the light out of other people who are not protected well enough."

For much of her career she has worked with women in correctional facilities and women who were victims of abuse. For a while, she ran a women's homeless shelter. Many of the women there were drawn to the light within her.

Patty says talk about Armageddon, or the world ending, is nonsense. "I believe there are going to be some changes and that frightened people are going to stay frightened. The rate that we are consuming and creating garbage and using energy is not sustainable. I believe that a shift is coming – it's already happening. My heart tells me that Mother Nature is rearing up and she is saying 'Love me. Do not rape me any more.' I really see it as a green shift to more sustainable lifestyles and sustainable communities. I have been part of the environmental movement for twenty years and it's a dream come true to see all of these people talking about organics. It's already begun. What nature tells you is to respect one another."

The angels want to remind people that we are not very good at respecting the earth and one another, and what they really want is for everyone to treat each other with love, kindness and respect.

Patty and her daughter studied Buddhism for about a year before Mary got sick. She describes her faith as a plentiful buffet where she takes a little bit from all religions. "My favourite line from the movie *Auntie Mame* is 'Life is a banquet and some poor suckers are starving to death.'"

And this, Patty says, is the case with many people in their spiritual lives. They are spiritually starved because they have not fed themselves with everything that's available in the spirit world, including angels. She has committed herself to a life that glorifies God with everything she says and does. The message she has received is that there is no reason to fear, that we can walk in the light, feel powerful and that anything is possible. The act of surrender is very difficult for most people. To let go and to trust is a very difficult thing for many. But when you surrender you gain more control, Patty has discovered. Once she learned to let go, she became very powerful.

"In the grand scheme of things I, physical Patty, am nothing. I am an open channel of universal love. I realize my insignificance and that is so freeing because I don't have to take responsibility for anything except what comes and goes out of me. The premise is flow. I think my life's lesson, my whole spiritual journey, has been to learn how to flow – to stop trying to impose my will. The world will unfold as it is supposed to, regardless of what I want or think I need. When you stop placing judgment on things and people, everything falls into place joyfully."

She calls on angels every moment of every day, even in her dreams, to help her in her life and work. She recalls a time when she was working with women in shelters and corrections – she called on the angels to help her with a particular client.

"She had a long history of violence. From the moment I met her, I said there is one button I have to push in order for her to step beyond that anger and that abuse. Before I went to bed one night I planted that in my mind. I needed to know what that button was so she could cross into the light. I woke up and I had a plan. I went to group that night and I pushed that button and she exploded. She said, 'You're fucking lucky I love you,' and she stormed out. It was a couple of days before she came back and she said, 'I need to talk to you right away. How did you know to say that to me? How did you know that? Are you in my head? Do you have magical powers?' And I said, 'No, I prayed about it and Creator told me.' She believed me. She was going to church so she was open to me saying that. I said, 'You know the universe wants you to find your joy, to find your bliss.' I trust implicitly the information I download from the universe. I trust that more than my humanness because it is never wrong. I may not always like it, but it is never wrong."

If it weren't for her connection to angels and her faith in the Creator Patty says she likely would have died from a drug overdose or alcohol poisoning years ago. As the mother of a child who's died, she says if it were not for the angels and Creator, and what she knows to be true, she likely would have taken her own life out of pure grief.

"That was a constant thought of mine. I thought it would be easier if I was dead because my heart was broken. I felt a pain I can't even describe, indescribable pain. Of course, it's psychological pain. Both of my parents that I adored have passed away and my grandmother. I have lost friends. I have lost pets. I have won and lost more than most people in a lifetime, but nothing prepares you for, or even compares to, the depth of the pain you feel when it's your child. The moment I would think it would be easier for me to die, somebody would ring my door, call me on the phone, show up at my house and love me; total strangers paid my bills, my mortgage, service clubs gave us money."

And all of those people were like angels coming to her in her time of great need. Patty says all of us have the opportunity to heal ourselves and others. All of us have the ability to connect with our higher power. Some might believe you have to have special gifts to do this, but she says this isn't so. All it takes is an open heart and mind. We all have the ability to talk to, hear from, and feel the presence of angels, as long as we are willing to open ourselves up to it. Reiki, in her opinion, can help with this, because it allows you to become attuned to the energy of angels and spirit. "Whether you want them to or not, the guides come and they do that when you allow that energy to come into you. It's a huge shift."

Alice Finnamore Explains Angel Activities

Therapist and author Alice Finnamore of Fredericton, New Brunswick, believes in angels and she thinks they, and the spirits of our deceased loved ones, come to us in our dreams. Even in nightmares, what we perceive to be something frightening can actually be messengers and allies that come with information and gifts for us but we don't recognize them as such. "Until we face that scariness, we are not going to get that message and we will keep having those repetitive scary dreams."

Raised in a Baptist home, Alice has always viewed angels as Divine beings. They were part of her religious teaching from her earliest memories and she always felt she had a guardian angel. Her maternal grandmother told her that after she lost children to premature death angels came to bring comfort.

"She had a visit from what she called an angel each time one of her children was dying. She lost several children. Most of them were infants. When one of her adult children was ill an angel came to warn her that her daughter needed help. She urged her husband to find her. She said to my grandfather, 'Evelyn is sick. You've got to go to her.' It was in the middle of the night and she knew. So she sent my grandfather to find her and sure enough she was very sick. I don't know whether it was a dream of an angel coming or whether she had a waking experience."

Alice, who has a keen interest in dreams, believes dreams are a communication tool angels and the spirits of our deceased loved ones use them to deliver messages to us. This is far more acceptable to most people than having angels and the dead appear to us during our waking hours. "Angels don't necessarily show up with wings and looking like an angel. You may not know you're being visited by angels. Even the Bible says that sometimes we entertain angels unaware."

She may have an angel that helps her with her daily scheduling. "It's almost invariable that I have an opening in my calendar and I don't know why that day isn't filled up with clients. The day will come and it will be somebody's funeral or something I have to attend to that otherwise I would have to reschedule clients for. I very rarely have to reschedule clients because it is already done for me."

She typically doesn't call upon the angels to help her with things in her life because she speaks directly with God about whatever is on her mind, but for many people it may be less intimidating to speak to angels than directly to the Creator.

In her book *The Glory of Being: A Biblical Journey into Abundance*, Alice talks about the purpose of angels. Originally, their purpose was to reflect God's glory. From her research for this book, through her study of the Bible, and from her knowledge of other people's experiences with the Divine, she believes angels are real, as are the spirits of our loved ones who keep watch over us after they die. "It says to me there's go to be something to that. That's why I don't discount any of these stories."

In Alice's experience, after our loved ones die, their spirits will often come to spend time with us in our dreams. When we die and our souls leave our bodies, we do not cease to exist. In spirit, we exist in another dimension. She compares it to television channels. Just because we switch channels doesn't mean the one we were watching previously no longer exists. "The way I think of ourselves is that we are spirits in bodies. When we are in the body we have to slow ourselves down, change our vibration to be able to exist in the physical form. When we are released from the body we're able to speed up again, in other words, get on a different vibratory level."

If we had a remote control we could press that would switch us from one vibration level to another, we would be able to see into the world of spirit. This, she explains, is what happens when we dream. Our energy vibration rises and therefore we can connect, or switch, to that other television channel. When we are in a dream state we are able to achieve a higher level of energy vibration, making it possible for us to connect with the other dimension where angels and the spirits of our loved ones exist.

We all have abilities we either aren't willing to practise or aren't aware of. Some people are better able to hear a voice, see things or feel the spiritual realm than others. Alice listens to the internal voice within her, which she trusts to be the voice of God.

In her opinion there is a definite difference between angels and the spirits of loved ones who watch over us. Once someone dies they don't become an angel. There is also a difference between being an angel and doing the work of an angel. "The work is being a messenger. Anybody can be a messenger. When you are dealing with spirits you have to realize they are not necessarily perfect because they are dead. You've got to be careful about what you are hearing and what you are connecting with."

Although she has no proof that the spirits of our loved ones sometimes watch over us, she believes this to be true from her own experience. She had a dream about her mother who had passed. In the dream her mother returned to tell her she was fine and was experiencing lots of wonderful things.

"Mom told us she was ready to go on a journey. In my dream she showed my sisters and me a little gadget that reminded me of a university calendar. It had different courses or activities that you could do and each course had a button you could push to go to that course. She showed us the button that allowed her to come and be with us. She showed us she was going to push another button and she was going to go on to the next thing she wanted to do. So she did and when she pushed the button she floated up off the ground a couple of feet and floated backwards across the field and away. That told me my mother is off doing all sorts of interesting things and that she can make a choice to come and hang out with us when she wants to."

Spirit Guides Visited Cindy Brewer's Mother As She Died

In December 1999, Cindy Brewer's mother was dying of cancer. Cindy, a registered nurse, decided she needed to be with her mother in the weeks and months that remained. A single mother with young children, she took a leave of absence from her job, packed up what they would need and moved her family into her mother's home, where they would remain until her mother's passing. With the help of home-care nurses, she helped care for her mother in the final days of her life. "We had an extremely close relationship before she got sick, but it intensified as she got sicker."

Every night she would bring a cot into her mother's bedroom so she could sleep beside her. It was a time of love, tenderness and connection. One night, two weeks before she passed away, Cindy recalls her mother was alert and knew what was happening. "She said, 'Cindy, look up in the corner. Do you see them?' I said, 'What do you see, Mom?' And she replied, 'There's three beautiful faces smiling at me.'"

Cindy thought her mother was hallucinating because of her pain medication. But when she thought about the dosage and when it was last taken, there wasn't a chance she could be seeing things because of the drugs. The woman's face, normally twisted in pain, was relaxed. She was at ease and happy. "She was smiling up at that corner of the bedroom. I asked her to describe them and she said, 'I can't really see them. But I know they are faces and they are smiling at me. Don't you feel the heat?' Then Mom went off to sleep. All night that corner glowed."

The home was in the middle of cottage country, where there were no streetlights. The only illumination in the room was a night light but the glow in the corner was something else entirely. Every night, Cindy looked at that corner of the room where there was a definite glow. At the time, she had no idea what it was. Now, looking back, she believes it was either angels or the spirits of her mother's loved ones who'd come to help her make the transition from earth to Heaven. Her mother told her and the rest of the family that the entities were waiting to help take her "home." But her mother wasn't ready to cross over until she had the blessing of her husband, children and grandkids. When her mother was close to death, Cindy recalls, she was completely at ease with what was to come.

The doctors had given her mother nine months to live, and told her she wouldn't see Christmas. But this determined woman told them she would spend the holiday with her family. Sure enough, she did.

"Mom was waiting for us to give her permission to pass away. She saw those faces frequently over a three-week period. She kept saying, 'They're waiting for me.' She wanted to go but would not leave until my father gave her permission to go because she wanted to make sure he would be okay.

"On December 27 she rallied out of a coma and was just as bright as a button. The whole family was there. She called every grandchild into her room, talked to them and told them something from her heart. She called my brother and me in separately and spoke to us. Then she called my dad in. Finally, she called us all in to surround her bed and said, 'Please, let me go.' My dad just broke right down and he said, 'I can't' and he left the room.

"On the 29th my brother, my dad and I were all standing around her bed as she was coming in and out of consciousness. My dad looked at her and he said, 'We love you. It's time to go.' He held her hand and she looked at me and I said, 'Mom, we love you. It's time to go.' She looked at my brother and he said the same thing. Within fifteen minutes she was gone. She knew she was loved. She knew she had permission from her family to leave this world and that there were others waiting to help her make the journey from this world to the other dimension."

In 2006 Cindy had many encounters that she believes were angelic. She asked her oldest son to clean the basement because she had invited friends for a visit. The job wasn't up to her standards so she decided to redo it. First, she went to the basement's kitchenette where she scrubbed the floor. "I turned around and, honest to goodness, there were ten brand new shiny pennies on the floor. I thought, 'Where did those come from? I just washed the floor.'" She picked up the pennies, then went on to vacuum the living room floor and furniture. "I turned around and the whole carpet was covered with brand new shiny pennies."

Next, she went into her son's bedroom to change the bed linen. When she went to place the quilt on the bed she noticed the entire bed was covered with pennies. She picked them up and put them in her pocket along with the others she had gathered from the kitchen and living room floors. Angel reader Pam Nadeau told her these were pennies from heaven. "She said sometimes when angels want to get your attention they kind of hit you with a two-by-four."

In her oldest son's bedroom there was an inexplicably cold area that puzzled her. When she spoke to her younger son about it he told he knew exactly what it was.

"He said, 'Haven't you felt that energy downstairs before? I feel it all the time. There's someone in the corner of Gordon's room. He wants to tell Gordon something, but Gordon won't listen."

Her youngest son, she says, is very intuitive with the ability to hear and see the spirits of the dead and communicate with the angelic realm. At that time, he wrote a message to his brother in a different handwriting than his own, instructing him to cut himself off from friends who were experimenting with drugs; otherwise he would get into trouble with the law. Once her older son read the note and changed his group of friends the cold, heavy feeling in his bedroom disappeared. "It left enough of an impact on him that he changed his entire peer group, which in turn changed his life."

In May 2009 when Cindy remarried, the ceremony and reception were held at a local curling club. She wanted to make sure there was nothing but positive energy in the space, so the night before, she went there and prayed. "I called all the angels into the room and said, 'Angels, fill every corner of this room' and I called Archangel Michael to take all the negative energy from the room. I gave them the time that I wanted them there and said, 'Just shine on us.' Every digital picture given to us is filled with angel orbs. I couldn't believe it. There were people attending the wedding who are very intuitive, and they said the energy felt warm, comforting and like a fuzzy hug."

Cindy talks to her angels daily. She often mediates and when she closes her eyes angels appear in her mind's eye. "I just see the outline of what they are wearing. I can see their hair. I can see what's on their feet, if they are carrying anything. But I cannot see faces. I don't hear words but I know what they are saying to me. It just comes to me. If I have a problem I will often ask for help. They will answer a question or give me an idea of which way to go."

When she gives Reiki treatments, she cleanses the space with sage, says a prayer and asks angels to come into the space to help her. She recalls a particular treatment with one man who had been experiencing back pain.

"I said, 'I am going to tell you even before we start, sometimes I get these images in my head and I hear things and I have to tell you what comes to me because it is usually a message for you.' I started to cry. I felt overwhelming pain and grief. I was really listening and tuning into why I was feeling like this. I said, 'You're suffering right now with grief.' And then he started to cry. I said, 'She wants you to go upstairs into your bedroom and on the bureau where you keep all of your newspapers, underneath all these newspapers is a little box. It's hand-painted with little flowers on the top and engraved with initials. Inside there is something special and it's something she wants you to have."

He came back the next day. He asked, "Is this what you saw?" It was indeed a little handmade wooden box, painted with tiny flowers. His and his wife's initials with their wedding date were engraved on the top. Inside was a pewter heart with her name, his name and their wedding date. "His wife had passed away one month before from breast cancer. She wanted him to have that memory of her."

When Cindy receives such information, she feels it's angels telling her things she needs to know. She doesn't believe she is intuitive all the time, but when she really concentrates, she receives information. "That shocked me when he brought that box because it was exactly what I saw. He came to me almost every week for about six weeks afterwards and his back pain was the result of the stress of losing his wife."

Knowing she is always surrounded by angels is comforting, calming and soothing to Cindy. She knows we are not alone in this world and that we are here for a purpose. Humans are spiritual beings here on earth to have experiences. The angels are here to help us as we travel on our journey. "If we are supposed to take a left turn and we are going right, well, maybe they will try to guide us more to the left."

Prior to becoming more spiritual she was a single mother, a nurse, and taking care of two ill parents. She had so much responsibility, sometimes she felt as though she was going in circles. Now she has slowed her life down and takes the time to meditate and commune with her angels. She trusts her intuition more than she trusts her logical thoughts. Cindy believes everyone needs a sense of spirituality and the strength that comes from it, because of all of the fear and uncertainty in the world.

"Every morning I wake up and say, 'God, please shine your love and light into me and may the light shine through me.' I will stop and talk to homeless people on the street and give them a smile. It could be a test for us too. My life is so much richer now that I have this belief in angels and archangels. It's more of a feeling, and I can't put words to the feeling. I think people are becoming more aware that there is something out there."

Angels Kept Mary F. From Committing Suicide

Mary F. was only a few years old when she began having conversations with angels. Her parents would often find her sleeping under her bed in the morning. When they asked her why, she told them she felt safer sleeping on the floor. The angels always reassured her she was safe and that she shouldn't worry about anything. "That's where I could converse with them. That was my safe place. I didn't hear them but I would see them. For me they looked like human beings. Like the people who were familiar to me."

Once she started school her angels came to her less. She thinks it was because she shut herself down spiritually. She was raised in the Roman Catholic Church where angels were acknowledged but not a part of daily life.

When she was nine, she went through a severe trauma – a young man molested her then told her not to tell anyone. "I confided in the angels. I remembered the feeling of protection they brought to me when I was a young child and so I knew I would be safe. I told them what happened and how I felt. I never told my parents anything, but I confided in the angels. It gave me a feeling of peace and serenity. The angels took care of it. It was almost like I forgot about it."

She had no more encounters with her angels until she went to university, where she lived in an apartment off campus. She knew the angels were around and could feel them but she didn't speak to them again until she was twenty-two and living in Fredericton. "I was raped. Once again I asked for guidance from the angels. I told them to just take it from me because the burden was too hard. I didn't want anybody to be involved. After I told the angels what happened and asked them to take the burden away, I felt a peace." Like the molestation from her childhood, the memory of the rape was erased from her mind and she was able to move on.

In her early thirties, she became ill and frequently felt dizzy. Once, when driving on a very busy road, she lost her vision. She was in a great deal of pain. It was like a lightning storm in her head. Somehow, when her vision returned, her car was on the side of the road. She has no idea how she managed to get her vehicle there without having a collision but she believes angels guided her. "I feel like they nudged me to the side of the road. I felt a sense of peace. I didn't panic when I lost my vision."

She was very dizzy and unable to drive. She got out and crawled on her hands and knees. A stranger stopped to ask if he could help. She told him she needed to be driven home. She didn't know him but somehow she felt no fear. "For me, he was an angel because he came and rescued me. I never saw that person again. My personal feeling is the angels sent somebody to help me."

Mary underwent many tests and misdiagnoses, but after twelve years she learned she suffered from cluster migraines. Shortly after her grandfather died in 1998, she started to have dreams of the molestation and rape. Then she discovered she was expecting her second baby. She had a sense there was something wrong with the child growing inside her body. When she was six months pregnant, she and her husband planned a trip to Digby to celebrate their wedding anniversary. She had experienced some cramps but thought she would be fine to make the trip. While she was there she saw a church and felt drawn to it. She felt a strong need to go inside and pray. She met a priest who knew many of her family. He asked if he could pray for her children. When he touched her, she had a real sense that the baby she was carrying wasn't going to be with her long. "I knew she wasn't supposed to be with me. Two days later I lost her."

Once again she called on her angels for help. They gave her comfort and allowed her to get through this devastating time. Immediately afterwards, she had more dreams of the sexual assaults she's endured. By now her son had started school and an aunt she was very close to passed away. It was too much for her to bear. The angels allowed her to feel these emotions, because it was time for her to deal with the pain she had buried for so many years.

"It was too much on me. I didn't feel I could bother my family with all of this. I was going to end it all. I was going to commit suicide. I had a plan. I was going to drive my car into the Mactaquac Dam head pond." While parked in her car she placed her foot on the accelerator and then put the car into drive. She thought it would take searchers a long time to find her body. Then she heard a very clear voice telling her what she needed to do at that moment. "It said, 'We are not done with you yet. Please go home and tell your husband what you are feeling.'"

She was shut down emotionally, in a dissociated state, and the voice brought her back to reality. She turned the car around and drove home. When she walked through the door she collapsed on the floor and told her husband she needed help. When she received treatment for clinical depression, Mary met a psychologist who helped her to relive everything that caused so much pain in her life.

"I forgave the person who molested me. I didn't forgive the rapist, but I forgave myself, which was a big thing because I was still blaming myself for the incident. [The psychologist put me into a meditative state] and I saw my daughter and she was beautiful. She was absolutely gorgeous. She was a baby. She was my little girl. I knew she was where she was supposed to be. I named her Isabelle. She's my angel. I know she is always with me and she is in the right place."

Mary had her first a vision of an angel in 2003 when she worked at a school in New Brunswick. She walked into a classroom to deliver a message to the teacher. "To the right of me I saw this huge wing. It took over the whole wall of the classroom. I looked again and it was still there. I talked to the teacher, gave her the message, turned back around and it was still there. I walked out of the classroom in a daze. It took my breath away."

A couple of weeks later she learned the fathers of two of the boys in that classroom had just been diagnosed with cancer. For Mary, it was a sign the angels were there to protect the boys. She prays often and speaks to her angels, asking them to send comfort and healing to people. "Ninety percent of the time my prayers are answered. I have a personal relationship with God and I always have. I truly believe that people are recognizing prayers are powerful and when you pray miracles will happen."

She speaks to her angels every day and asks them to protect her family and friends. She has a sense of angels around her constantly. Sometimes while she is driving, she zones out and cannot recall how she has gotten from point A to point B. "For me, it is the angels taking over the wheel. Sometimes they will send you something like a bird crashing into your windshield to wake you up."

She feels closely connected to Archangels Michael, Gabriel, and Raphael as well as the Virgin Mary. As Michael is the warrior angel, she calls upon him to protect her family. Gabriel is the messenger angel whom she asks to bring messages to her and her loved ones when they need them. Raphael is the healing angel and she calls on him when someone she knows is ill and needs help to heal their body. The Virgin Mary is all about unconditional love, and she turns to Mother Mary often.

Mary learned Reiki over the past four years but doesn't believe this energy healing brought her any closer to angels, because they were always a part of her life since her childhood. "For me, Reiki is something that helped me to heal from my depression. If more and more people experienced Reiki in their lives, there would be less depression and they would be happier."

Angels are thrilled when people seek them out and want to communicate with them, because so many people have spiritually shut down. But when people gather together for the good of everyone, angels come by the hundreds and thousands and they are happy. "Miracles happen every day. The fact that we are alive is a miracle, that we are healthy. The fact that we have families that love us is in itself a miracle."

Rachel Quigg Learned About Angels Through Numbers

Angels exist in Rachel Quigg's life. She speaks to them frequently and calls upon them for daily help and guidance. Angels started to manifest in her life in 2005 when she was in Canmore, Alberta, visiting a friend.

"She pointed to the time and it said 1:11. She said, 'Do you know what that means? That's the angels speaking to you.' When you see this number, you really need to watch your thoughts because you are creating what you are thinking about."

It piqued her curiosity. She researched angel numbers and their meanings then began to notice triple digit numbers on digital clocks and license plates. She gathered a library of books and angel oracle cards, which she describes as a divination tool that helps her to receive messages of guidance from angels and ascended masters, great spiritual teachers such as Jesus, Buddha, Krishna, and Quan Ying.

She now reads angel oracle cards for others, as this is one of the many ways angels try to make contact and communicate with us. All of the messages are positive, encouraging and filled with love and light.

When she came to the realization that angels communicate through numbers, she started to see these numbers frequently. So much so that she looked for numeric angel communication almost obsessively for several years. Now these numeric messages appear naturally to her, and she is relaxed in knowing that the angels are present and speaking to her in this way. *Angel Numbers* by Dr. Doreen Virtue helped to clarify the meaning of the numbers she was encountering.

The number is a message from angels that we are to have trust and faith that the seeds of whatever it is we have planted as intentions for our lives will grow. For example, the number 333 is a sign that you are very close and connected to the ascended masters, who are present in your life and want to help you.

Rachel also uses a pendulum as a divination tool. It is a string or a chain with a weighted object at the end that helps her to measure energy and tap into speaking with angels, her subconscious and her spirit guides. "I used the pendulum for a long time before I started getting the angel numbers." Now she uses the pendulum in conjunction with oracle cards and the *Angel Numbers* book, in what she calls the 2000 Plus Library, to help her when she does angel readings.

In 2007 Rachel was in Victoria, British Columbia, when she had her first auditory experience with angels. She was in great emotional despair as her boyfriend had told her he wanted to end their relationship. "I was hanging on by a string."

She left their apartment and got into her car but had no idea where she was going. With tears streaming down her face, she drove along a Pacific coastal road. "I had the feeling that I wanted to give up. That my life was over because I was no longer with this guy." A part of her knew she shouldn't be driving when she was so upset because she was not in control of her emotions, but another part of her was determined to keep driving on this very crooked road.

"I had no idea where it led and I didn't care. I just wanted to kill myself. I remember praying to the angels. I said, 'Angels, please get me out of this.' Not even five seconds later I heard a voice that said, 'Rachel, pull over.' It was very strong and very authoritative and I will never forget those words. That's all it kept repeating: 'Rachel, pull over.'"

The voice was so loud it was as if someone was in the car with her. It felt as though someone grabbed the wheel and turned the car into a parking area where her car stalled and stopped.

"I heard the voice again that said, 'Get out of your vehicle. Get outside.' I said, 'No.' I'm bawling my eyes out and having a dialogue with this other voice. I stepped out of the vehicle and sat on a nearby bench. I was in shock. I continued to have a conversation with that voice for about an hour and a half. It was almost like I had a life coach right there with me. I walked down to the beach and sat on a log."

She didn't want to return to the home she shared with her former boyfriend, but she didn't know where else to go. She asked her angels where she should go. They asked her to describe what she wanted. So she gave a detailed description of a place where she could live temporarily. As she was walking back to her car, she had a sudden thought that she needed to go to a friend's home on Bowen Island. She made the ninety-minute drive and took two ferries to get to her friend's house. When she arrived, her friend took her in and cared for her for five days.

"When I came back to my ex-boyfriend I was in a really positive place. There is no doubt I heard a voice that I knew had to be from the angels. There was a light inside all of that darkness."

Rachel has spent the past several years tuning into her intuitive abilities so she can help herself and others. Angels, she has discovered, give love unconditionally and are available at all times. "They are our cheerleaders who never give up on us."

David and Kelly Rennick Experienced Angelic Encounters

For twenty years David Rennick worked the night shift at the Saint John, New Brunswick, *Telegraph-Journal* as a printer in its press room. He would drive home at three a.m. to Hoyt, about an hour away. "I can remember numerous times, especially on a stormy night in the winter, when I felt there was a presence with me. Like there was someone sitting next to me in the other seat. I would look over to see if there was somebody there, but I couldn't see anyone."

In all those years, he says, there were only two nights when the driving conditions were too poor to make the trip home. There were many nights when the road home wouldn't have been plowed but despite the poor driving conditions, he never had an accident. For him, this is proof he was never alone while making the drive. "It's a conviction that angels are there. They take care of us."

David says he believes angels surround him and his family and prevent accidents from happening. "How many times could I have fallen when I was up on a ladder? There have been many times I have sensed somebody there. I presume it was an angel."

All of his life, David has believed in angels and he believes more people are becoming sensitive to spiritual things, partially because organized religion has failed to meet the expectations and needs of many who are looking outside the church to find their spiritual fulfillment. "And God has chosen another avenue or another vehicle."

Kelly, David's wife, has always felt angels around her. She also believes angels have prevented her from having car accidents. "While driving I have felt that presence. They will jerk the wheel back when I am out of control. Once, I was sliding out of control one day in the winter and the wheel just jerked back on its own. That, to me, was God sending angels to help us."

On one occasion driving near her home, she had an urgent sense of needing to slow her vehicle's speed. "I slowed down and was crawling along far before I got to the stop sign. A big transport truck was coming too fast for the corner and coming into my side of the road. Had I been where I normally would have been at the stop sign, I wouldn't be here. I didn't know if I heard the warning or felt it in my bones."

Sometimes she will hear audible whispers and sometimes it will simply be a knowing about something and this, she believes, is information from God or angels when she needs to be aware. Her experience with the spiritual world is becoming stronger, and she believes this is true for many people. There is a collective spiritual evolution happening, and the collective consciousness is being raised to allow many people to be able to tune into the spiritual realm and to experience the presence of angels in their lives.

It may be difficult for some people to see the connection between this world and the spiritual realm. For this couple it is impossible to separate the spiritual from the earthly. Kelly is an intuitive and says she will get a sense of when things are about to happen or when she will see people. "Sometimes I will know who is going to call before the phone rings."

Kelly often sees the deceased in her dreams that come to her with messages. She believes these are messages from God.

She says it's important to know that even though angels exist and are here to help us, we have to take responsibility for our lives and our actions. "I think there's a responsibility we have as spirits in the flesh. We are supposed to be stewards of the earth and we are not doing really well with that. That's what the angels are trying to tell us. We have to step up. I believe God works through us. I believe the other genre of angels is human beings [earth angels] who are walking God's way, who are guided by God to do His work. The angels are here to direct us in the great work, because it is work. We are going to get our hands dirty and it's good for us. God uses the people who are willing and able to be used for His purposes."

Kelly and David believe their meeting was divinely inspired. She had been living in Fredericton Junction when she moved into a new home. A friend suggested they go to a restaurant for some dessert. David was there, though he normally didn't go to that restaurant. They both share the same spiritual beliefs and have a passion for working the land on their farm, and living a sustainable lifestyle.

Children are naturally in tune with spirit but most get distracted and conditioned away from nurturing it. Seven-year-old Hannah Rennick tells her mother she sees balls of light which she says are angels. Her mother and David don't want to do anything to suppress the spirituality they see in this girl. "We're pretty open and God is a priority in our lives. I'm open to [angels and the spiritual realm] so I speak openly with her about it," Kelly says.

Cecile Boudreau Has Felt Angels Near All of Her Life

Cecile Boudreau has had a lifelong connection with angels. Now in her eighties, she was raised to believe in angels and to pray to them. Her grandmother taught her a prayer that helped her to feel their presence and protection. She still says it before she starts each day. She believes angels serve as God's messengers and help in His work on the earth, and prays to the angels for herself and others in her life.

"I say this prayer every morning: 'Guardian angels, watch over those whose names are written in my heart, guard them with every care and make their way easy, their labour fruitful, dry their tears if they weep, sanctify their joys, raise their courage if they weaken, restore their hope if they lose heart, their health if they be ill, truth if they err, repentance if they fall. Amen.' Often I say it during the day, if I feel that one of my family members needs help."

Cecile believes angels protected one of her grandsons when, as a toddler, he was about to tumble down a long flight of stairs. "He was at the top of the stairs and it was almost as if he was going to walk on air. But he made it down and he turned around and smiled as if he was smiling to his angels who protected him from falling. We believe there was some power that kept him from being hurt."

She is quick to acknowledge that God is all-powerful and the angels are His servants. She believes angels are always near to help her when she asks for their assistance. Her home is filled with dozens of angel ornaments, reminders of the angels that surround her, guide her and protect her. She keeps a deck of angel cards with messages on them, which she reads each day. She believes these are messages from her angels and she finds them very encouraging. Cecile believes people of all faiths and those who before now didn't believe in anything are going through a spiritual reawakening. "I feel it is coming but it wasn't that long ago that people would not even discuss things such as this." She thinks it's because people are discovering that there is no lasting happiness and security in the material things in the world. "It has to come from within. I know it's the grace of God."

Her Grandmother's Spirit Comforted Pam McCaughey

Pam McCaughey was sixteen when she experienced what she believes to be a comforting presence in a time of great sadness. Her grandparents, who were in their fifties, had been severely injured in a car accident in 1971. Her grandmother Nettie was hospitalized in Charlottetown because she needed round-the-clock permanent care. Pam was very distressed that her mother didn't allow her to remain at the hospital when Nettie was near death.

"My mother banished me to the nearby Kirkwood Motel, where I stayed by myself while she went back to the hospital with my father." As she sat in the hotel room she was extremely distraught. Exactly at 3:30 p.m., despite being in distress over her grandmother, she no longer felt alone. "I felt as though there was a presence there. The presence was there to say to me, 'It's okay. I'm all right. This is what has to happen.' Then that presence left. I found out later that my grandmother's death had actually occurred around 3:30 in the afternoon."

As a teenager, going through what she describes as one of the major losses of her life, the feeling of the presence in that motel room took away a lot of the fear about her grandmother's impending death. "It gave me hope. It made me realize that a person's death was not the end of things. I believe, when I was in that motel room, the presence I felt was my grandmother leaving her body and coming to me because she knew I would be upset and I needed closure. I needed one last communication from her."

The presence she felt was more of a knowing than anything, she says. It was as though she could feel something settling in her mind and touching her heart. Her father told her later that on the Sunday afternoon her grandmother died, a youth group came into the hospital to sing and play hymns. They had asked if they could come into her grandmother's room to play a song and say a prayer.

"My father said all afternoon my grandmother never opened her eyes. She was in a comatose state. He said when the young people finished the song and the prayer, she opened her eyes and looked at someone he couldn't see – she smiled, breathed one last breath, and it was all over. My father wondered whether it was God, Jesus, an angel, or one of her family members who had come back to guide her across, so she wouldn't be afraid, so that she would willingly go."

Some years later, upon the death of her grandfather George Millar, she experienced a dream in which he asked her questions about finding his will, and how her mother intended to dispose of his house, car, property and other such things. It was a great comfort to have that dream conversation with him. Because such questions were so totally in character for George, she knew it was a real visitation.

It seems dreams have been an important spiritual connection for Pam. On May 15, 2003, she dreamed of the Holy Mother Mary, wearing a blue robe with an intense light around her, who said, "You are my child. You belong to me. I love you and I look after you. I want you to know this is the case."

"I didn't want that dream to end. It was all the joy, peace, happiness and total tranquility that you could ever feel in your lifetime being poured into one situation. This impacted my life in a major way. I am still feeling the impact of it today. It intensified my spiritual life."

Pam's views changed radically as a result of this event. As a child she was raised in the Presbyterian and Baptist churches. Over time she has become more spiritual and less tied to religious dogma. She believes people around the world and of all religions are striving for the same thing – "I do think the preponderance of human beings on the planet have had a desire to reach for that divinity within themselves as well as the divinity outside of themselves."

She has explored the Wiccan religion, which she says is the most misunderstood and maligned religion there is. It is not connected to Satanism in any way, as some unenlightened people may believe, she explains. It is a very natural, organic and healthy belief system; angels and spirit guides are present in the lives of people who are followers of this faith as well. "They don't necessarily use the term angels; they use the term beings, presences or messengers. There are a whole lot of different euphemisms for it in the more pagan faiths, but it still boils down to the same thing."

Nowadays, Pam follows a pagan faith more akin to that of the ancient Egyptians, and, like them, believes strongly in life after death, reincarnation, and the unseen world of spirit that guides and protects. According to Pam, these spirit beings are more elemental and more closely connected to the earth in some cases, but they still serve as messengers. "In my own faith, I tend to see an angel as more of a being of light that has a presence and a power and something that's either seen or felt, as opposed to being heard. If you come in contact with one of these beings, you may be the only one who sees it."

While she has never seen or felt one of these angelic beings, she has felt protected at various points in her life. "I felt there was something there, but it was unseen. I do think a lot of what goes on, in terms of us being protected, is unseen. I believe there are messengers out there. And I believe our deceased family members may take over jobs as guardian guides or spirit guides. Just because they leave this dimension of existence doesn't mean they cease to exist or cease to remember the connection."

She still has a strong sense that her grandmother is with her in spirit as a guide to watch over her and to help her in her life. She also has a sense that she has other guides around her who are also deceased family members. A couple of years ago she visited a home that once belonged to her great-grand-mother Matilda Millar. The owners who now occupy it called her in 2007 to ask if she was interested in buying it. She went to see the house for the first time since 1976, when Matilda had passed away and the home was sold.

"When I went into the house I could feel her presence there and I don't consider myself psychic. She had a very powerful personality. There was no doubt about it. Three deaths occurred in that house: two of her children and her husband, my great-grandfather John Irving Millar. And the other presence I could feel was my grandfather George, Matilda's only son, who'd been born in that house in 1913. Oddly enough, I felt him not as an adult, but as a little boy. I felt if I turned my head one way, I'd see him on the stairway wearing his little sailor suit. I swear, out of the corner of my eye I could see him on the stairs, jumping down the stairs." She feels her great-grandmother, grandmother and grandfather very strongly in her life.

When Pam's father passed away, she was with him. She saw him take his last breath. "I didn't know what to expect. I didn't know how I would feel and I didn't know how the end would come for him because he was in a great deal of pain, so they had him heavily medicated. I remember it was not a laboured thing. There were a couple of breaths and it was over. It was such a peaceful thing. It was such a simple movement from one place to another."

She has been visited by her father's spirit too. It happened about a year after his death. "He was always a trickster and a joker. I was in bed. It was in the wintertime. I have chimes hanging in my window. There was no heat on in the room. I woke up about three o'clock in the morning and I most clearly felt his presence, but moreover, somebody had grabbed the bottom part of that chime and was shaking it. I think that was his way of saying, 'I'm here, I'm okay.' That's something he would have done. Even the temperature in

Angels and the Afterlife   111

the room changed. It was really, really hot. I remember lying there thinking, 'Thank you. Thank you very much.' I needed this.

"I think the spiritual climate is allowing people to discuss these things more openly. There was a time when, if you talked about these things, the church would practically burn you at the stake. People are reaching out and recognizing some of what is going on in a spiritual sense. I also wonder if maybe the world of spirit is moving closer in some dimensional way to the world that we inhabit."

Although unconcerned about the future and the fears surrounding the end of world some people say will come in the form of Armageddon, Pam believes something is coming but it won't happen in the physical world. Rather, it will happen in subtle ways in the spiritual world. She believes many people are searching for something more meaningful, deeper, and a sense of spiritual fulfillment that's lacking in their lives.

"I think there is a big difference between being religious and being spiritual."

We may be divided in our opinions of religion and which is the right path, but one of the unifying things throughout the world is the belief in and people's experience with angelic beings.

Pam fears nothing. "There is more to us than just the physical body. There is a Higher Power out there by whatever name we call it. That Higher Power sends spirit guides or angels to guide us, to protect us, to help us, to calm us, to console us."

When she prays at night to the Great Mother, she never asks for things, because she knows her needs will be met even before she knows she needs them. She knows there are many pathways to the Divine Being. It doesn't matter what spiritual path we choose to take, what matters is that we are willing to make the journey in the first place – that's important. The life path we are on is the one we've decided to take, even before we were born into this world.

Many people haven't given themselves permission to follow the path they feel led to take in life, and the angels are here to help us take a step in faith and follow whatever spiritual journey we choose with the understanding that whatever path we choose, it's okay – we will get to the Divine in our own time and in our own way. "Remember Jesus said, 'Other sheep have I not of this flock.' Jesus is just one of many very enlightened people who came into this world to teach us things."

Pam believes angels are here to relay messages back and forth between us and the Divine, to protect us, to guide us away from negative things and to guide us towards positive things. "I even think they are here to guide us to certain people or circumstances that we need to be in." Angels may even come in the form of other people or animals that, at times, can be angelic in their behaviour and actions to help people in their time of need, she says.

Dennis Atchison Has Felt A Presence Since Childhood

Dennis Atchison grew up in the Eastern Townships of Quebec. He could sense someone was looking after him since he was a youngster. It's always been this way.

"I constantly felt someone was there, over my shoulder or off to the side hovering above me; I thought it was kind of fun. I wasn't afraid. It was fascinating."

When he had thoughts of what to do and where to go in life, the things his inner voice was saying would make sense to him. "There's different ways of knowing. We call it intuition because we struggle. We want to put labels on things. We want to make them linear, you know?"

Different things happened to him that made him understand he wasn't alone and was being protected in dangerous situations. "Someone was looking out for me. Whether it was driving a car: getting on a certain side of the road late at night when another car comes driving down the wrong side of the road – the car just misses you. Why did you shift over at that moment in time? You don't know, but you did and it saved you from a head-on collision."

Dennis is sure he's had a guardian angel watching over him through-out his life. He has always felt the presence just when he needed it in times of danger to give him a nudge in the right direction. When he was in his early twenties, he really started to pay attention to that inner voice. He feels it intui-tively and physically. He is aware in his daily life that there is a being around him and also that it inspires and motivates him in directing him on his path.

The purpose of an angel, he says, is self-explanatory. "They are there to help you through your moment in time, if you are open to it."

The presence of an angel in his life, he says, has affected both his private and professional life. He didn't take a traditional route when his twin boys were younger. When he was married, he and his wife decided she would work outside the home and he would be a stay-at-home father after a long and successful career as the organizer of the Special Olympics in New Brunswick. For five years he cared for his boys while his wife worked on her career. While he cherishes every minute he spent with his sons, he hated it when people questioned why he stayed at home with the children, while his wife went to work for their income. His angel helped him to get through the rough times, even in the worst of it, while he went through the process of a divorce.

"Something inside of me just moved and said, 'No, I never want the boys to lose their relationship with their mom.' I was being guided at that moment because it was a really intense time."

He spent a year with the New Brunswick Trails Council, then his next job was with the Family Resource Centre at CFB Gagetown. For eight years he worked extensively with the provincial New Democrats. Now, he is a communications specialist with the New Brunswick Union of Provincial Public Employees.

Dennis is unconcerned about what others will say once they discover he believes in another realm and the existence of angels in his life. He is very open to speaking publicly about his spirituality. "Most people would go, 'Oh no, no. That's private or separate.' I think that's part of the problem."

He sees a societal shift happening now. People are looking for something of great spiritual depth. He believes people are fed up with the ritualistic aspects of organized religion and increasing numbers of individuals are looking for something of greater spiritual meaning. He was raised in the United Church but it has nothing to do with his daily spiritual life.

"We all have a need to believe. We all believe in different things, but the human need to believe is powerful. Unfortunately, it creates conflicts and wars. I'm raising my boys to look at all of the religions of the world and I tell them not to ever go thinking one is better than the other."

He isn't concerned about what happens to him when he dies. He says he has always believed in the physics principle of infinite energy. Energy changes forms but it doesn't go away.

Dennis believes angels exist to protect us, to love us, to guide us but are never to interfere because humans have free will. Angels want us to know there is no need to be afraid of whatever may come and that while we are on this planet, it is important to help and love one another. "That's it, switching it to love from fear." The fact that angels have been acknowledged around the world and throughout time is proof of their existence, he says. "It means people need to believe in how they structure their reality."

He gets excited when he talks about the possibility of a world where everyone puts others' needs first and society's needs above their own. The concept of earth angels appeals to him. "Wouldn't it be so nice if everyone did that in their own way, in their own house, on any given day? It's conscious. It's not random, it's conscious."

Dennis thinks people are more open to the possibility of examining their own spirituality now because they've either had personal traumas through life, or are contemplating the end of their lives as they age. Or maybe, he says, it's because they have lived in the material world for so long and are unsatisfied that they are turning inward and examining their spirituality.

Debra Debano's Home Is Guarded By Angels

Debra Debano's family lives in the Philippines in a gated community, guarded by a private security company. Every night between 11 p.m. and midnight, a security guard checks every house on her block. One night, a couple of years ago, the guard double-checked her home and the lane she lives on. That's when she realized the uniformed guards weren't the only ones keeping watch over her home.

"When he checked the second time, he only checked my house from afar, about twenty or thirty metres because he saw a man who was standing in front of my gate, a man like a security guard, but he didn't know this man, so he thought we hired a private security guard specifically for our house. He saw him standing in front of my gate for two days. When I was ready to go on vacation with my husband and two daughters, we stopped at the security post and the guard asked us whether we hired our own security guard. Of course, we said no. But suddenly my heart beat so hard. I felt the presence of the Holy Spirit among us. I knew that it was an angel who guarded my house and us.

"Starting that day, I heard so many stories from my maid and a girl who gives me massages at home. Both the maid and the masseuse are Muslims. On Sundays, they have the day off."

One Sunday afternoon while Debra was attending church services, the maid and the masseuse walked past her home. They saw two big men inside the front yard sitting on the stairs, chatting with one another. "So my maid and the massage girl thought I was at home and was entertaining guests. They were confused and wondered why I had given them the day off when I had invited guests."

The next day, her maid asked her why she didn't need her if she'd planned on entertaining guests. "'What guests?' I asked her. So she told me the story. I started to be aware of the angelic activities in my life after that day. I feel so overwhelmed and pray a lot to get more understanding of the character and the assignments of these angels."

Debra saw an angel when she was in her bedroom in the middle of a conversation with her husband. She saw a man standing behind him. He was very handsome with long red hair – he looked much like the main character in the movie *Braveheart* starring Mel Gibson.

"This angel looked exactly like Mel with the same long hair. He wore a Roman-style knee-length tunic and sandals and his eyes were like a flame. He stared at me. It seemed that he wanted me to know his presence in my bedroom. I was so shocked to see him, I stood there frozen. I couldn't speak or move my body. My husband looked around but saw nothing. So he waited until I could speak and asked what I saw. I said, 'I don't know.'

"I prayed and asked God who the angel was. He revealed to me, this angel's name was Caesar and that he will be with me all the time to protect me, to guide me to my destiny. I don't know if I'm already in my destiny. Sometimes I can feel and see Caesar around me and I'm so glad to know this."

Mammie Murphy Connects With Her Angels

Mammie Murphy always had a sense angels were near, but until a year ago she didn't pay much attention to them. "I am somewhat intuitive."

Mammie has premonitions that come to her in her dreams. She dreamed of the assassination attempt on Pope John Paul II a week before he was shot on May 13, 1981. Then, she dreamed that the Challenger space shuttle exploded minutes after takeoff a week before that disaster took place on January 28, 1986. Both incidents frightened her badly. She chose to ignore those dreams and didn't pursue them.

In 2008 Mammie started to have premonitions in her dreams about friends and family. She felt the presence of angels very strongly and realized she could connect with angels through meditation. And angels, she says, are everywhere in her life. "I feel them. I don't see them. I think it's because I have asked not to see them; I told them I am not ready to see them. I get goosebumps. It's the same way I feel my mom or my dad or any other spirit."

When she went to the hospital for some routine tests she felt an angel in the car beside her. "His name was Hector. I asked him who he was and the name Hector came to me. I knew there was somebody beside me because I could feel the presence. I had a knowing." She doesn't believe he was her guardian angel and isn't sure what he was doing in her car, but she knows for sure he was there.

"My guardian angel is Gabriel and I have met her through meditation. In the last month or so I have been asking for the angels' help a lot."

She asks for guidance and help with problems by writing messages to them. Since connecting with her angels she feels much calmer. Once, when she was feeling down after an argument with someone close, she thought she needed to feel safe and that someone cared for her. What she really needed was a hug, she thought, as she left her home to go shopping. The cashier at the store stopped what she was doing and spoke to her. Mammie is sure the angels used the cashier to send her a message. "She told me everything was going to be okay and then she gave me a hug. When I got back in the car it was like somebody wrapped themselves around me. I knew it was my angel, because before I went to the store I had asked for help."

She believes angels work through other people and people are listening and looking for signs of them. "There's a shift in the energy of the universe. I feel it all the time."

In her opinion angels want to connect with us because they want to prepare humanity for the future. Mammie is able to feel the emotions of other people. She believes many people are living in fear and they have been raised to believe the end of the world is coming.

"I don't believe in that. I believe something is going to happen, but it's nothing to fear – easier said than done sometimes. The angels are all loving. They are protecting us. If we ask for protection they will protect us. Sometimes I wonder what it is that the angels want us to know. I would like to think they are helping me to be a better person and to live life to the fullest."

Tuning to the presence of the angels in her life and accepting who she is has changed her for the better, Mammie says. Others have told her they notice she is much calmer – many say she almost glows with positive energy.

Angels Bring Out Barbara Gill's Creative Side

Barbara Gill describes her upbringing as Anglo and Protestant. While she was always in touch with nature and drew her sense of God through it, she never had any connection to angels. But that all changed in 1990 when her father was diagnosed with terminal lung cancer. She was in Vancouver at the time on business. She'd called home and spoke to an O.R. nurse who told her the sad news.

Naturally, Barbara was very upset. A work colleague told her she should take a trip to Grouse Mountain, where there was a multi-media production and a story about an eagle. "She said, 'You must go there before you leave Vancouver. You will find solace there.'"

The healing began as she ascended to the top of the mountain. As she entered an amphitheater she was surrounded by sights and sounds. The song "Our Spirit Soars," sung by Long John Baldry and Ann Mortifee, played. She was moved by aboriginal carvings but it was the voice of Long John Baldry that was the greatest balm to help heal her wounded heart. Inspired by her experience she wrote a poem for her father and mailed it to him.

My Father Flies like an Eagle

Climbing
the strong-limbed stands of
evergreen
we search the vast ocean
for eternity
midst rolling bursts of fog and sunshine
rugged rock
that jags the sky;
Grouse Mountain calls
the child calls me
to fly with the eagle.
My spirit soars
reaching
my father lifts me
on his wings
powerful and free

releasing
his piercing love song
to last eternally.

"When Dad received this poem he picked up the phone and called me. He said he loved it and also loved me. We enjoyed a beautiful year as he prepared for his death. Two days before my father died, I took cedar clippings from the trees that surrounded my home; the family business was known for its cedar fencing. I wanted Dad to enjoy the fragrance of this evergreen in his palliative care room. He drifted off to sleep.

"As I sat beside his bed, I leafed through a magazine provided by the hospital, the only reading material in the room. When I opened it, I discovered a story about Grouse Mountain and the Eagle. I could not believe my eyes. He woke and I showed him. 'Look,' I said. 'This is where I wrote your poem, Dad.' He glanced at the picture and acknowledged it with a nod of his head.

"He and I stood at his bedside to exercise his legs. We held each other's arms; I told him it was the first time I had the pleasure of waltzing with him. When Dad resettled into bed he reached for his notebook and pen. He said, 'Time for my cocktail,' and motioned to his veins. Even in my father's dying, he eyed the clock. Others could set their watches to his routines. Always.

"I shared The Eagle with the minister who would preside over my father's funeral. He told me the eagle was biblical, and at the graveside, following the burial, he pressed this scripture into my hands: They that wait upon the Lord shall renew their strength; they shall mount up with wings as eagles.

"Later I expressed my gratitude to Long John Baldry. He came to my hometown of Fredericton and performed at the Harvest Jazz and Blues Festival. Following his pub concert, one of his crew approached me. 'Long John likes to meet people from his audience. Come on back and say hello.' I was surprised at being singled out. I hesitated. But this gentleman was persistent. Away we went. I told Long John about the impact the song "Our Spirit Soars" had on my father and me."

Barbara feels her angel with her constantly and has since shortly before her first bout with cancer in 2001. This is when she started to write in the voice of a being she calls Shandarrah. "That scared me to death when it first happened to me. About five years ago, I reached out to an aunt of mine and she said, 'You are going to find that this happens in your life.'

"I thought I was going crazy, like literally going nuts. I can get very creative and be seen as a little off the wall anyway. I'm considered eccentric by a lot of people. It used to bother me. It doesn't bother me a bit now because I'm old enough. I've gone through cancer twice. It's good that I'm even alive."

Her sense of angels grew steadily from 1991 and remains to this day.

Where does the presence she calls Shandarrah come from? "Some people said I was channeling Shandarrah. I said if I had to name my soul it would be Shandarrah. Shandarrah is walking with me. She is a voice of innocence. I don't see her but I feel her presence all of the time."

She also hears the voice of Shandarrah, who she thinks is an angel. "She reminds me of things all of the time. The innocence we need to see, the innocence in life. We have lost it."

Barbara believes angels are here to heal. Her writing too, is spiritual. She started writing before her first illness and since that diagnosis, she has also been painting. Many of her works are displayed throughout her home and have an ethereal, angelic quality about them. There is one painting of a waterfall in her home. She says it is how Shandarrah came to earth from what she describes as the high and holiest of places. Here is a poem she wrote through her connection to Shandarrah:

'Tis From There We Flew

Our high and holiest of places
Reveals the many varied faces
Of you, of me, as we pursue
The parts of each to each most true.

Our high and holiest of places
Guides now the core of our basis;
Integral to all we must do
Compassion enveils ev'ry cue.

Our high and holiest of places
Embodies our reflective paces;
We make choices, understand too
Our souls acknowledge to renew.

Our high and holiest of places
Ensures we'll not weave tangled traces
Protected there, where we first drew
Our place of love – 'tis where we flew.

Does she think the presence of Shandarrah came to help bring her through her times of illness? Perhaps, but it is far more than that. "If I allow her voice to come out, it will be a voice that can heal many. Because people who have read the poem have felt healed; they've felt very innocent. They've felt very childlike."

Shandarrah, Barbara says, is with her all of the time. She says this angel has shown her that as a person she can sometimes be harsh and cynical. She doesn't have conversations with her angel, but she says she feels her presence and feels her urging peace, quietness within herself and laughter, love and the innocence we as humans have lost. The compassion is what we need. At their core people are very good, she says. She believes everyone has angels around them, but people have to be receptive enough or lucky enough to allow it to happen. "I think with trauma, things often tend to open up. It's unfortunate but that tends to be the way. There are some of us who are more sensitive, more tuned in terms of the forces around us."

When Barbara feels her angel around her, she feels warmth and love and a carefree existence. Because life can at times be very dark and negative, it is very important for people to try and make a connection to the light and to the positive energy that comes from God and the angels. And she says when she tries to make that connection to the light and to be the positive energy that comes from God and the angels, she meets many people whom she feels compelled to help.

"This is the type of experience I've always had. I bump into people. Or they bump into me. I think we all do. Whether we listen to a plea for help is another thing. As a registered nurse I served and was paid to do my job. While I often went above the call it always felt good to nurse. However, my real serving has been outside of nursing. It is the people I bump into. They always come. I have been told I am an exceptional listener. Perhaps that is the key, although I talk a lot too!"

Angels Are All Around Ruth O'Brien

Ruth O'Brien's mother believed in guardian angels and she was raised to believe in them too. "My mother was Protestant and my father was Roman Catholic. She always believed there was someone looking after us, whether it was angels or passed loved ones. If we were struggling with something she would say, 'Well, ask your guardian angel to help you.'" When Ruth was very young, she could see the spirits of the deceased. But, because it frightened her, she blocked those visions.

About six years ago her connection to spirit and angels returned. It was just after her husband, Gilbert Fauvelle, had been medically discharged from the military. The family was struggling financially and they were both under a lot of stress. In their home, she says, there was a lot of negative energy. "I didn't like it and I didn't want it to continue."

A co-worker directed her to Mary Lou Firth-Irving, an alternative health practitioner who does a lot of energy-healing work.

Mary Lou explained to Ruth that the body is made up of energy fields and if those energy fields are out of balance, as a result of trauma, it can cause a lot of problems such as back problems, shoulder pain, headaches, and migraines. When those energy fields are realigned those problems cease to exist. And they completely ceased to exist for Ruth once she figured out what the trigger was – she needed to figure out what the emotional strain attached to the trauma was.

After her treatments she had more energy, her back and leg pain were gone and she felt an overall vitality she hadn't felt before. From there, she was introduced to angel channeller Pam Nadeau, who did an angel reading for her. Ruth says in that moment everything made sense.

Since then she's learned more about angels and calls upon them to help her in her daily life. When she travels, she asks them to come with her and to surround her car to protect it and her. She also asks for easy parking wherever she needs to go. She says something as simple as a parking space or the saving of a life are all possible and are done by angelic intervention every day. "Nothing is too big and nothing's too small."

Ruth always asks the angels to be with her throughout her workday as a hospital communications clerk. When there is a presence, she sees a haze, like heat radiating up from pavement on a very hot summer's day. "I still haven't figured out whether it's an angel or someone who's passed." When the angels are present she gets a feeling of calm, peace and joy.

When she is near others in the hospital who are closely connected to angels, she can hear angels too, in the form of an inner voice. When she first heard it, she thought she was having a psychotic episode. But she has come to understand these are the voices of angels who bring her reassurance. She knows they are with her. "If I ask for guidance, for a sign, or if I have to make a decision, I will either get the message through numbers, seeing the same numbers over and over again, or I will get a 'Yes, it's okay.' It depends on the situation."

In the hospital where she works, she believes angels are there to help guide the nursing staff. A lot of nurses who work with her are also Reiki practitioners and those who do hands-on energy work for patients who are willing to allow them to do it.

"Reiki is the laying of the hands," she explains. "If you go to the Bible and see where Jesus laid his hands on the lepers and the blind man, that's what it is. Reiki is energy that comes from the universe, or God, or whatever higher power you believe in, through you – you being the vessel – out through your hands. The energy is wise. It knows what it needs to do, where it needs to go, to start the healing process."

Ruth says angels are there to help the energy flow when she gives Reiki treatments. And sometimes, she has felt the presence of Jesus Christ working through her – she knows it is Him. When the angels are working with her during energy treatments, she feels the energy flow and her hands get warm but she doesn't feel the intense heat that she does when she knows Jesus is working through her. "I sweat when He works through me. I don't sweat any other time, other than when He is there. And I can't move my hands any-where other than where they are supposed to be. I feel really grounded when Jesus works through me."

As our world is so complicated and hectic, she believes people are in search of something reassuring. Like others, she believes there is a huge shift in people's desires from the material to the spiritual. She thinks people are looking for something that will bring them a sense of fulfillment, happiness and calm. "It's not any religion. When you bring in the angels, spirituality, your higher power, the universal energy, whatever you want to call it, it's also your inner higher self that you are bringing in. That is much more fulfilling than anything. You don't need the big car and the big house and the expensive clothes."

Her need to call upon angels is greatest in her role as a mother and when she fears for her children. She knows the importance of trusting that the angels are protecting her children in everything they do. "For myself, I know this is my hardest time to release and let go and to trust that all will be well. But it doesn't happen right away, because I go into 'mommy mode' instead of standing back, taking a deep breath and releasing. When you do it, I find it happens almost instantly that the angels fix things. When you procrastinate and hold on to the fear it will take longer. You will hit more road blocks or brick walls."

She calls upon Archangel Michael when she is releasing fear. "I ask him to come and put the fear in a basket. I see those fears going into the basket and then see Archangel Michael taking the basket away. You usually feel a release inside. You can do that visualization and then say, 'It's gone. He has it. I have total faith that he will look after it.'"

Ruth does this often for the safety of her three children and for anything her family might be going through. Now, her family's life is so much better. They no longer live with negativity. She says her husband also believes in angels. His belief started after he saw the changes in her. "I became calmer. I didn't stress over the little things. I have learned to let it go. Because what does it really matter if a sock is picked up or not? There is more peace in the household. My husband is happier and calmer now too."

They no longer worry about things that come up. They trust that money will arrive when it's needed. Because she is human, sometimes she will allow fears and worry to overwhelm her, but as soon as she reminds herself to allow the angels and God to take over, she slips back into a sense of calm. "It's funny, because if I stay stuck in worry what comes is just more problems." But the minute they let go, the problems seem to go away too, she says. "It works every time. It might sound crazy but yes, money comes from Heaven. If we get into a rut and money's a bit tight and we start to worry, my husband and I will both say, 'Okay, let's let it go and let the angels take care of it.' They are not allowed to intervene in your life unless you ask. It's all about free will."

She talks about guarding angels and archangels daily to her children and encourages them to call upon angels for help. Her sixteen-year-old son James was having difficulty with a school bus driver, who was constantly finding fault with whatever he did. The teen built up a lot of resentment towards the man. Whenever he spoke of the bus driver he had such anger in his eyes, his mother recalls. She told him to go to his room and call on Archangel Michael to take away the anger. The skeptical teen went to his room to try and visualize the angel taking away the resentment. When he came back to his mother he told her it worked, that he had seen Archangel Michael in his visualization. But when he described the angel, his mother knew it wasn't Michael who, she says, she has seen many times.

"The girls at work have a joke that Archangel Michael is like that actor Fabio with long blond hair, a strong muscular body, gold-tipped wings and a sword. James wasn't describing what I had seen. I have a book of the different guardian angels and archangels." She found an angel that matched her son's description. It was Phaleg, the angel of resentment. Ruth had told James to visualize a ball of anger and resentment and then ask the angel to take it away from him. "He says his whole body felt a release. Physically, his whole body felt lighter." After this experience, her son's resentment disappeared. He was able to let go of the anger and his relationship with the bus driver greatly improved and there was no longer any conflict between them.

Ruth takes precautions at work and at home to keep from picking up viruses by following common sense proper hygiene methods such as washing her hands frequently with soap and water. But she doesn't worry about the chances of becoming ill, for she believes she is protected from illness because she affirms good health.

"Every day I say, 'My body enjoys optimal health. My body is perfect. Nothing can harm my body.' I rarely get sick. I have to be run down and not practising my affirmations in order to get sick. Those who really fear disease are likely the people who will become ill, because you are telling the universe that's what you expect. The angels are part of the universe; whatever higher power you have is part of the universe. Whenever you have a positive thought, it is positive energy that is going out into the universe and it comes back as positive energy. But if you have negative thoughts, it goes out as negative energy and it comes back to you as negative energy. What the angels are hearing is, 'I want to be sick.' They help us with everything that we want. They give us this so we can learn to shift. They will give us more of these miserable brick walls so that when we finally hit one of them we go, 'Okay, enough.' And then we make the shift to the positive and get away from the fear and get away from the negative energy."

Angels Are Working Through the Healers in Our Hospitals

Jocelyn Clark has always believed in the concept of God but she never had a strong church upbringing, although she was confirmed into the Anglican Church and attended services on and off throughout her life. Angels had no place in her life and were only something she'd heard about in Bible stories. She went to a medium several times in the 1990s, when she was seeking guidance on some issues in her life, but her real awakening to the idea that angels exist and are with her happened in 2004.

When a back injury left her bedridden for about six weeks and suffering excruciating pain, her sister brought her books about angels to give her something to read. "I was negative and unhappy. I was to the point in my life where I needed a change. In my experience, God gives you a few taps on your shoulder and says, 'Okay you need to make a change,' and if you don't get it, He knocks you off your feet. It's either through an accident, through a physical illness. For me it was my back."

She was unable to do anything except remain in bed and read the books about angels. She started meditating, got in touch with what she calls her higher self and opened herself up to the angelic field. "I started asking them for help to change my life. I didn't realize I could go inside of myself to get answers. I stilled my inner chatter in my head and I was able to get guidance from my wise self. Every one of us has God in us. Soul guidance is a good way to put it. I hear information in my head. It's like a voice."

Over the past five years she's experienced a life transformation. She says she has clairsentience. She describes it as a knowing about someone or something. She believes she gets information from what she calls the "other side" from people who've passed away. "I get information from my spirit guide and also from angelic sources."

She spends a lot of time being quiet and meditating while soaking in her bathtub. It's her quiet meditative place. She stills herself and asks for guidance. Sometimes she will connect with Archangel Michael or Archangel Ariel. "I've connected with Jesus. I know that He's out there. Some people would find that really wacko, but I know I connect with Him. Basically I will have a conversation with them. I will ask questions. Usually it's when I'm in a quandary in my life and need guidance on a certain subject. I ask what is it that I need to do to resolve the situation. I'll usually get some wisdom from them.

It's like a back and forth conversation. Sometimes they talk and they will just give me information. It's thoughts that come. It's not words I'm hearing."

When she follows those thoughts, she says it always works out. She has always used what she calls her power of discernment and has never connected with anything she felt wasn't of a divine source. Angels will also connect with her in symbols. For example, before she agreed to talk about her angel experiences for this book, she received three messages from three separate people asking her to contact me.

In Jocelyn's experience everything angels are and do is based on love. "They want us to be happy. They want to provide comfort. They don't want to see us struggle. It's not necessary to struggle. When we are having trouble in our lives and when we are experiencing resistance, it's because we are basically going against our paths."

There are so many unhappy people in the world. They are filled with fear, bitterness and anger. Since angels have come into her life, the negativity and unhappiness have gone away. Not only has her life been transformed, but many of her work colleagues have seen a change in their lives too. "Our whole work environment has transformed. I've been there nine years and it's become a place that's fun, enjoyable and respectful."

Six out of the eight people in her workplace believe in angels and have had angel experiences. She was the first to have an angel encounter. When the negativity and unhappiness left her life, others noticed and were drawn to her positivity and wanted to know more about it. "I offered them information on people to go to. Once they started their own physical and emotional healing, they decided they wanted to learn more. It's amazing how you can totally transform a work environment just by having like-minded people. I think I have attracted these people to me because it was not like that when I first went there. It used to be a very negative environment."

She has no idea how many angels are around her, but she knows there are many. They are around her all of the time and she can see them in the form of flickering sparks, like fireflies, inside her house, usually in the evening when it is darker.

Angels have never let her down. Even in the smallest of ways, they are there to help her in her life. "I use them to help me find my keys, a parking place." Many people would ask, Don't angels have more important things to do than to help someone find their missing car keys? But Clark says angels are not like humans in that they can be in many places at the same time.

According to Jocelyn her entire life is based on angelic experiences. She feels the world is ready for this. "I really feel the world needs it and people need it. I don't allow fear and negativity to enter my life. I work in the health field and see the number of people who are depressed and who are on medication for depression. I see the amount of people who are angry and people who are just plain sad and lonely. They are looking for a way out of it. It's really not that hard. It happens when you are ready to be on your path. I could have started in the 1990s when I first went to a medium and first realized there was more to life than the physical existence, but it wasn't meant to happen to me until 2004."

Jocelyn sees the door opening and more people who are willing to explore their spirituality. As a nurse, she also trained in healing touch and Reiki. She works in a place that would never have been open to such things in past years. Recently she was teaching a parent how to do healing touch on a child who'd developed seizures. As she explained about people's energy fields she told the woman about positive and negative energy fields.

"You know when you are near somebody and it feels good to be around them? But sometimes you will be around somebody who is not happy, who is angry and you can feel it. It's all energy. Everybody knows what it's like to be near somebody who is happy. You want to be near them all of the time. You know what it feels like to be around somebody who is not nice, is not fun, and is not happy. You don't want to be near them."

She believes angels bring that happy, calm energy. She feels them around her constantly when she's at work, and she sees miracles happening almost every day. She sees God and angels at work in the hospital. She believes she is able to do what she does as a nurse because she is connected to angels.

"I think I stay more physically and spiritually well because I work with the angels. I think the people who come more from their head are the ones who are going to find it difficult to maintain lengthy careers without physically breaking down. You can't replenish your spirit like that. If you want to connect with somebody's heart or their spirit and want to help them, it has to come from the place of the heart and this will sustain us over the long term."

Are there earth angels? She believes God puts people in the right place at the right time to help people. Health care professionals who have a desire to help people rather than being in it only for the money may be some of God's earth angels.

"It can happen in many ways and I think we are all here to help each other on our paths. We all have our bad days. There are times when people piss you off and you get angry. That is part of being human. We have been planted on earth to come down and do our learning. We're in school. When we are in school we can't be perfect. You can be an earth angel but you still have your imperfections and your issues."

As a nurse she sees fear in people's eyes every day. She says if people were more connected spiritually and knew angels were there to help them, their fears would be lessened. Where she feels it's appropriate, and when someone is open to hearing about this, she will connect with them and refer them to others who can help them learn more about angels.

"I think a lot of times just touching somebody and showing them you care is enough. Everybody has their path. For me to say they need this or they need that would be judging. But if you see someone who is suffering emotionally and you feel guided to share with them what has happened to you, I think that's great. That's what we try to do where I work. We try to care for people and show them they are worthwhile and they are being cared for – they are not just a number. I think that's what's changed our workplace, because before it was more like you were just on the conveyor belt, just going through the motions."

Angels and her spiritual walk have become part of Jocelyn's daily life. Every day she wakes and knows they are with her. She knows there are others who are hungry to make some kind of spiritual connection in their lives. "I have seen a lot of people who I thought were not on board with any of this stuff, who are turning around."

Madonna Bennett – Angels Are With Her at Her Job

Madonna Bennett is a nurse who says angels are all around her and with her in her work. She has always felt the presence of angels, but since she changed from one hospital unit to another, this feeling has intensified. She used to be an emergency room nurse. Five years ago she felt overwhelmed by the constant pressure of her job. It robbed her of her true self.

"I felt I was becoming someone I didn't want to be. I felt like I wasn't as patient. I didn't have the compassion I'd always had. I have always been a very caring person and knew I wanted to be a nurse from the time I was little, but I was just not the nurse I wanted to be. I have always prayed. I said,

'Please God I need something else. I need to have a job that's less stressful. I need to stop doing shift work. I need to spend more time with my family because I feel I am missing out. Please find me a job that I can go to work and come home and not hang on to everything."

In less than a year, her prayers were answered. She saw two job postings in another unit of the hospital, applied for them both and was hired. She was thrilled and says it was an answer to prayer. Madonna is not alone in her belief in angels and her knowledge that they are at work in this hospital unit. In fact, all but a few nurses on the unit are in tune with angels. "We came together in that place because we all wanted to be happier and more caring. I think God has put us there to do work."

They see signs of angelic presence daily and she will hear angels. "I hear voices and words. When I am doing treatments I get messages. If I ask a question, I will hear the answer. What I'm getting is that angels are very happy and fun, and they want us to have fun and enjoy life. They want us to lighten up."

Madonna explains when our energy levels are high, then we feel good, but when they drop, then negative things start to happen. People need to understand that angels can and will help with anything we ask. "There is nothing too small or too big. I am teaching my children to know the angels are there and they can ask them for help." From the time she wakes until the time she goes to bed, she asks angels to surround her and her family and to keep them safe.

While she doesn't see angels, she will get the sense that deceased loved ones of her patients will come around them out of love and concern for them. Because many of the nurses she works with are connected spiritually, she says she knows what she feels and hears is true. In the unit where she works there is a place they call the angel room. A woman who channels angels has told the nurses this is a room where angels like to spend time. If a patient who is having a difficult time comes to the unit, the staff will place them in that specific room.

"That just seems to be a room where things happen. Sometimes, we will just get a feeling that a patient needs to go in Room 20. We put them in that room and they will be in there longer than normal. It's like they are getting healing in that room. That's what we feel. People come in and are in that room all day long, and for some reason they end up having their surgery canceled and go home. I feel the angels are in that room to heal people. We find that all of a sudden they are feeling great and they are ready to go home."

As a result of her work on this unit and the other like-minded nurses who work with her, she feels full of compassion and at peace. She is where she is supposed to be, doing what she is meant to be doing. She and the other nurses who are believers call themselves light workers. They are doing the work of the angels in the physical form. "We are just hands and we are working for God."

She will call on angels whenever she needs help with her teenage children. She finds she can also call on them for calming herself, even when one of her children tries her patience.

Angels have also helped her come to terms with her fear of flying. "I used to be petrified to fly and had to take medication." Before a trip to the Dominican Republic someone asked her if she had taken anti-anxiety medication. "I said, 'No. I don't need that anymore. I know my angels are there and I feel at peace. I don't have to worry about anything because I know I just have to ask."

The angels are always there to protect us, to strengthen us, to encourage us and all we have to do is ask, she explains. When she travels, she always asks angels to surround her vehicle and keep her safe from harm while on the road. Once the angels protected her from colliding with a deer herd.

"I was driving home from work and it was dark. I saw a group of deer and they started running across the road in a herd. I said, 'Oh, my God! Angels, help!' I slammed on the brakes. I couldn't believe how many there were. There were so many I couldn't count them. I was in shock, so I had to sit there for a minute and calm down. I started to drive again and there was another group that ran by me up the other side of the road. It was like they swarmed me but I didn't touch one. That was protection."

Yvonne Mersereau's Connection to Angels is a Personal And Private Journey

Yvonne Mersereau's encounters with angels didn't begin until later in life. She was raised in a fundamentalist Christian home where the rules of life were strict. The idea of personal communication with angels would have been frowned upon, she admits. But several years ago, after reading some books on angels, she opened herself up at age seventy-two to the idea that angels were around her and started to tune into their presence.

"I like angels. I know they're around. I don't see them. Angels are around you all of the time; you just have to work at opening up to them a little bit. It's just a very deep knowing inside, that is so deep it's probably part of my DNA."

Recently, while lying in bed, she breathed in a wonderful aroma – a beautiful scent but one she had never smelled before. She lay as still as she possibly could. "I thought I don't ever want to open my eyes and I don't ever want to leave this spot."

She isn't sure what the aroma was that lasted for only a moment, but she believes it was a sign from angels or from the spirit of her mother. Friends who are strongly connected to angels, have suggested it's possible it was her mother coming to check in on her or it was a guiding angel. Sometimes Yvonne hears her name called when no one is around. Once, she asked aloud who called her name, and the voice of an angel told her the angelic realm was trying to get her attention. "There's a peace that comes with it. They are your guides. If you can be in tune with them periodically, your direction seems to run much smoother and have more meaning."

Whenever she finds herself in a situation she doesn't know how to handle, she will pray about it, and usually will hear an inner voice that makes suggestions about what she should do. When she listens to that voice or a sense of knowing, things go smoothly, but when she doesn't listen to that still, small voice within, she is lost. Yvonne talks to angels daily in a non-verbal way. "When you are communicating on a spiritual level, it's internal. It's your spirit to their spirit. I just know there are angels here to guide everybody."

Since she's become tuned into angels, she has experienced a real sense of peace in her life and none of the turmoil that makes life confusing and frustrating. With retirement, she has more time to stop and listen to the voices of the angels. And she doesn't worry about doomsday scenarios. "Jesus said, 'I will walk before you always. Be not afraid.' And we completely ignore those three little words 'Be not afraid.'" God sends His angels to comfort and to reassure us that we are not alone.

Some believe they are incarnated earth angels but Yvonne likes the idea that everyone on the planet has the capability to be an earth angel for others. "Just because we don't have wings and a halo doesn't mean we can't be there for one another."

She believes interest in angels is on the rise because increasing numbers of people are searching for something of greater spiritual meaning. They are trying to get back to what's truly important in their lives and are on their own spiritual journeys.

"It's so important that they don't see this need as a fear, because fear is one of the most debilitating emotions we can have and it's the most prevalent one. Most of the news is based on fear. Everybody's afraid and they're afraid of everything. But when you understand God, and not man, is in control, there is nothing to fear. If you just stop and say, 'Lord, I can't handle these fears any longer or I can't handle the situation and I need some help.' Then, if you wait, the help will come and it will come in the most unusual way, and maybe it will come in the form of an angel."

Gloria Paul Makes a Deal With Saint Francis

Gloria Paul doesn't see angels but she feels their presence always. She has a strong sense of them being around her, especially when she goes to sleep every night.

"A friend of mine says there are so many angels around us all of the time that when we walk we push them aside. Isn't that a lovely image? I have no trouble believing in that."

Gloria's belief in angels started when she was a young girl. When she was eight, her older brother told her there was no such thing as angels. "So I said to my mom, 'Are there such things as angels?' And she said, 'Yes Gloria. It's written that every child's face is brought by an angel before God.' That was the only thing about religion I ever heard my mother say. But it stuck very firmly."

All of her life, she has invoked the angels when she's needed help. Last fall, for instance, she saw something run in front of her car. She'd struck a tabby kitten. "It had blood coming out of its mouth. I put it in the car and

I tried to find a vet." No vet would agree to treat the animal unless they knew who owned the cat. She'd named it Job. Already attached to the injured animal, she was desperate to find someone who would provide treatment for its injuries. On the way home she called on every saint and angel she could think of.

"I said, 'Okay Saint Francis, you said you loved animals – well here's an animal and I hit it and it is bleeding from its mouth and it's going to die. I was responsible, but you can save it. And Archangel Gabriel, if you're so important, what are you doing up there? This cat is in the back of my car now, bleeding to death and it's my entire fault.' I had tears pouring down my eyes and I invoked every angel whose name I could think of all the way home. This cat should have died. I hit it, bang."

One vet who looked at the cat decided it was a feral stray and agreed to do what she could to help save the little cat's life. The cat had two fractured teeth, which were extracted. The cat remained at the veterinary clinic while it was neutered and recovered from the surgery and vaccinations. The vet tried to find the cat a home but no one wanted it. So Gloria agreed to give Job a home. When she went to pick him up she expected to pay at least $600 for his treatment. She was amazed to discover there was no charge.

"The vet said, 'Not a penny. We have an orphan's fund.' So I brought Job home and he is a happy little cat now. I look at him now and I say, 'All the angels are watching over you.'" Gloria is sure the angels were listening to her that day. She believes if she hadn't asked for their help, the cat's injuries would have been far worse and it likely would have died.

She talks to God and angels whenever something is bothering her and she needs an answer. While she is working on the grounds of her twenty-three-acre property in Hoyt, New Brunswick, she will often ask God to send angels to give her body the strength she needs to get the physically difficult job done.

In her opinion, more people have an awareness of angels because many believe we are coming to the end times, including her. "I don't see how we can carry on the way we are carrying on. We've become very knowledge-able but we are not using that knowledge for good. When the end time is exactly, nobody knows."

The world is in a state of turmoil with wars, economic crises, and the ever-present threat of global warming, natural disasters and disease. Many people are afraid of the future and what will happen to them and the world. Gloria isn't afraid because she knows she is loved and protected by God and angels, and for this reason there is no need to fear. She says they are trying to make us turn our attention back to what's truly important – our spirituality and to spend time in the Creator's presence.

"I don't worry about things I have absolutely no control over."

There's a real peace that comes with the knowledge that whatever happens in the world, she is loved and protected by God and her guardian angels. "Why worry about end times? Oh my word, no."

She and Yvonne Mersereau received YMCA Peace Medallions in 2007. While they were pleased with the honour and accepted it with humility and grace, the women were more excited about their plans to go to a spiritual re- treat to reflect on what's truly important. Often they will feel a need to go on retreats so they can focus on what's real and true in their lives, which is God and the angels. Often they quote the passage from the Bible, "Be still and know that I am God."

After they get away to a quiet place, they are able to rededicate their lives to God and to peace work. Finding peace within helps them to do their work throughout this province, the country and the rest of the world. Both retired nurses, Gloria and Yvonne are also women of strong faith. They have a deep-seated desire to follow scriptural teachings, especially when it comes to living peacefully. "There's one phrase that runs through my mind all the time and that is to love God and your neighbour. Unless you can do those two things, you're going to have problems with peace," explains Yvonne.

For sixteen years they ran a retreat they called Pilgrim House, a place where thousands of people came seeking quiet time and reflection. Now Yvonne and Gloria are in their mid-seventies. Several years ago they decided to close the doors of the retreat because the work became too much for them, but they still welcome people there to walk the grounds to commune with God and to talk to the angels. While she walks through the property's many trails and stops to rest among the large pine trees, Yvonne says she feels closest to God and the angels. She has a knowing that angels are around her constantly.

Both women remain committed to working for world peace. Gloria is the chair of the Fredericton chapter of Project Ploughshares, a member of the Fredericton Peace Coalition and is dedicated to seeing an end to all wars. At a time when it seems the world is at its most unstable with terrorism and war, these women remain hopeful for a better, brighter future. "Ultimately we both believe that truth and good will out. It has to," says Gloria.

Chriss Tricoteux Is No Stranger to the Presence of Angels

Chriss Tricoteux has always felt and seen angels around her since she was a very young girl. While riding her bike, going on walks or exploring in the woods, she could feel someone or something with her and that always made her feel safe.

"It was big, the size of an adult. I thought maybe it was a guardian angel. They had shoulders, they wore long flowing robes. I didn't see expressions but I felt expressions. I saw happiness, a feeling that I didn't have to be worried or scared about anything."

She had a real feeling she was loved and protected when they were around her. "I still see them every once in a while, depending where I am and who I'm with. When I'm in a place alone or there aren't many people around and I could potentially be unsafe, they're there. I don't know whether they are protecting me, or just keeping me company. I know I have relatives who have passed on that are with me. My grandfather is with me and my great-grandmother, my mom's grandmother, is there. I know my grandmother is with me as well." These past loved ones are with her to help her in her life as spirit guides.

On a typical day she is too busy to see, hear or feel their presence. It is in the times while she's meditating or giving Reiki treatments to a person or an animal, that she knows they are with her. "I can see a tall being there. Sometimes I see one, sometimes two. They are there to help me. That's the feeling I get. Whether I am giving Reiki, or walking through the woods, they are there with me."

Chriss recalls visiting a friend who was terminally ill and in palliative care in the hospital. She was administering Reiki treatments to give her comfort from the pain of cancer. "She didn't want to die in the hospital. She wanted to go home to spend her last days with her family. I had gone in every day for a week to spend time with her and give her Reiki. One day she said, 'I have to make a decision.' I said, 'Well, that's good because you have an angel here. He's sitting on the ledge, swinging his legs and he's saying, 'Make a decision, make a decision' – about whether she was going to die in the hospital or at home. She needed to tell the people who mattered the most to her. Not one of us wanted to see her die in the hospital." Chriss's friend chose to die at home. She did one week later.

Chriss wasn't at all surprised to see that angel in the hospital. She sees them frequently during Reiki treatments. Sometimes they take the shape of animals and sometimes they are very tall entities. If she is giving Reiki to animals, their spirit guides come in, often in the form of other animals. Once she was treating a large animal and she saw a duck come as its spirit guide. "As it turned out, he had ducks at home."

"I know when I am doing Reiki, spirit guides come in and they are also guardians of these people. I know they are around. I know my husband has two guys hanging around him all of the time. I've told him about that. They come when I am giving him Reiki. They want us to know we are loved, we are protected, and we're safe, because often people don't take the time to say they love each other. They don't have time to stop and say they love their kids and a lot of us, in the world of working, live very scattered lives. I believe they are there to comfort us and to let us know we are loved."

She's careful about whom she talks to about angels and spirit guides, because it can be overwhelming for those who are not open to this. But when she is in a group of people and the conversations turn to angels, she tells them about her experiences and as others share their stories, people start to open up.

"I think the more we get out there and the more we talk to people, the more people will be able to relax and say, 'I remember that, or that happened to me and I'm not weird. Maybe I do have someone protecting me.' And maybe they will be able to feel love more."

She's found angels will come when they are needed in an emergency. When she worked as a teacher on Prince Edward Island, she often drove to Fredericton, New Brunswick. Several times she drove through snowstorms and wondered how she managed to keep her small Austin Mini on the road. "I would see transport trucks going off the road and think, 'Please help me through this, and please help these people – I don't want them to be hurt.' I would just be able to see far enough to get through the storm."

She calls on angels to help in her life every day and to help others. Whenever she does Reiki she will call on her angels and spirit guides as well as those of the person she's treating to assist her. Chriss says Reiki will come faster and it's like there are more hands on the person and more energy healing power flowing through them. Clients often tell her they feel more than one set of hands.

With everything happening in the world, it is nice to believe there are angels around us helping, guiding and protecting us so we are not so frightened. "I don't have any fears because I know I am protected. We can all make ourselves ill with worry."

She dismisses the thought that 2012 is the end of the world. Rather, she says, this is the end of the world as we know it and the beginning of a whole new way of thinking, where many more people will be open to seeing, hearing and feeling what's happening in their spiritual lives.

"The shift is coming in that more people are seeing, thinking, feeling angels. The shift is coming as more people are meditating and relaxing and reaching out to other people. It's a paradigm shift. They are starting to see that they can do without a lot of material things in their lives. There are many things that these spirit guides and angels can teach us. Why carry worry and the weight of the world when you don't need to?"

Throughout her home she has angel pictures and ornaments that help remind her of the peace angels bring into her life. It helps her to feel energized and calm. The bumper sticker on her SUV says "protected by angels." She says most people like this and ask where she got it or some of her other angel collectables because they are drawn to them. Chriss estimates she has more than fifty angel ornaments and pictures in her home. People give them to her as gifts because they know she likes them.

Chriss feels we all have the capacity to serve as angels on earth to others. She views people such as Mother Teresa as earth angels. Those who are selfless in their behaviour do what they can to make the burdens of others lighter and they do not seek attention, much like angels. We all have the capacity to do this and it's so easy to help someone without letting them know you have acted on their behalf. You don't need to tell anyone you have done something nice. It is so rewarding, she says, to see the relief on someone's face when their burden has been lightened, because of something you may have done to help them. Small acts of kindness are angelic.

"We can have more grace. We don't have to be uptight and negative and critical. We can be more kind to others."

Angels Surround Mavis Lamont

This registered massage therapist and Reiki master's home and office is graced with angels in many sizes, shapes and colours. Walking up the front steps of her home you see several winged beings standing and sitting among the lush foliage and flowers.

As Mavis Lamont welcomes guests into her home, she takes the time to make it an inviting, special experience. Instrumental music that she calls angel music comes from her stereo. Jasmine tea and cookies are served and she offers a napkin with two cherubs that are too beautiful to wipe away crumbs. Angels peek at you from tables, shelves and the hardwood floors in the dining room, living room and second-storey bathroom.

Like the very nature of angels, the decorative ones gracing Mavis's home are subtle. They don't demand attention but you can't help being drawn to them. Some appear very delicate and fragile; others very strong and powerful. All have significant meaning to this lady, who received most of them as gifts from friends and clients after she started her practice in 1996. "When I started my massage therapy practice I had a Christmas card with two angels on it and that was one of the first things I used as part of the decor of my room." It is now framed and kept near the people who come to her for massage therapy.

She collects angel ornaments. She'd see them in stores and know if they were meant to come home with her. "I'm drawn to them. It depends on how they make me feel. Some are very serene. Others are sweet. Others are very beautiful. Some are simplistic. You don't choose them, they choose you. If I see them I will look at them. I don't seek them out unless I'm looking for one for a client. Sometimes I'll buy specific ones for someone who is going through a very difficult time and they are very touched. It's usually during a very significant time in their life."

The angel decorations in her home represent a time or an event in her life. She has given many of them away when the time seemed right and she felt someone could benefit from one in her collection. The ones she has kept close to her are personally significant, reminding her of aspects of her own existence that she says serve as a steadying force when life can be full of disruptions. At other times, they serve as a gentle reminder of the beauty of life. All of the angels in her home have a name and a story. She finds them intriguing, beautiful and comforting. And all of them are placed with a lot of thought. "You choose the space that honours them. I love to look at them and I am very touched when I receive them because they are always given with love."

She has come to believe that people's interest in angels and collecting them in the form of decorative items is growing because of the difficult times in which we live. In a time when Canadian soldiers have been deployed to foreign theatres and killed in wars, when people are faced with natural disasters, when they lose investments with an economy in crisis and suffer fears over disease and death, she thinks people are grasping for anything that will make them feel some amount of peace, security and comfort. Many find comfort and peace when they look at angels, because they are symbolic of what's good in life: love, peace, serenity, and compassion.

"As people look for bigger jobs, better jobs, bigger houses, better cars, when they close the door at night they find it doesn't give them the comfort they thought it would. When push comes to shove, when disaster happens or when bad things come about in their lives, unless they have a faith, it's very challenging to find much comfort in that new piece of furniture."

The number of angels that surround Mavis depends upon where she is at any given time. At work she knows she has eight in her waiting room and seven angels that work with her every day in her Reiki practice. "It's so beautiful. When a client lies down there is an angel on either side of their head. They place their hands on the side of the person's head and they whisper to them that they are there and that the person is safe."

At times she bumps into beings. She steps back and asks who it is she's bumped into. "The very first time I bumped into one, I was in my old office space and I stepped back from a client's head, bumped into something and said, 'Excuse me.' And I turned around and of course there was nobody there."

Most of the people who come to her for massage therapy, Reiki or other energy work are open to the idea that there is another realm and that angels exist in their lives.

"There's an awful lot of fear and control in this world. When you see someone who is angry usually it's because they are not being listened to. Why aren't they being listened to? It's because the people they are dealing with are coming from a place of ego.

"I deal with clients who are going through burn out. I work with clients who are dying. I work with parents who have lost their children and

I work with people who just can't cope with their lives. They have everything and yet they have nothing and they say, 'I don't understand.' They come to me initially because they can't sleep, they can't eat, and their body is failing them – they are sick. What's behind it all are their hearts. That's the source. Peace, comfort, a sense of calm. Meditation will take you there, but first you need to clear some stuff from your life."

She says the world is experiencing a huge shift and we are in the process of a great cleansing. By 2012 we will be at the pinnacle of that time. In her opinion the world will not end with a big bang. Rather, she says, the world is evolving and it is happening a little at a time, which is why people are being slowly awakened to a more beautiful way of living. She makes the point that God is trying to get our attention and the angels are assisting us. "No matter how you choose to live your life, whether you are one nasty piece of work or whether you are one of the most beautiful souls that ever existed, you will always have your guardian angels with you and they will always bring you those choices about how to live your life differently."

When Mavis had an angel reading in 1999 the angels that came through spoke in an analogy. "They said, there's a ship coming in and a plank will drop down, and the earth people will have a choice whether or not to accept the fact that there is an opportunity to live in a more benevolent way and on a higher vibration by being more kind and more compassionate, or they can keep on being as they are, seeking after material things and scratching their way to the top. But there will be a choice and those who get on this boat will be those who have chosen to live a more benevolent and kinder life. The others will still have their guardians, but they will be separate from the others."

Some people say the world will come to an end one way or the other: through a meteor strike, a flood, or a man-made disaster such a nuclear warfare. But Mavis, who says she communicates with the angels, says this will not happen. The world will end as we know it, but it will happen as an energy shift, and in the way people conduct their lives. "It's a choice. Everyone finds happiness perhaps in different ways. But in the end happiness comes from within. It is within you. There isn't a piece of anything you can hang on to, sit on or carry with you to create happiness within you. It's yours."

She says she believes the earth will continue to exist and so will people, but they will live differently than they do now. God and the angels are not happy with what people are doing to the planet. "We are really screwing up, but we can change it. Turn off the lights. Don't throw things away. We're really being challenged because of what people have done to the earth, but it isn't too late to change it."

Whether you are a person who goes to church or someone who doesn't belong to any particular faith, she says you can offer prayers and ask that everything that happens in your life be for your highest good and for the highest good of others. The angels will protect you until it is your time to die. If you ask for help, or if it is a life-threatening situation, they will come without your request.

"We have become physical beings to fulfill our own personal destiny, and that is to be the absolutely most beautiful beings we can be. With that, we have many temptations, we have many opportunities, we have many times we can choose to go left, to go right or down the centre and it's all to do with ego, choice or it's to do with service for the highest good."

God brings us here to this planet to evolve and progress in a loving and compassionate way throughout our lives. Rather than performing random acts of kindness, Mavis believes we should be doing conscious acts of kindness always. If everybody put themselves second and the other person first, the world would be so much better off.

"We're getting there. That's the shift. People are starting to turn away from self and ego and are looking to see what they can do to make this world and this day and this moment a better place for others."

Her home is filled with the aroma of jasmine, an incense she has chosen to welcome guests because, she explains, it is the scent of the angels. When angels are present you may also smell roses. Mavis used to work in a concrete building located in a parking area. Once, she walked towards her car at the end of the work day and smelled the most beautiful perfume. It happened again the following day and a number of times since then. "People will say: do you smell that? It's so fast. You don't even know what it is."

During our interview, when I asked if there were angels present in the room with us, she told me there were three: Ariel, the protector of women, along with Archangel Michael and Archangel Gabriel. What were they doing? Watching over us and listening to our conversation about them, she explained.

It is important for parents not to discount children when they come with stories of seeing angels and spirits, as all children have a sense of angels. Mavis pulled out photos of her infant grandson, where it was clear the baby was looking at something or someone other than his grandmother. "He could be seeing my aura. He could be seeing angels."

When she works with clients, she is flooded with the presence of the saints and angels. Some are overseers, some are speakers, some are guardians and some are the ones who do the healing work. While she doesn't typically channel the voices of angels, she can do so. One main angel, saint or guide will act as a moderator, so she can hear one voice at a time. She's seen Christ in her mind's eye while she is doing healing energy work. "I don't see Him a lot but when he does appear, Mother Mary is often here too. I have a prayer that I've been given that I say before I even leave my bed. I ask that God be present with me this day, that I am blessed."

Mavis also has seen the spirits of the departed. Just before her mother died, the spirit of her father was in the hospital room. He was sitting on a chair with his legs crossed, waiting for her mother's spirit to leave her body so he could help her make the journey to the other realm. Archangel Michael was at the window and Gabriel was at the door. As her mother died, Mavis held her hand. "I said, 'Mom, it's okay, you can go. Dad's waiting for you.'"

When we die, where do we go? Many people's spirits don't leave this realm for another dimension. Sometimes they have unresolved business or don't want to go. Others don't know they are dead. Mavis explained about the spirit of one man who was in her home for a while – a young farmer who was deeply in love, but had been very controlling of his wife. The woman, who couldn't stand being controlled, left the marriage and the area. He died not knowing what happened to her. "He was heartbroken. He roamed the area looking for the woman he never stopped loving. He's been roaming here for generations. If you were to ask people who live in the area, they would tell you strange things happen in their homes. Doors will open and close."

While some spirits are friendly, others can be angry, negative energies and nothing to be toyed with. She has seen demons in the home of a friend. Once, she received a phone call from two women who were terrified and needed her help. When Mavis arrived, one woman was screaming and the other was crying. Then, a beast-like thing, with fiery eyes, flew down the staircase towards her. "I said, 'I don't think so.' I told the women to come to me and we said The Lord's Prayer. Then I said, 'Where two or more are gathered together in the Lord's name there He is in the midst.'" The evil spirit left in that instant.

Barb Burnett Hears and Feels the Presence of Angels

Barb Burnett became interested in angels about a decade ago. They played a big role in a difficult time in her life – a divorce from her husband. Her son was ten years old at the time, and she really needed something to hang on to. It was because of this spiritual journey that she knew there was something more in life and she would be okay.

Barb is a Reiki master and teacher. The room where she conducts these energy-healing treatments is filled with angelic ornaments and photographs. It is a place of profound peace and healing. She knows there are many angels and kind, gentle spirits who come to help in this healing work. A bookcase is filled with all manner of books on angels, which she uses as research material to educate herself. Many are written by Dr. Doreen Virtue, a noted angel expert who Barb has studied under.

She can hear angels and feel their presence too. "I see them occasionally, but I have to work hard at seeing them. They are shapes. I think one of the blessings I have been given is that I have no doubt."

The voices of angels come through to her as an inner voice. Sometimes angels will come to her in the form of automatic writing. Their words will flow through her when she allows her mind to be still. She closes her eyes and allows her fingers to go where they will on her computer keyboard. When she opens her eyes and reads what is on the computer screen she has no doubt that it is a message from the angels.

Barb had long suffered terrible pain from a condition in her jaw called temporomandibular joint disorder. She wore a mouth splint designed to help relieve pain associated with TMJ, which happens when your jaw is out of alignment. While she was attending an angel conference she had a feeling in her gut something very special was going to happen to her that day. She felt jittery and was unable to focus on anything that was happening at the four-day conference.

Then she met Mary Lou Firth-Irving, who approached her and offered to help through hands-on energy work. As a Reiki practitioner Mary Lou knew and believed it was possible to fix TMJ this way. "She treated me through vibration kinesiology. From that day – April 1, 2006 – I haven't worn the plastic splint and I haven't had any pain."

Barb says everyone receives messages designed to help them on their life's journey but many people choose to ignore those messages. People who choose to listen to and follow the messages they receive are blessed.

Laurie McNeil-Connors Was Ten When An Angel Appeared

It was the 1970s and ten-year-old Laurie McNeil-Connors saw an angel in the sky while she was in her parents' car. "I said, 'Look Mom, there's an angel in the sky and she's flying around.' It was an image of light. It wasn't humanized. It was a spirit being and I felt it was an angel. It was in the form of a person. As a child I believed I did see wings. My parents didn't see it but they called in our priest because I was having many sightings of angels around this time."

The priest told her parents it was simply the imagination of a child but nothing they needed to be concerned about it. Her parents never mentioned it again and they didn't believe her, so she spiritually shut down. But over the past five years, she has seen and felt angels around her again.

"I started to accept who I was. I went through a lot of trauma in my life and was very suicidal. I was in a pit, down on my hands and knees on the floor. I was just done. I spoke straight to God and said, 'God, please help me. You have to take me out of here. I can't do it on my own.' And a voice said, 'You can do it. I know you are strong enough. I know you can do it. I can't take you out, but I am going to hold onto your hand.' I felt more power after I lifted my head up and realized I couldn't kill myself. I believe I have come for a higher purpose and I wasn't meant to go. I remember feeling there were a lot of spirits and angels around me, but I was directly talking to God. I felt I heard the voice of God in my mind."

Since that time, she has sensed angels round her. As she's been willing to open her mind to the possibilities, she has visions of angels again. "I walked into a hospital room a couple of months ago as my sister-in-law's father was passing away. As soon as I walked in, I said out loud, 'There are three angels standing by his head.' I think they were his guardian angels." The angels appeared as they did when she saw them as a girl – white forms without facial features. Now she is hearing the voices of people after they have passed into spirit form and exist in another dimension.

Two weeks before her first encounter with the dead, Laurie heard from her angels she would receive a gift at the end of April 2009. The next month her sister-in-law's father passed away. A week later, he spoke to Laurie and told her he had a message for his daughter. "He wanted to reassure her he was fine and was watching over her."

She says she sees angels every day. "I believe they are all around me." She feels especially close to Michael, who serves as the protector, Raphael, the healer, Metatron, the angel who watches over children, Gabriel, and many others she calls upon whenever she needs their help.

During a very difficult time in her life Laurie was constantly praying for protection and relief from the trauma she was experiencing. "It was the hardest time of my life. I would wake up at three or four in the morning. I was under a lot of stress."

She has angel oracle cards which contain images of archangels such as Michael, Gabriel and Raphael. One night she woke and saw an apparition which looked like Archangel Raphael. "I didn't see his face but I saw his whole body. He must have stood there for at least five seconds. It was long enough for me to know what was going on, who it was and that he was telling me I was safe and he was there with me."

She was filled with a sense of peace and the knowledge that everything was going to be okay. It was also confirmation that the angels had heard her prayers and wanted to reassure her they are present in her life and want to help her and everyone who asks for their help. Angels, she says, are her life and they are here with us to help us through this time of change we are experiencing on the planet. "To me they are beings that love us unconditionally."

In the past six months her life has been completely transformed. She has undergone a major spiritual growth. When she calls the angels into her presence, she makes sure she takes the time to prepare first. "You have to ground yourself. You have to think of roots into the earth, because when angels are around it's a different form of energy – it can be very strong and hard on you, you can become sick and ill. It's stuff that shouldn't be played around with. People should know what they are doing because this is energy, this is real."

The angels have told her the world is in an energy shift and we are headed into a new era of light, love and joy. "What's happening now is that God is preparing those of us who are healers to help people when the time comes. What the angels have told me is there is going to be a lot of chaos and fear. People need to get in touch with their spiritual sides because that's what lives forever. I totally believe we have turned around and gone the wrong way, and we need to go back to our Creator. I know love is the only answer."

Her view is no matter what people believe, what their religion is, wherever they live on the planet, they are all creations of God and all paths lead to the Creator.

She doesn't believe there will come a time when the world will end. "I think God has spared us. I think we are going to recreate what was supposed to have happened but didn't happen [with Eden]. So now we are going to recreate it and that's what we are doing. We are on our way to the new light era. I'm so excited, but I know I have to wait and I have to have patience because this power and this light that is coming into the world is going to manifest in people in so many beautiful ways. The angels are going to be known more to people."

As she talks about what she has seen for the world's future, she experiences goosebumps. This is her verification that this information comes from the angels who are very excited about the future of humans. "Yes, they are excited, because we are going to be able to see them more. We are going to be able to hear them too. It's going to be much easier to heal ourselves and to live in love and in the light of God."

In her opinion, there is so much fear in the world because people fear what they don't understand. We need to get out of a place of ego and into a place where we can live in faith. "You have to go inside to feel. God is not outside anywhere."

As soon as she wakes up, she says a daily motivational prayer to the Divine, including God, the angels and her spirit guides. "Every morning I get up and I say, 'Dear Divine, dear spiritual guides and teachers in the physical and spiritual world, I love you. Could you give me guidance and a blessing for my work and service today? Please bless me with your love and light. Give me the energy and intelligence to allow me to do a better job of serving humanity. Thank you, thank you, thank you.' I usually ask Archangel Michael to protect me. If I am around a lot of people I become emotionally and physically drained."

She has had many encounters with angels. While driving in her car she has seen flashes of light that she believes are angelic protections. God and the angels have helped her to heal from the many traumas in her life, including sexual abuse as a child and the emotional pain after an abortion. "I have totally forgiven myself and everyone around me that caused any of it. That's part of healing. I have been given so much in return." She says it is wonderful to feel God's power and to know she is loved and protected. She believes

God has chosen his brightest lights at this time in the history of the human race, and she has been told she will be helping humanity in a very large way. "At this time we need a lot of protection, because there is a lot of negativity on the planet and it needs to be lifted. We have to come back only with love and healing."

The message of the angels is love, she has been told by angelic messengers during her meditations. Many people have tried to fill the void inside their hearts with things. But the satisfaction that comes from those things isn't permanent. Connecting to oneself, God and the angels every day is what makes her feel peace, love and contentment. When we can learn to connect each day with the Creator and the angels there is a peace. Going deep inside is where we will find the peace, love and fulfillment we long for because this is where they are waiting for us. "When you do it they are there. Being on the planet is hard because we are not in the spirit realm. We are not in Heaven and we need to bring it here."

Laurie is so in tune with her angels she's sure they are with her at all times. She feels them always and sees them at different times. Even though she doesn't doubt their presence, she will sometimes ask for confirmation that they are around.

The number four is said to be an angelic number. While driving away from a seminar on angels one evening, she felt frustrated. She wanted confirmation of the presence of her angels. She wondered aloud why she never saw sequences of the number four. So she asked the angels about it. "I said, 'Why don't I ever see fours? Why don't you ever give me that?' I was kind of upset at them and said, 'I know I am upset and I am sorry I am mad at you, but you never give me fours. I never see any.' I said, 'Tell me that you are here for sure.' I came to a stop sign, looked down at my odometer and the numbers were 4444. And I said, 'Okay. That's all I needed.'"

Laurie also believes there will soon come a time when we all will be able to see our angels and our loved ones, because the veil that separates this dimension from the other side is thinning. "The more spiritual we become, the more the veil is opening and thinning. It's not just us preparing for this time. The other side is also preparing because we are all one. It's awesome."

Angels Helped Joanne Gruttner as a Child and Saved Her Life as an Adult

When she was three, Joanne Gruttner was diagnosed with juvenile rheumatoid arthritis. But in those times much of her comfort was Heaven sent, she recalls.

"Holy Mother Mary, Jesus and Joseph were always around me. I used to think it was in my mind, which it was. They would come and talk to me. Jesus would play with me. He was a little boy with curly hair. It was in my mind's eye, I think."

When she was diagnosed, doctors told her family she would never walk again. She recalls having an out-of-body experience where she could see Jesus and the saints telling her it wasn't true.

"I had surgery on both knees. I was riddled with arthritis in my whole body and spent a whole year in the hospital at age three doing hard core physiotherapy and being told not to expect anything. I had my little friends [Jesus and the saints] with me and I remember we would just play and they would cheer for me."

She walked with crutches from the hospital. As soon as she walked through the door of her family home she threw her crutches down and ran after her sisters. Joanne believes she was divinely healed.

"There is no separation between God and me. I knew that as a child, but our society says, 'How dare you even think that!' There is no separation between God and me. God is in me. The angels were my reminders and my cheerleaders. They were reminding me that the mind is what separates you from your divinity, where you are from and what you believe you can do."

She was raised in the Roman Catholic church. Her parents were alcoholics, but her grandmother and aunts, including one who was a nun, had a big influence over her spirituality while she was growing up. She remembers the rules and religious dogma and a fear of God, but inside she felt the love of Jesus, the saints and the angels. It was really quite confusing to her as a child.

"That's where I drew my strength from. People used to say, how have you been raised the way you were and then end up the way you are? Out of my siblings I'm really the only one who has a strong spirituality and faith. I always knew there was something or someone with me. I always had a support system, even though it was not in the physical world."

As an adult that childhood experience was confirmed as real and not an imagined thing. She experienced a deep seven-year depression but refused medication because she intuitively knew she had to take a holistic approach to healing and recovery.

"I had a dream one night. Christ was standing beside me and the room was yellow. He was showing me to put hands on someone and I woke up the next morning and I thought, what was that? I know they called it the healing of hands in the Biblical days, but what was that?"

During an illness, Joanne had heard Reiki treatments could help her, so she took a course so she could help heal herself. During her study, her Reiki master stood beside her in a yellow room, which reminded her of the dream.

In the eight years Joanne lived in New Brunswick, she went to university and earned a bachelor's degree and a master's degree in adult education. Over the years, she has become a Reiki master and a master instructor of integrated energy therapy. Energy flows through her and out of her hands into other people. The reason so many people in the alternative healing practices have had angelic encounters is because they are more attuned to a higher energy frequency than most people, so they are able to connect to another realm. That includes angels and the spirits of those who have died, but have yet to cross over into the spiritual realm.

Recently, she has been seeing an angel by her side. "They are in my mind's eye. Sometimes I will see a shadow. It's not only angels that I see – I also see discarnate souls. The angels use me to help these souls pass over. They don't know they are dead and they are lost. The angels appear and guide me and tell me what to do. Basically, what I am doing is providing a bridge for the discarnate souls to go over to the angelic realm."

Angels and spirits of people who've died are two separate things, in her opinion. "There are people who have passed on, who are lost and don't know how to get home. Then there are your ancestors and friends who come back to guide you, spirit guides. And there are the angels who are Divine beings."

She once encountered what she believes was her guardian angel after she underwent an emergency hysterectomy. During surgery she lost a lot of blood but didn't want a blood transfusion because she was worried about contracting HIV or hepatitis C. The doctors and nurses urged her to take the transfusions, warning her that without them she would die. She was very weak, near death, when she heard the voice of a woman tell her she had to take the transfusions. She wanted only to close her eyes and sleep, but the voice told her if she did close her eyes, she wouldn't wake up and it wasn't her time to go. With the last bit of strength inside her, she whispered to the nurses, "I need blood." She received the transfusions and survived. Joanne is sure that was the voice of her guardian angel urging her to live.

Mary Lou Firth-Irving Has Seen Angels and Spirits

Mary Lou Firth-Irving's grandmothers read tea leaves. From the time she was a child, she has been able to see into the future and realize what was going to happen. Angels have been with her all through her life.

"After a child reaches the age of eight or nine parents will say to them, 'Oh no, you can't be saying that,'" she explains. "Pay attention to little children. They are in their bedrooms and the angels watch over them. We have angels and spirit guides. Kids with imaginary friends really have angels around them."

When she first realized she has the ability to see angels and the spirits of those who have passed, she didn't want to share it with anyone because she worried people would think she was mentally ill.

"I can actually see them. I can see them after someone has died and they will come in with a message for you." If she hesitates to share these messages with people she gets pain in her ears.

Ten years ago her father passed away. Three days before his death, she knew he was going to die. She was in her car when the air both outside and inside filled with fog, "It was the eeriest thing I've ever felt. I was told on the drive home to say goodbye to him." The angels and her spirit guides speak to her in an inner voice, and the angels explained her father would die and it was time to let him go – he died three days later. "So I've always paid attention when I have this mist around me."

Not long after her father's death she had to drive to Ontario. Before she left she went into her bathroom and looked in the mirror. She saw the same mist and the same inner voice told her to be very careful. When she left with her sister and her children at eight p.m., her sister got in the driver's seat while Mary Lou decided to recline in the back of their van and closed her eyes.

"A voice inside my head kept saying, 'You need to drive. You need to drive.' I knew I wasn't going to rest so I said, 'Shelley, I need to drive.' My son got in the front with me. We were driving along and there were two transports around me. A car pulled up beside me on the 401 highway and I looked at it and thought, 'Oh God! Don't say a word.' There was nobody in the car. Not a soul. The lights were on and you could see in the car because it was almost dark. It scared the bejeezers out of me but I thought I'm not going to say a thing. My son, who was nine at the time, said, 'Mommy, there's nobody in that car.' I said, "I know, babe, but we're okay.' My sister and my daughter both sat up and were freaked out. The car pulled up, put the signal light on, pulled up beside us and slowed us down while the two transports went by. The words in my head were 'Change the pace. Get off the road.'"

Just before they made the next exit off the highway she says the car with no driver left the road, drove into a nearby field and disappeared out of sight. "That was an angel telling me what to do."

She pulled into a gas station, put six dollars worth of gas in the car, then she heard the voice again, telling her they were okay. They got back on the highway and discovered, just four miles further, that the two transport trucks she had been driving in tandem with had been involved in a crash along with five cars. Mary Lou believes this was her father's spirit helping them get safely to their destination.

Angels, she believes, can be Divine beings as well as people who have crossed over after death. People can return to earth as angels and can come back in their own human form, but only for a very short time. She recalls the time her stepfather, whom she called Poppa, was terminally ill with cancer in a Moncton hospital.

A man, who appeared to be a street person, was in the bed next to him. Mary Lou's mother was rather distressed about the man who was sharing the same room with her husband. "I said, 'How do you know that isn't an angel of God sent down to look after Poppa?' That turned her tune right around. The man took Poppa to the bathroom and he was a God-send to him."

Mary Lou wanted to send a letter of thanks to him, so a nurse gave them a mailing address, but no such place in Bathurst existed. A nurse told her the same man had often been admitted and placed in the same room with someone who was dying and needed comfort. This is just one of many spiritual encounters and experiences she has almost on a daily basis and angels have protected her from harm many times.

Whenever she sees the mist on the road while driving, she knows angels and spirits are warning her to pay attention and to be careful. Once, while travelling from Moncton to Campbellton with her niece, she saw a shooting star fall from the sky and the familiar spirit mist sprang up on the road. She slammed on the brakes just as a moose appeared and crossed the highway in front of her. "This mist is my protection from my father."

Mary Lou has travelled around the world as a board member of EnKA, the Energy Kinesiology Association, an international group based in the United States. At one conference, she met a man from South Africa who told her he has always had the ability to see dead people but until he reached adulthood he was unable to discuss it with anyone, because he knew people would think he had lost his mind. "He gave a course the next day and it blew my mind about who took the course, because these were people who were very well off and very well known throughout the U.S."

But now there are more people who are willing to openly discuss angels and spirit guides in their lives. We are entering a time when it is becoming socially acceptable to open yourself up to what's known as the "Third Eye" – your intuitive abilities which allow you to connect with spirit. It is becoming more acceptable to acknowledge angels and spirits because there is also a conscious movement underway.

Mary Lou says it isn't that more people are having encounters than in the past. Rather, people are more willing to talk about the encounters they have had with the angelic realm. There is a shift in people's thinking and she views it is a conscious awakening: almost like remembering the things we knew when we were children. She makes the point that we are starting to remember the things we had forgotten because we are opening up the intuitive side of ourselves that we had been forced to close down long ago. The message she hears from the deceased for the living is that everything is fine, there is nothing to fear and we all go home to God when we die. "There's no doubt in my mind that when we die we go home. I have seen that. I held my dad's hand when he passed away and my subconscious saw where he went, that there was a beautiful golden light."

The angels are here to reassure people of all faiths around the world. So many people live in guilt and fear. The angels want people to know they are here to help release them from those feelings of guilt and fear. Like many, Mary Lou believes the veil between the earthly and heavenly realms is thinning and is another reason more people may be experiencing spirit and angels.

Another interesting point she makes is that waking in the middle of the night between three and four a.m. puts you in what she calls "the angel hour" – a time when angels are most often present with us. "They are around to check on you at nighttime. Different angels do different things. Different spirit guides are for different things."

Mary Lou also practises automatic writing, which are the words of the angels coming through her. She will sometimes write six pages and then read what she's written, not recognizing it as her words at all, because it isn't. Instead it is the words of wisdom from the angelic realm.

When she does energy healing work she knows the angels are with her, serving to protect her and the client. She travels a great deal but never worries about her safety because she knows the angels and her spirit guides are with her to keep her from harm.

Deana Barnes – In the Company of Angels

Reprinted with permission of Deana Barnes, www.newinepouring.wordpress. com

"In the fall of 1996, I was on my way home to Nampa, driving on I-84 from Boise, Idaho. It was sometime after 10:00 p.m. and I had just left the chapel of the medium security prison. We had a great service. God had moved mightily and I was so excited!

"The flow of traffic was about seventy miles an hour, and it was pretty heavy. Suddenly, I noticed that cars ahead of me were swerving to change lanes in an erratic manner. Before I knew it, I was driving up headlong into the back of a school bus that had just merged into traffic.

"For some reason the bus crossed over into the middle lane at a crawl. It couldn't have been going more then fifteen miles an hour. The other cars in front of me were able to swerve around it, but I had no where to go. A pickup truck, oblivious to the predicament ahead of me, flew past my car, close to ninety miles an hour.

"To avoid crashing into the back of the bus or moving into the path of the speeding pickup, all I could do was crank the wheel to the right, as far as it would go, slam on the brakes, and shout out the name of Jesus. I did this because I believe that there is power in His name, and it has been proven true time and time again!

"The car slid sideways as oncoming traffic lights blinded my eyes. I turned the wheel to the opposite range, and did a complete 180 in the middle of the interstate, sliding again, sideways, as I shouted out the name of Jesus for protection.

"Somehow, to my amazement, I was able to drive out of what could have been a horrific car crash. I drove around the yellow deathtrap crawling at fifteen miles an hour in the middle lane. I prayed to God no one would smash into it. It was a whirlwind; it was surreal, like a dream.

"In total amazement, I thought to myself, 'How did I get out of that?' The world around me kept moving like nothing had ever happened, yet I felt like I had crossed in and out of some kind of parallel universe. I was in shock and had to pray for God to help me drive the rest of the way home. I had a few miles left to go, and I was thanking Jesus for allowing me to go home to my three children that night.

"I also had to wrap my brain around the other thing that occurred in the car during the peak moments of God's Divine intervention to save my life. During the time that I was cranking the wheel of the car, and shouting out the name Jesus, it really was as though time stood still. I saw an angel sitting next to me in the car. He was sitting quietly, with his hands resting on his lap. And even though I have seen them dress like modern men, he was wearing a robe.

"He had the face of a man with normal male features; however, above his temple and forehead, his head flanged out into the shape of a crown. I'm not saying that he was wearing a crown, but that his head opened up and out like a crown. He was not a solid 3-D figure, but was more in an outline form, and the color of mist. The crown-like flanges wisped out and then vaporized. He just sat there the whole time, quietly, next to me, shoulder to shoulder.

"Later that night at home, still shaking my head in utter amazement, I began to ask God about the angel. Why was he so still? I mean, you would think he would have been doing something dramatic, like maneuvering the car around, or covering me up with wings or something. What about the shape of his head?

"Until this day I really don't understand all of what this angel was but there are some things that God showed me not too long after the ordeal. When I asked the Lord why the angel was not moving or doing anything, the Lord revealed to me that my eyes were only opened to one of many angels that were there.

"The breakthrough that took place in the prison ministry had been battled over weeks prior and the enemy's plan to take my life had been thwarted. People have asked me how I know all that and I just tell them that in the same way God opened my eyes to see the angel, in that same way, he opened my understanding to know the story behind it.

"When we see angels it is because God shows us them and He does nothing without purpose. The angel I saw was the Spirit of Wisdom. His head flanged out open to the voice of the Father; he only speaks what the Father speaks. And God said, 'This angel is assigned to you to assist in ministry, and show you wisdom.' Did you know that we need wisdom from God on how to administrate His anointing in our lives? You know, like who to pray for, and how to pray?

"Only God could have given me wisdom to handle that car the way I did that night like a stuntwoman from Hollywood, in a scene out of *Vanishing Point*! I have a hard enough time parallel parking! On the outside of the car was another story – angels kept it from rolling, and hitting numerous cars that were all around me. The second miracle that night was that my spun out tires made it all the way home. The next morning they were flat – in the driveway. Praise God for his mercy endures forever."

Years later Barnes was outside an elderly friend's house cleaning up her yard. This is a story she relates about another encounter with her angel:

"I was cleaning up my neighbor's yard while she was in town. This was in the mountains. I had my hair up in a bun. I began to feel something on the top of my head and thought, it must be my glasses.

"Well, this went on for quite a while, feeling this sensation, but I was too busy to pay attention. I walked into the house and milled around, and I reached up to take the glasses propped up on my head off. However, the sensation of something on my head remained and began to slide towards my forehead. Thinking it was a leaf or something, I bent way down towards the floor and plop! Off my head the biggest, greenest, grasshopper-looking thing I had ever seen. Well, God in Heaven knows I love him, but some of His creatures really freak me out, and this huge leaf with legs was no exception. In a microsecond, in time held still, while my melt down was just about to kick in, my eyes were open to my angel and he was laughing.

"He was laughing and you know I started to get half mad at him because that thing was on my head for quite a while but he saw my reaction and knew I was going to go into a tizzy over it; his laughter dropped to a grin and he reached up and touched my shoulder.

"The vision stopped but his presence remained. The fear melted off of me into a beautiful calm. And then I began to laugh. And I laughed, and laughed, all afternoon. I put a jar over my green, crawly visitor until my husband arrived to let him go. He put the little (big) guy out on the awning and touched his belly, and that creature made a sound we always wondered about. He made that southern insect sound that starts chirping come summer."

Angels Encouraged Katherine Kehler's Father

Katherine Kehler is an innovator and entrepreneur who has developed and launched many successful ministries. She is also the creator of a website called www.thoughtsaboutgod.com. This is her angel story:

"An angel from heaven appeared to him and strengthened him" (Luke 22:43).

"When my mother was forty years old she became pregnant with twin girls. I was twelve years old at the time and there were four other children. Living on a large dairy farm, there was no end of work to do.

"It was a hard pregnancy and six weeks before the twins were to be born, Mom was hospitalized with toxemia. My dad was now taking care of five children as well as managing our large dairy farm. Mother's prognosis did not look good. The possibilities of her dying were very real. Perhaps there would also be two babies he would have to care for by himself. Dad was very discouraged.

"One morning, after all five of us were in school, two men knocked on the kitchen door. Dad had never seen them before and wondered who they were but he invited them in. They came into our kitchen and lovingly read to him encouraging verses from the Bible. After they prayed for him, they left. He never saw them again, but was sure they were angels. Their visit filled him strength and hope.

"Several days later, Mother gave birth to twin girls and was home again in a week. She was fine and so were the babies. Other than having two small sisters to babysit, life returned to normal.

"Angels are sent from God. It happens all the time. More often than we realize. During the past few years, so many people have told me stories of God sending angels to protect, strengthen and encourage."

Angels Took Angie Aldridge's Grandfather to Heaven

Angie Aldridge describes an encounter with angels. "In 1995, my grandfather passed away October 30th. It was a pretty emotional time, as my grandfather was always just up the road from me. The day was cloudy with rain misting outside. We were all at the funeral and the minister was just saying a few words to us about death and losing a loved one. He had a container of holy water and he sprinkled it on my grandfather's casket and said (to the Lord) to let His light shine and to take this man home. Just as he splashed the coffin the brightest beam of sun shone through the window and down onto the coffin. It startled the minister so much he actually ran outside to see the sky. It was still a miserable day. That light came from nowhere and I believe it was my grandfather's angels coming to escort him home."

Angels Save Marjorie Jewett From a Serious Car Accident

Marjorie Jewett knows angels have saved her life.

"I had a car accident a few years back. A bee flew in through the window of my car, which terrified me. I went to swat the bee to get it away from me and the car swerved and rolled twice. The windshield popped and I had some dust on me but that was it. The car landed back on its tires. I know there was an angel there, because I should have been killed in that accident. The car was a mess. It was a write-off."

In that moment, when she knew the car was out of control, she had absolutely no fear. Once the car stopped rolling and landed upright, she got out, changed one tire that had been flattened and drove the wreck home. The car was damaged beyond repair but she didn't have a scratch on her body.

"When I looked at the car, I couldn't believe I'd walked away from it and that I had actually driven it home. Everyone has a guardian angel. You have as many angels around you as you want."

Marjorie cares for children in her home. Sometimes, she says, they will see things in the room adults cannot see. She believes they are seeing angels, spirit guides and the spirits of deceased loved ones who drop in to watch over everyone in her home. As children we are born with all of our memories of the other side. It is possible for children to see the spirits of people who have passed over and to see angels, because they are new to this realm. "They are

new here and their minds aren't closed off. As you grow, your mind gets closed
off and that's where you have to start searching again to see things that you
were always meant to see."

Her interest in angels and the paranormal started in her twenties.
Over the past thirty years she has paid close attention to it. Marjorie was raised
in a fundamentalist Christian home where the family went to church six times
a week for services, choir practices and youth group meetings. Many of the
sermons she heard were of hell and damnation. "It terrified me. I thought all
they ever preach is doom and gloom and fear. I kept thinking this isn't right.
How could God damn us to hell forever if we did something wrong? I was so
afraid of dying and going to hell, if we had a thunderstorm I would think that
was the end of the world. I was paranoid. I was scared to death even in my
teens and young twenties."

Through reading and exploring other views, she came to realize
God was not wrathful, angry and ready to damn her to hell. She has come
to understand the Creator is a loving being who doesn't judge. Instead, the
Almighty accepts us where we are, as we are and is ready to embrace us in
love, sending angels to help us on our life journey.

Angels, she says, helped her with her mindset. They encouraged her
to look further and in other directions and not to be afraid. She feels them
around her often as a very warm, comfortable presence. While this woman
sees and feels angels around her, she has only once heard what she believes
was an angelic being. "I was walking down the street and I heard my name
being called. I looked around and there was absolutely not a soul there. It was
a male voice and I assume it was an angel. I think that happened to let me
know that if we listen hard enough we can hear them."

Whenever she has a decision to make, she says, angels will gather close
to her. They come in the form of birds and will fly very near to her. Angels,
she believes, can come in many forms including humans, animals, birds and
butterflies to let us know they are around to help us.

"I think God is pretty laid-back. And I think angels are around us all
of the time to help us; all we have to do is to ask."

Her daughter had a close friend who died in a two-vehicle accident
(the man in the other car also died). If guardian angels exist, then why would
God allow something like this happen? Marjorie believes humans are eternal
beings who come to earth to have experiences. "I believe before we are born,
we have written our own charts of what's going to happen. We have so many

days that we are going to live. When our time is up, our time is up. It's something we decided before we came here. We have always been a part of God. We are all sons and daughters of God. God created us. We will always be a part of Him."

Angels have always been around, however many of us have ignored them. "But as we are becoming open, we are starting to see and feel and hear. We are evolving. It was meant to be." Angels, she says, are everywhere. They have always wanted to make contact with us and, with our minds changing, it is becoming more possible for them to do so.

Marjorie has also developed her intuitive abilities. She sees images in her mind's eye and sees things before they happen. Once she told her husband she foresaw the image of a newspaper article which said 'Three Canadian soldiers Killed in Afghanistan.' Three days later that same article appeared on the front page of the local newspaper. She is grateful it doesn't happen often as she finds it very disturbing.

She doesn't believe there is anything to fear in the end-of-the-world scenarios that are being talked about these days. It is especially bothersome to her when she hears her twelve-year-old grandson talk about not wanting to make an effort in school.

"He said, 'I don't know what for, Nana, the world's going to end anyway.' I said, 'Who told you this foolishness?' He said, 'Everybody is saying it. It's all over the Internet.' I said, 'Then throw the Internet away, because it's not the truth.'"

The only end, in her opinion, is the end of old ways of thinking and a new awareness of caring for the planet and for one another. If there is an end of the world, it will likely be the end of the world as we know it, and the beginning of a whole new way of thinking and living. "I think you will see this come about when people get signs and messages from angels. I think if anything is going to happen, it's not going to be negative – it's going to be positive. There's nothing to worry about either way."

Marjorie's son-in-law is a soldier who has served three tours of duty in Afghanistan and is slated to return there. There is nothing to describe the fear that comes with seeing a loved one go to war. She prays for all of the soldiers there and asks the angels to surround her son-in-law and all of the soldiers in this time. She says she will call on Archangel Michael and thousands of angels to protect all soldiers serving in war zones.

"I sent angels to help heal my girlfriend's mother in Germany, who is diabetic and has been hospitalized with diabetic complications." Her friend noted the time Marjorie said she would ask angels to go to her mother. The woman knew when it happened and told her daughter, "She said, 'Canada was here last night. I could feel it come all the way through my body and my feet felt so warm and tingly. I fell asleep and I felt so good.' She could feel the healing energy I was sending and the angels. It took her from being house-bound to being well enough that she could start walking to the market."

For years Marjorie worked in nursing homes with palliative care patients who were very afraid to die. "I would call the angels to come to them and give them comfort." In her experience, angels are always near when people are close to the end of their time here and help our spirits cross over to the other side.

Joie Pirkey Sees and Hears Angels and Demons

From childhood, Joie Pirkey has always been able to see and hear what she describes as angels and demons. She remembers her mother being in the kitchen singing when she saw an orb of light hovering over her head. "It wasn't the first time I had seen this, but it was really distinctive because it was very large and very bright." It was a difficult thing to talk about because her mother dismissed what she saw and heard as nonsense. "One time she took me to an eye doctor and told him I was seeing things and focusing on things that were not there. He said, 'Her eyes are fine. I think she just wants attention.'" Her mother then took her to a pediatrician, who said he didn't know what the problem was and maybe she should pray about it.

She also knows when relatives are about to die. It happened the first time when she was in middle school. She had a vision of her Uncle Joe's death from a heart attack. Two weeks later he suffered a heart attack and died. She saw her grandmother's passing in advance.

"That's happened many times. I know God has given me a gift. I think it is the gift of seeing. I see orbs of light. Sometimes the orbs of light will come and there will be quite a few of them, and then I will start to see sparks of really silver-white light around them. Only a few times I have seen a man. I have come to find out that those men are angels. I know also demons can show up as angels, because demons are fallen angels. There were a set number of angels and a third of them fell from grace. They are still angels, but they are simply following Satan."

Joie can tell whether they are angels of God or the fallen ones. "They are around people. Sometimes they are in people. You can see a person who is saved. They have Jesus in them. And you can see when a person is possessed. They have a demon in them. That's rare. But I can see them. And then I can see demons stuck on to people. Just like angels of God will sometimes sit on the back of people's heads. Demons are here to torment people. They try to kill, maim and destroy them."

Most angels are Divine beings who were created, and are very much separate from human beings. Angels minister to us and comfort us, but Joie does not believe they guide us. "I believe God specifically sends messages that guide us or messages that require us to do something. Angels are His ministers, His messengers. God sees people when they grieve. He hates that. God feels it deeply when we grieve so He sends angels to us for comfort. So you will see a lot of angels around people who are grieving. Whenever I see angels around people, I think to myself that person has just lost someone they love."

When a person is worried, Joie often sees one or two angels around them, maybe as many as five or six. But when a person is worshiping, depending on their level of worship, there can be literally thousands, because angels join in our worship.

"I have seen them many times when I am worshiping. All of a sudden I will look up and see thousands of them in rows in front of me. It's as if they are showing me that when we worship as human beings, we literally join the angels before God in worship. They really like that."

When people prepare their hearts to worship, they cause angels to start appearing around them. Joie says in all of her years of seeing and hearing angels she knows this for sure. Angels are not concerned with themselves, unless they are the fallen ones. "They are concerned with God and His will. So if they are coming to speak with us, it is to accomplish God's will in our lives. They are pointing us to God. His way is their goal. Many times I don't even notice the angels because I am waiting for the message from God. The message is more important than the messenger. The comfort comes from the Holy Spirit and they [angels] are ministers of that comfort. From my own experience they don't want attention. They want our attention to be on Christ. The angels are listed in the Bible a couple of hundred times. In the Book of Matthew you will read the first couple of lines and there are angels popping up everywhere.

They are part of the story. To deny them is just sort of stupid, but to make them the focal point shows that you don't get it."

Angels come and go very quietly when they appear in a human-like form, and it can be very frightening, she says. "You can't have something show up in your house that shouldn't be there and not have it scare the heck out of you. There are times I will literally jump over my husband and begin to push him towards it because I am so afraid."

Each time she has seen angels that appear in a human-like form, they have curly hair, are about five-foot-nine, have regular features, are lanky and dressed in white robes. They are very, very graceful. Every movement is choreographed because they are so graceful. When you see an angel, it is so overwhelming you can't talk and you can't believe what you are seeing. In her experience, being in the presence of an angel has a physical affect on your body like you have taken some kind of muscle relaxant. You have such a relief of stress and tension, you feel like you have taken a drug with no side effect.

"I was trying to describe to my husband when I was seeing one, and all I could say was, 'It's so beautiful. It's so beautiful.' When they approached me there were about a thousand of them, and there was so much light I couldn't really see individuals until they got up close to me. It literally looked like an army. Then they moved off to the right and began to ascend what looked like a ladder. It was unbelievable what I was seeing. The light is so bright you'd think you have to cover your eyes, but the weird effect is that your eyes want to drink this in, so your eyes open wide, like your eyes want to drink this light in, even though it is very white and very bright. When they cross their arms there will be silver-white light and it will spark. It is really something to see. I saw one that was very large and it looked like a black man. He was huge, like that *Green Mile* guy, but bigger. One had blond hair and big gold wings. My son also saw that one."

Joie believes people's minds are opening to the spiritual realm now because many are spiritually starved and are searching for something that will fill them. She also believes that emptiness started when humanism entered our world view. Many of us have literally thought God out of existence in our lives. As a result, in her opinion, people have become starved for Him.

She believes others are having experiences with angels but are not speaking about it. Some may have realized the profit that can be made from people's interest in angels and are saying they are having visions of angels when really they are not. "I have been in meetings and I have people saying,

'Joie, can you see those angels standing at the back wall?' and I am thinking, 'What is this guy trying to do?' It's not like I am some kind of angel expert, it's not like I can always see them, because I can't, but I know when somebody is being phony."

Joie believes there are many people who are fakes – who claim to be able to see, hear and feel angels because they are looking to profit from society's growing interest in angels. And yet, there are others who are really experiencing the Divine and the presence of angels, but say nothing about it because they are ashamed, don't want to be affiliated with this, or worry that people will think they may be mentally ill. People may have always had angelic encounters, but many now are more open to this, and we have the ability to connect with literally thousands of people in one day through the Internet.

Joie has seen things spiritually that she is not willing to discuss publically about the end of the world. "That being said, I do not believe the world will end in 2012 – not even close. When people talk about the end of the Mayan calendar and 2012, I think they are just playing up the fear. I think people have to live as if the end of [their world] could happen at any time, because it could happen at any time. But I do not see it coming in 2012. I know there's a lot of talk about it, but all I can tell you is that God keeps telling me it's nothing like that. There may be catastrophes, but it's not going to be the end of the world. The world will continue as is, past 2012. That's my prophecy."

Regardless of what will or will not happen with the future of this planet, Joie knows this for sure: when we die we live on in spirit.

Monty Lewis Has Encountered Angels and Demons

Monty Lewis knows beyond any doubt that angels have saved his life many times. For his first thirty years he lived hard and fast. He was born and raised in New Waterford, Cape Breton, a coal-mining town where people worked hard and played harder. His home life was dysfunctional, with his father beating his mother in alcoholic rages. He hated the violence. But children learn what they live and it wasn't long before he started to drink and fight too.

He had his first street-fight before he started school and drank rum and smoked cigars before he entered kindergarten. He'd even drink in school. He was a smart kid who did well in his classes, but as a teen he was more interested in drugs and alcohol than education. He carried a .38 Smith and

Wesson and made money by selling stolen liquor and doing whatever he could to support his drug and alcohol habit. He would write his own prescriptions for narcotics on stolen prescription pads. Still in his teens he was on a first-name basis with organized crime leaders. His drinking and drug abuse intensified and so did the level of crime he committed. He crawled inside society's underbelly, moving back and forth between Cape Breton and Toronto.

Long before Monty turned his life over to God, he heard voices but they weren't divine. To most people this man appeared to be fearless, someone who wouldn't back down from anything or anyone. But inside, he was terrified of the demons that tormented him ever since he was a small boy. "I would feel them and hear them and see them. It made me more aggressive and on the defensive towards everyone then. They [the demons] would tell me people were going to get me. I have seen manifestations of demonic angels."

He'd spend many nights battered and bleeding, after brawls, in drunk-tanks. In Vancouver in 1973, heavily into crime and drug abuse, he had a near-death experience when he overdosed on heroin. He was in a rented room in a flophouse with a couple of other drug addicts who hit him up with much purer heroin than the stuff he was used to injecting into his veins. Immediately he felt his soul leave his body.

"I'm up above, looking down at myself slumped in the chair and I knew it was me with my head on my chest and they were having a conversation about me being dead. The girl said, 'Well, what are we going to do with his body?' Halifax Jerry, the other guy in the room, said, 'There's nothing we can do about him. They'll find it later and they'll lug him out.' I'm up in the corner trying to tell everybody how good I feel and how I've never felt as peaceful in all of my life. I couldn't move and I was trying to tell myself from up there, 'Lift your head up, boy!' I was looking at the situation, hearing every word they were saying. I don't know how long it was but after a while I came back into my body.

"I never thought anything about that until years later when I was being transported from the Cape Breton County Correction Centre to Dorchester Penitentiary by the sheriff I'd grown up with. He said, 'Monty, in all of your travels and experiences what's the thing that stands out in your recollection?' So I began to tell him that story of my near-death experience. He said, 'Wow. You had an out-of-body experience. I've been studying them for years and that was an out-of-body experience – where your spirit left your body and your spirit was going off to eternity. For some reason it was all stopped and your spirit was put back into your body.'"

Monty now believes he didn't die as a result of that drug overdose because God had other plans for his life. He cannot count the times guardian angels have protected him from death – from car accidents, fires, hired killers, drug overdoses. He feels God saw him through so many dangerous situations by surrounding him with guardian angels.

"God sent them whenever I needed them, all of my life. Just look at how I lived for thirty-some years. He kept me from that, and from being beaten to death with weapons, left to bleed to death in forty degrees below zero weather, soaked in gasoline, slashed open. I came out of fires in cars. I used to call it a hunch or a sixth sense when I heard a voice say, 'Don't go down that alley' and I'd find out later they were waiting to do a contract on me. I've been in places where I know people sent me out of a cab and they waited outside because I was supposed to be shot dead. When I went in the house was empty. Then out of the kitchen came these two girls and one guy and I know they had a gun and I knew, for some reason, they couldn't do what they were paid to do. I believe now, as I look back, the Lord was there and prevented them from killing me."

Most of his arrests and charges never stuck until he was arrested and found guilty of, among other things, assault causing bodily harm. On December 30, 1976, at age thirty, he was sent to Dorchester Penitentiary to serve an eight-year sentence. While he was there the federal government started offering university courses to inmates. He decided to study and passed with top marks. While he was growing up, his father always told him he would never amount to anything. For the first time in his life he realized he was an intelligent person with potential. He was the go-to guy for everything and anything prisoners wanted, including drugs. It gave him power. He had a reputation. "They called me Crazy Monty Lewis. They knew if they messed with me … I played until the end."

He was transferred to the minimum-security Westmorland Institute. Then, while on parole, he applied to the University of Western Ontario in London and was accepted. He was doing well until he started to dabble in drugs again. It wasn't long before he had a needle in his arm and was back in his old life of crime. He'd just committed a huge drug score, but the police were tipped off and his parole was revoked. This time he was sent to Kingston Penitentiary. His mother prayed for him until the day she died, asking God to help her son turn his life around. Sadly, Helen Lewis never lived to see it happen.

He was stripped of his clothing and thrown into the hole. While in solitary confinement, the voices in his head told him to kill himself. He cried out to God. "I prayed and the love of God came over me and in me and through me and filled that cell. I just wept and wept and wept." The next morning a Salvation Army officer came to see him. Lewis prayed the Sinner's Prayer and invited Christ into his heart. Once a con man, Monty Lewis was now Christ's man. He made a commitment to live the rest of his life for the Lord. He started Bible studies with his fellow inmates. It was the beginning of what was to become a ministry known as Cons for Christ.

Released from prison, he got a job digging ditches. He hated it but was determined not to go back to his old life. He worked all day and would go to AA meetings at night. On Sundays he could be found at Salvation Army services. In every spare moment he shared the salvation message and his story whenever he got an opportunity. He's been clean and sober since November 21, 1977 – the day he prayed with the Salvation Army officer in the hole. He met his wife Lynda in 1978, shortly after he'd been released from prison. She was a Canada Post worker and recently separated. "We were just friends for about a year but then there came a time when a handshake was not enough."

They married on December 27, 1980. Their first child, Lana, was born in 1982. When she was a little girl, he says she used to see angels in their home. "When I used to pray for Lana, God showed me angels around her and He said, 'Don't worry about Lana, my angels are around her.' I could literally see angelic beings around her and I never had to worry."

In 1984, Adam arrived. Working full-time and supporting a family, Monty was a million miles away from the life he'd once lived. "It was great. I started to realize who I was. God began to show me who I was. I wasn't a mistake and no good. I believed the lie for thirty-five years of my life."

These changes in his life were wonderful, but he wanted to reconnect with two daughters he hadn't seen in nine years. When their mother realized he was a changed man, she agreed to allow Juanita and Cheryl to get to know their dad. He even managed to let go of the pain and hatred he felt for his own father. His dad was desperately ill and not expected to live, so Monty made the trip home to Cape Breton from Ontario to visit him in the hospital. The once fierce Marshall "Buddy" Lewis was now old, frail and struggling to breathe. As Monty washed and massaged his father's feet and back, love and forgiveness replaced the pain and anger. "I stood up crying, asking him to forgive me for all of the disgrace I brought upon his name and for robbing him and beating him. And he forgave me and started crying and asked me to forgive him for how he treated me and my mother."

While working at Canada Cement Lafarge in 1985 Monty was also conducting a full-time ministry. When it got to be too much, he prayed about what he should do. "God spoke to me. He told me to quit my job, sell my home and move here, to Fredericton." He wanted confirmation that what he heard was truly God's will. He never said a word about a possible move to New Brunswick to anyone. So when Lynda asked him when they'd be moving he thought perhaps it was God's will. Still, he wanted more reassurance this was the right plan. So they decided they'd move if someone offered to buy their home without them advertising it. His neighbour offered to buy it for exactly the amount they wanted.

On his last week at the cement plant he was working a night-shift. It was that night, he says, he had another encounter with a demon. He walked from the top of the plant to the locker rooms and when he entered he felt a cold, overwhelming presence.

"I looked around and here was this thing hovering in the air. It was hairy and brown with claws. It had a round face, with pointed ears and big teeth, with its mouth open, and beady, fiery eyes. It stank. It was very imposing and threatening. I ran out of the locker room outside of the building and around in front of the offices with its big plate glass windows. My intent was to run around to the main entrance. This thing was chasing me and the smell was unbelievable. I was really running. I was fearful. I ran inside and it was out at the plate glass window."

His aim was to get inside and take the elevator to the third floor, where the building's security guard was located. "The spirit of God spoke to me and said, 'If you go on that elevator, you will be running from that thing the rest of your life. I want you to go out there and face it.'" Monty walked outside. He says he could feel and hear the growls. "I was cold, ice cold. So with fear and trembling, I walked towards it and all I could say was, 'Praise you Jesus, praise you Jesus, praise you Jesus,' with my hands up. And as I got closer it started to back up and then it was gone."

The experience strengthened his resolve to move to New Brunswick. "We ended up sleeping on a church floor for a week." They were living on the money they'd made from the sale of their home, while they were looking for a place to build. Then a member of their new church family said he felt compelled to give him two acres of land. Other church members offered to help build their home. Monty was amazed at these acts of generosity. And he says God continued to bless them. The baby of the family, Stephen, was born in 1989.

Over the years, God has supplied all of the family's requirements and those of the ministry just when they were needed most. Monty never worries about where the funds will come from to continue his ministry work. God always provides. In 1993 he was given more land and built the Bar None Camp for Kids, which has been running since 1995. Cons for Christ remains in operation and he and his ministry team also run Bridges of Canada, which spans the entire country reaching out to everyone. Now, some thirty years later, he remains committed to this ministry. There is no retirement for this man. He will continue to serve God until the day he dies. With him, there are no half-measures. Whatever he commits himself to, he does it fully.

Over the years Monty has taken part in exorcisms where he says demons were delivered out of people. "I have had many times where Satan has spoken through a person and said he was going to kill me. I have had people who are demonized literally attack me, bite me and come right over the desk. The RCMP, investigating satanic worship across this nation, came to interview me about a person because she was found covered in blood in a nightgown on horseback by a pastor's house talking about sacrificing babies."

After Monty finished a twenty-six-day water fast, he says Satan manifested himself through other people for several months. While at a retreat in Bridgewater, Nova Scotia, he encountered one of those demons. He recalls going into his travel trailer where he found his wife and a woman who was also taking part in the Christian retreat.

"The children were hungry and Lynda was going to make them something to eat. She said, 'I'll cook you some chicken.' And this lady said, 'No, save it for the feast.' Lynda said, 'Oh, is there going to be a barbecue?' And the woman said, 'No, there's a feast.' Lynda got frightened and sent the children after me and I came up. As soon as I came into the motor home, the woman was sitting at the table and her husband was there too.

"As soon as I looked at her, I knew what was wrong. I walked in and sat by her. As soon as I sat by her, her eyes began to spin and her tongue began to dart out of her mouth. And a voice that was not hers, it was a man's, said, 'Monty Lewis – I'm going to kill you.' I knew it was the enemy and I burst out laughing. I said, 'Satan, you fool. For thirty-some years you tried to kill me when I didn't know the Lord, and it didn't work. In the name of Jesus of Nazareth, come out of this lady right now.'

"Well, she fell down on the floor. My wife and children ran to the back of the trailer. Then she began crawling on the floor like a snake and talking in two voices. In one moment she sounded like a sweet, innocent little girl. In the next breath, she spoke like the devil. She began talking about seducing pastors and sliding her hand up on my leg. I just kept rebuking the spirits out of her. I got a couple of other people there and we were there late, because there were so many spirits in her and demonic activity in her. God delivered her. She and her husband were very wealthy Dutch farmers in the area. They became missionaries. Then he passed away and to this day she is still a missionary in Africa."

Another time, a pastor and a woman arrived at Monty's office. The pastor asked whether he believed in delivering people from demonic possession, then left Monty alone with this stranger.

"She's looking at me across the desk. A tiny little lady with round, beady eyes looking right at me. I kind of felt uncomfortable. I didn't know what to say, so I said, 'Well, praise the Lord.' When I said that she just sprung right out of the chair and right over the desk screaming. She sunk her teeth in my neck. She grabbed me by the necktie. The chair went upside down. She bit me all over. And all I'm thinking was, I didn't want to touch her inappropriately while trying to defend myself. She cleaned the shelves of big leather-bound Bibles. She tore the watch off me. I was thinking if this lady doesn't soon slow down, I'm going to knock her out because I didn't know what else to do. In the process the door got kicked ajar. Here she and I were on the floor tussling around. [A colleague] walked past the door and I said, 'Judy, get help! Get help! Get the pastor!' It was quite a tussle and she made a mess of me on the floor there. Well, he walked in and said, 'Madame, you need Jesus.' Well she didn't want Jesus."

The woman was taken to the psychiatric floor of the hospital in Fredericton, where Monty saw her twice and then lost track of her. A couple of years ago, he says, he got a letter from her. It said, "Dear Monty: you probably don't remember me, but I just want to say thank God for you and your book. When I saw you last I was satanically possessed. I had been in the church and something happened with me and the pastor; nobody believed me – they believed him – and I got cut off and ostracized. I became very hurt and angry and I got into satanic worship. I was a Satanist when I met you. I got my life together with the Lord Jesus Christ after reading your book [*The Caper: The Monty Lewis Story* by Joanne Jacquart]. I thank God for your book. Enclosed is a cheque to pay for whatever damage I may have done many years ago. I want to thank you for loving me and praying for me."

Angels are all around us but few people have experienced the actual presence of God. Monty explains, "It's one thing to hear from the Spirit of God, but it's another to have the living presence of the Angel of the Lord representing Our Heavenly Father come into your room. I've had that happen twice."

Once it happened when he was in deep prayer. "The presence, the actual presence of God began to come into the room and fill the room, and fill it to the point I couldn't take it any more." The holy presence of God was so good, so pure, and so intense, Monty was overcome. "I had to start begging God to stop. It was like I was going to explode. I thought I was just going to blow. It was beyond anything human. I fell on the floor from a kneeling position and all I could do was lay there and wait for the Lord to leave. I couldn't take it. I would have died. Angels are real – there's no question about that, none whatsoever. I don't have any question about that."

So why would God send His guardian angels to protect this man, once angry, a drug addict, alcoholic and thief when some very fine men and woman who never harmed so much as a flea have died prematurely in horrific deaths? There are some things, including why he is still alive and others who lived good, clean healthy lives die young, which are unexplainable. Monty says there is no possible way to try and understand it all. "There are things we won't know or understand until we get to Heaven with the Lord, and then they won't even matter."

His heart is filled with compassion. But Monty always had a heart for the underdog and he always had a desire to change – he just couldn't find a way on his own. He says his life is proof that no matter how down and out someone is, there is hope for something better. There is no doubt in his mind that he has experienced both God's angels of light and the demonic angels that are the followers of the anti-Christ.

"As the Apostle Paul said, 'We war not against flesh and blood but against spiritual powers and principalities.' One of the things I know for sure is when you open yourself up to a long period of drug abuse you open yourself up to another spiritual dimension and I know that experientially. I understand why, after three or four days of doing chemicals, I would start to hear voices and see things," he explains.

While science would say this is simply the result of altered brain chemistry, Monty comments the brain's chemistry is being altered, but it is being altered spiritually. The spirit is the root of the man. You lift the spirit out of the man or the woman, and you just have a body.

Now in this time of great uncertainty and fears over terrorism, the wars in Afghanistan and Iraq, global warming, hurricanes and other natural disasters, world economic crises and disease, people are more open to the possibility of angelic presence and manifestations in their lives. Monty suggests if you look back to the Old Testament of the Bible, there is evidence of angels trying to get people's attention through times of trouble.

"God Himself says these words: 'I even sent the drought and the famine and the blight from the locust and you still didn't turn from your wicked ways and turn back to me.' So a drought and a famine speak of economic brokenness. I believe everything that comes like that is God is trying to get our attention as a nation, so we can turn to Him, so we will not be part of the mass destruction to come when the presence of the Lord actually leaves here."

Angels are trying to reassure us that we are protected and loved by God and we have to turn to God. All through the ages we've seen evidence that in the worst of times people will see, hear and feel the presence of God. "We are coming into the end times."

People are searching. There's a real shift in mindset. Over the past decade people have seen through natural disasters such as Hurricane Katrina, massive fire storms in Australia, terrorist attacks such as 9/11, and world-wide economic break down, just how quickly all of the material things in life can be taken away.

"God got the world's attention after 9/11. It was easy to pray with people after 9/11. It really shook a lot of people. I read an article in the *Toronto Star* written by secular scientists that said, 'We are not trying to prove the existence or non-existence of God. We don't care about that. We're not believers.' But the way current events are taking place in the world today, we need to take a closer look at what the Bible has to say about the end times."

With TV channels running shows about Doomsday scenarios and Armageddon and major films with themes including the end of days, Monty believes this is all part of God's plan to get people's attention. It doesn't surprise him that hundreds of people around the world say they have experienced angelic encounters. Is it possible for God to put people in the right place at the right time to help others in times of crisis? The Bible says to welcome strangers because you may be entertaining angels.

"I landed in Thompson, Manitoba, one time in the middle of winter, at two or three o'clock in the morning and I was sick from drugs and booze. I had half a bottle of wine, no money, no toothbrush, nothing. After about four days, I stopped shaking enough to make it downtown. I sat on a bench. I was still sick and broke and I was a mess. A young guy came over and sat beside me. He was an eighteen- or nineteen-year-old First Nations kid. He just sat there. He didn't say anything and I didn't say anything. He got up and he left. He walked about fifteen, twenty, thirty feet and he turned around and stopped and he looked at me. He came back over and he put money in my shirt pocket and he turned and he walked away and didn't say a word.

"I hollered to him, 'Hey kid, kid.' He stopped and turned and looked at me. I said, 'Give me your name or your phone number or an address, so when I get some money I'll send you whatever you gave me here.' He just looked into my eyes and he said, 'No. Wherever you go give it to someone that needs it,' and he turned and left.

"I don't know to this day if he was an angel. If he was, he was a Native angel. And every time I am able to give something I do. I forgot about that time, until I became a Christian and God brought it back to me. Was he a person simply performing a random act of kindness or was he really an angel?"

Eleanor Watson Saw an Angel

Eleanor Watson truly believes her guardian angel has protected her all her life from illness and injuries. "When I think back, yes, it is true, I have always been looked after."

When she was very young she believed in angels and sensed they were around her as protectors. In 1952, many people contracted polio and were left with lifelong physical challenges. When she was eleven she came down with it too, but never suffered any real lasting effects from the illness.

As a young mother and married to her first husband, the family was involved in a serious car accident. It happened October 29, 1972, on the way to a restaurant in Silverwood, near Fredericton, New Brunswick. A fully loaded tractor trailer hit their car on the passenger side. "People in the restaurant said there was fire coming right out of the back of our vehicle."

No one was wearing a seatbelt – not many people did at that time. (They weren't legally mandated in the province until many years later.) Her husband and young son weren't injured, but Eleanor was hurt so seriously that she was transferred to the Saint John hospital, where doctors were waiting to deal with her broken body. "My neck was broken. I had fractures in the lower back. Most of my ribs were broken or cracked. Then they discovered I was a few weeks pregnant."

Doctors told her she probably wouldn't be able to walk again, and it was unlikely she could carry the pregnancy full term and deliver her baby. Eleanor says she wasn't worried about herself or the baby, that she had a sense she was being looked after. "That baby is now thirty-six years old. I am not in a wheelchair and I had no side effects. It is a miracle."

Eleanor has a large collection of decorative angels in her home as reminders that angels are around her. "I feel they have watched out for me. I wanted the angels in my home and to have that feeling of protection."

Her first husband died at forty-four and in 1988 she married Bill Watson. In the mid-1990s she was very worried about his health. He had undergone a chest x-ray and there was some concern he could have a lung tumour. "I was very worried because he was a smoker."

In the early morning, around three a.m., she was having a restless sleep because she was worried about Bill, a security guard working the night shift at the Hugh John Fleming Forestry Complex in Fredericton. She was alone in their home. When she woke up, she saw what she described as an apparition in her room.

"It was floating by my bed. It went to the foot of the bed and it was like a transparent fog. I couldn't make out a face but over its head there was a shroud. There were white sparkling lights shining through it. The voice said, 'Why are you so afraid? Haven't I always looked after you?' I wasn't scared. I just thought, 'Am I seeing what I am seeing? Am I hearing what I am hearing?' It was a very peaceful feeling that came over me. I thought, I can't believe this is happening. Is this real?"

She asked the angel to protect her husband and keep him safe. She believes her guardian angel intervened. When further tests were done, doctors said they could see no evidence of cancer in her husband's lungs and it was simply a shadow on the x-ray.

Eleanor says Bill was already a believer in angels and miracles, and had experienced a couple of encounters with what he believed to be a divine being. While he was working at a parking gate at a hospital, a man who looked like a priest approached him as he was reading an adult magazine.

"Bill had never seen him before but he said, 'How are you today, Bill? You'd better put that stuff away. That's not what you should be reading.' Then he walked up the street. The next day the same priest appeared and told him he knew he was struggling with his faith. He walked out of the parking lot and around the corner and Bill never saw him again. He just vanished. Bill said he knew he needed to go to church, and it didn't matter where he went to worship."

She didn't discuss this with many people because she was afraid they would think she had a mental illness. But she is now willing to share her stories of angelic encounters because she believes people are more open to the idea of the presence of angels in their lives.

"I think for years people have been entrapped in religious beliefs and doctrines and they felt a lot of fear and guilt. People want more knowledge of angels and protection and about the afterlife. I think people are more open because all we used to hear was hell and damnation."

In 2009 she visited Pam Nadeau, who channels the voices of angels, to find out who or what the apparition was in her bedroom that night in the mid-1990s. Pam told her it was Archangel Gabriel. "She said, 'You and your family have always been under Gabriel's protection.'"

Angels are here to guide us and protect us if we ask for it, according to Eleanor. She asks them to help her in her life and to protect her and her family. Often she will hear an internal voice that she believes is the voice of an angel. "I will hear this very clear voice that tells me to call someone right away."

She listened to that voice when it told her to call an elderly friend. The woman answered, but Eleanor knew something was wrong because her voice was very frail. "She said, 'I'm terribly sick. Call my son-in-law.'"

Eleanor is certain the voice was an angel whispering to her. It often occurs. "I've had a sense of when things are going to happen for most of my life. I have elderly parents and I can tell you when they are going to call, and I sense when they are in trouble even before I get word."

When she hears this voice she knows she needs to pay attention to what it is saying, because it is truth. "When this happens and I listen, I feel at peace, but when I struggle with it, I feel turmoil."

Eleanor wants people to hear her story because, she says, a relationship with angels is a gift and there is no need for anyone to live in fear or in want of anything. The angels and the Creator want people to understand they can live in strength and power, and in the knowledge that they are loved and protected. Fear doesn't come from God or the angels. Rather, it is a fabrication of lies designed by negative forces to prevent people from living the true, authentic lives that they are intended to live. "You know what the definition of fear is? It is false evidence appearing real."

There are many reasons why people are afraid. People fear many things in the news these days, especially the future survival of this planet. There are lots of reasons for concern. But Watson no longer allows fear to prevent her from moving forward with her life, because she is safe in the knowledge that she is loved and protected by the angels and God.

"My parents are eighty-nine and ninety-two years old, and they've lived their whole lives in fear. I have shared some of this with them and they want it, but my father thinks I am off the wall. My mother says, 'Don't tell me this stuff because it makes me feel creepy.' But I tell them I find it very comforting."

Her husband Bill died on December 16, 2007. They had been married for nineteen years and were very spiritually connected. After he died, she went to a spiritual medium where Bill's spirit came through and told her he was with his family members who had died before him. "He said, 'I'm happy here.' He never had a good relationship with his mother and he said, 'My mother and I have made peace. We're now friends.'" The medium told her Bill wanted her to go on a cruise and would show her a sign he was with her. During that vacation, while she was in Orlando, she looked up in the sky and saw a sky writer in a plane making the image of a happy face and the words "Jesus Loves You." She believes it was her sign from Bill, that the message in the sky was from him to tell her he was fine.

Eleanor knows Bill's spirit is around her and he lets her know he is often near. The lights in her home will flicker. She says it's Bill's way of letting her know he's around. "Some nights, if I am down or lonely, the lights will blink. And I will say, 'You're here, Bill.' I feel comforted. My sister-in-law was here last year and he was blinking the lights in a lamp in the family room and she tightened the bulb and checked the plug. I said in my mind, 'Please don't do that anymore because she is getting spooked and she doesn't believe in any of this stuff.' She unplugged the lamp and sat down and then the light on the other side of the room started blinking. He was a kidder. He was a tease and had a dry sense of humour."

Before he died, Bill told his daughter he would visit her at Christmas in the new home she had built and that he wanted her to prepare a big wonderful meal for him. On Christmas Day, as the family sat down to their holiday meal, there was a knock at the door. When Eleanor's daughter-in-law went to answer the door it blew open, but there was nobody there. She believes her husband was coming to dinner. "I find that so comforting because life doesn't end."

She never worries about the future. All of the fears and worries she once had ended after she had the vision of the angel in her bedroom years ago.

Her guardian angel has saved her from yet another car accident. She was driving home with her friend Lisa on August 14, 2007, when they had an experience they are both sure was Divine intervention. "We left the church about 9:30 p.m. That particular night Lisa was driving and she said, 'I'd like to take the scenic route through Lincoln.' I asked her why and she said, 'I don't know, but I'd like to go the long way and then we can talk.' We came to a bad turn and she said, 'Oh my God! Look what's coming! There's somebody on our side of the road. What am I going to do? What am I going to do?' We could see the headlights, probably fifty feet away. She said, 'It's coming. It's coming right for us! I don't know what's happening.' And as she said that, the car went by us on our side of the road. It must have been going 120 kilometres an hour. I just froze because I had been in that bad car accident before."

The next thing she knew, their car was over on the side of the road. She turned around to see what had happened to the other car and it was still driving on the wrong side. "I think the angel Gabriel, who told me he would always protect me, must have picked that car up or got our car off the road." Eleanor believes their car had been lifted off the road so it wouldn't be struck by the oncoming vehicle.

"It felt as though it had been suspended in mid-air. To me that's what it felt like." Eleanor knows she and her friend were saved from that accident.

Angels Helped Guide Nate Miller's Life to a New Direction

When Nate Miller was a child, he saw, heard and felt spiritual beings that came to him at night. "I would wake up in the middle of the night and see presences in the room."

When he got older he didn't see or hear much of anything, and he believes he shut himself off from the spiritual realm because his parents didn't believe him when he told them about the encounters he had with spirits.

Nate had no religious upbringing, but when he was fifteen, he believes he had an angelic encounter in a dream. "This presence that seemed really real came down and kissed me on the forehead, and then it went up again like it was flying. I saw it. It looked androgynous, young with a youthful sounding voice. I woke up and I was startled because I could hear a voice. It was some kind of a calling and it said something like, 'I'm here,' or 'I'm waiting,' or 'I'll see you later.'"

He often dreams of angels. He thinks this is one way people encounter them. In 2004 his experience with the angelic really became evident in his life. He was undergoing a stressful situation at the time. Through a dream, he was shown things that would change in his life.

"It was like winning the lottery. I felt I was the luckiest being on the planet because I felt I was being guided. Now I know there are beings out there that are beautiful and will help out. Now, no matter what troubles I have in my life, I know they're there."

Nate says angels have guided him out of going in the wrong direction in life. When he was working in a job he didn't like he was shown that he should leave it and the city he was in. "I was going to college then, but I wasn't studying the right thing and I was stressed out."

In 2006 he decided to learn yoga and meditation. He heard a message from his angels that his life would change and things would be different. At the time, he really didn't want to make changes in his life. But as he studied Reiki, his sense of angels became more evident and they spoke to him more frequently and with more clarity. "I made a conscious effort to understand this better and to nurture myself."

Nate's life has changed significantly in the past several years. He has learned how to become much healthier in mind, body and spirit. Now he says he sees angels in his mind's eye, feels them and hears them speaking to him. "There are times when I will hear things in the room. It's very weird when it happens, but it does happen. It's exactly like hearing someone in the room but there's nobody there. I will look and I won't see anybody."

Angels are with him every day. As a musician, he's written the music for six angel meditation CDs. While involved in these recording sessions, he felt angels surrounding him. "I didn't know what to expect when I started. I would sit there and meditate and close my eyes; I felt like I was being taken to a heavenly kind of place. Sometimes I feel the angels around me in a circle."

Recently, he learned how to interpret the messages he receives from his angels. What he has come to understand is that when things seem dark and uncomfortable, they are not true, but the things that are uplifting come from angels.

Nate gives Reiki treatments to many clients. Before he begins, he calls on his angels and spirit guides to surround him with light and protection from any negative energy. He doesn't associate with any angel in particular. He simply asks his angels and guides to come to him and help him in his life and work.

He also believes people can serve as angels to others when they do things to make people's lives better. "I believe angels are people who have died and have dealt with everything and have learned all of the lessons they wanted to learn, and they no longer have to struggle with the stuff we struggle with in life. I think ultimately we are kind of like angels. We are made of light and energy." As he learned how to do energy work, he met many people who have had similar experiences with the spiritual realm, and this greatly reassured him.

Nate initially wanted to learn Reiki to become more physically and mentally healthy, but because of and through this energy work he's opened himself up to the spiritual realm. "Maybe now I feel like I have a relationship with angels because I am able to say I believe in them. I don't mind saying it."

The understanding that angels exist in his life has been a transformative experience. He is far happier than he has ever been. He doesn't struggle with things as he once did. He no longer reacts to the world as he once did. His life has improved and he knows he is on the right life path. "It's made my life a lot better."

Many of his family and friends do not believe in the existence of angels or in the Divine. Nate has had to learn not to care what people think about his belief in angels and his connection with them. "It might look really spaced out, but that is nothing compared to what I get out of it."

Some people say this is New Age but he notes that people have had angelic encounters since ancient times and that humans have drawn, painted and written about angels for thousands of years. No matter how educated or intelligent people may be, they still have pessimism and fears in their lives. Nate thinks many people have been pulled away from things spiritual because of the fighting between various religious sects. But angels are a unifying thing, because around the world, people of all faiths and even those people who might not follow any religion at all believe in angels, agreeing that they exist and are all about love. "When you feel love on a divine level that's amazing."

Angels Protected Carol Easton's Husband

Carol Easton believes in angels and says she knows they will intervene when they are called on for help. She experienced it when her husband was scheduled for a throat biopsy. On April 29, 2008, she asked Archangel Raphael to watch over him while he was in the hospital. Her husband encouraged her to go shopping with their daughter rather than sit in the hospital, but she had a very strong feeling she wasn't supposed to leave, as the surgeon told them he thought a lung specialist should be in the operating room with him.

Carol believes the angels saved her husband's life. As she and her daughter waited outside the operating room door at the Doctor Everett Chalmers Regional Hospital in Fredericton, the O.R. doors kept opening and closing.

"There was nobody standing on either side of those doors. They opened and closed many times. Those doors don't do that unless someone is standing right there. I said to my daughter, 'Those are the angels going in to watch over your father.' Why I said that I don't know. It just came out of me. The doctor wasn't in there five minutes when he came out and said, 'Carol, I'm sorry. The tumour is a lot bigger than we thought it was. We have to do a tracheotomy on your husband right away – we are losing him.'"

She believes the surgeon was divinely inspired to ask the lung specialist to be in the O.R. that day so he could do the tracheotomy. The specialist wasn't supposed to be there but if he hadn't been, her husband likely wouldn't have survived the surgery. She was told by several nurses and doctors her husband had come very close to death. "That doctor got the tubing to put in my husband. If he hadn't been in there to do the tracheotomy, my husband may not have survived. That doctor never met my husband until the Friday before the surgery. He wasn't supposed to be in that operating room. Normally you have to meet with a surgeon weeks before."

A couple of the nurses who believe in angels told her they were praying for her and had asked the angels to give her strength and energy. She said she immediately felt stronger. After surgery her husband was taken to the intensive care unit. In the window above his bed was a suncatcher of Archangel Gabriel. Carol saw that ornament and knew it was a message from the angels that her husband was going to be all right. Over the next forty-eight hours, while they waited for the biopsy results, she felt at peace. The results showed her husband had throat cancer. He was sent to Saint John for chemotherapy and radiation treatments. Today, he is doing well. She doesn't have a doubt that angels saved her husband's life.

Carol talks to her angels daily and has a real desire to connect with them. Recently, she attended a seminar on angels given by angel channeller Pam Nadeau. There were about sixty people in the room. Pam asked everyone to be seated and to place their bare feet on the floor to help ground the energy in the room. Then she asked everyone to take three deep breaths as she invited the angels to enter the space. When Carol closed her eyes, she sensed many other beings enter the room. "Everybody was seated and we were all in our bare feet, but I literally heard a group of people walking. When I told my sister she said, 'Well, I heard that too, but I thought it was someone moving around.' I got the same feeling as the day I was waiting outside the O.R. during my husband's surgery."

Carol explains these experiences have changed her. She is more open and willing to take more time for people and to really listen to what they have to say. She often has given words of comfort, even to people she doesn't know, and believes those words are divinely inspired messages to others coming from the angels.

Shelley Ling Has Always Felt Connected to Angels

Since she was about six years old Shelley Ling has felt a strong connection to angels. She had a sense they were around her but she doesn't recall having any encounters with angels at that time in her life. Raised Anglican, her earliest memories are of an active church life. While angels are known to be Divine beings here to help, they were not discussed at any great length, except for references in the message of the birth of Jesus Christ.

Unfortunately for Shelley, she says, she chose to marry a man similar to her mentally abusive father. But, she says, "Coming close to the end of that marriage I got into Reiki." It helped her to focus more clearly on where she was and where she was going in her life. At the same time, she came across Doreen Virtue's book *How to Hear Your Angels*. It sparked her interest in reconnecting with that side of her spirituality. Reading Doreen Virtue's book and taking Reiki courses led to a personal transformation.

"Everything seemed to click soul-wise. Life in general made more sense to me. The questions I always had about the Church, things in the Church sometimes didn't make sense to me. They didn't seem to be quite right. Something was missing. There was always something missing to me. I was taught that God and Jesus were above, and I felt they weren't. I always felt connected; that Jesus was my brother; that I was God and God was me."

Shelley travelled to Hawaii in June of 2009 to take a course from Doreen Virtue on angel therapy, where she learned how to connect with angels. Now she feels closely connected to the Archangels Michael, Raphael and Gabriel, who are with her at all times. "Michael is my protector. I definitely needed him with everything that went on in the relationship with my ex-husband, and Gabriel is coming more forward now with my writing and seminars I am preparing to give. You have to ask the angels to help because they cannot interfere in free will. So unless you ask, they cannot help."

Shelley is a Canada Post letter carrier working in one of the roughest areas of Saint John, New Brunswick. She says she tries to deliver light and love along with every letter along her route. She calls on the angels to protect her as delivering mail can, at times, be a dangerous job. People can be rude and animals sometimes attack.

"I've had a lot of people in the post office say they don't understand why I have my particular route. I think it's an overall protection that I request before I go out to do my walk. I have run into dogs that looked rather scary, but they've stayed away. I've never run into a person who has given me a hard time."

Every morning, when she wakes up at 5:30, she has a conversation with Archangel Michael. She asks him to surround her with light and to allow only those things that are of light and for her highest good to come through and that everything else be sent back to the sender with love and light.

Since Shelley has become more attuned to angels she feels their presence much more in her life. She hasn't physically encountered an angel, that she is aware of, but she has what she calls mental movies that play in her head of angels in various circumstances in people's lives. Giving an angel reading, she explains, involves tuning into a person's angels. The angels will answer the questions that are on a person's heart. She gets pictures in her mind's eye and uses angel cards to help her confirm the message for the person.

There is growing interest in angels and she believes this is because a shift is occurring in the world away from the external power, money, selfishness and the never-ending search for material things – they don't satisfy the spiritual starvation many people are experiencing now. "People are tuning in more to their inner selves. Their authentic selves are coming to the forefront and they are looking for answers."

Angels, she has discovered, will come if we ask them for their help. Since connecting with angels, she has experienced a life transformation. When she returned from the angel therapy workshop in June 2009, the emotional hurricane of life was still swirling around her, but she felt as though she was finally in the eye of the storm, the most peaceful place to be.

"Don't get me wrong, there are still times where I think I am going to lose my mind. But I come out of those times of stress quicker now, because I'm able to think about what I need to work on that's dragging me back into that place of stress. Then I am able to get back to that peaceful place a whole lot quicker."

She says talk of the end of the world and doomsday scenarios is nothing more than fear-mongering. "I think a lot of people who fear looking inside themselves perpetuate that to keep other people in a fear state. If we stay in a fear state then we are easier to control."

She believes God and the angels want people to know we are all on this earth to learn and to grow in harmony with one another. "If we all consciously got together, realized that, and eliminated the fear, this would be

Heaven. Everything is universal and there is one God, whether you call him God, the Universe, Spirit, Creator or Allah. I think it's all one."

With many pathways to God and many experiences to have along the journey of this human experience, Shelley believes with time and a willingness to explore the possibilities and the meaning of life, people will come to the conclusion that it's okay to follow the road to the Creator of their choice. And she is unconcerned about the time and circumstances of her own death. "I never have been. I was twelve years old when my sister's first baby died. I walked up to the casket and the baby looked like he was sleeping. He was about four or five months. He died of crib death. When I did an angel reading for her he came to me."

When Shelley does an angel reading she connects with Archangels Michael and Jophiel to help quiet her ego, and to make sure she doesn't doubt that the words she is hearing are coming from them and not from her own mind. Then she asks the angels to come to her to tell her whatever message they want her to deliver. She hears an inner voice; she sees pictures in her mind's eye and, at other times, she has a knowing about things that are happening in people's lives.

Shelley tells me Archangel Raphael is with me. "Because the work you are doing is going to be healing work ... This book will help people to connect with their inner knowledge and bring them together with people you are going to highlight in your writing ... They will have more connections and places to go to help them connect to their authentic selves," she explains.

When asking help from the angels, she recommends, "Just say, 'Whatever you can do to help me get where I need to go, let me notice the things that indicate the direction you need me to go in and bring the people to me that I need.'

"I want to start teaching people and that's what Doreen Virtue said – she was teaching others how to do that because she couldn't get to everybody. She said, 'Go teach other people to do what you do, because everybody can do it.' That's what I and other angel therapists are here for: to connect people with themselves."

Tapping into one's intuitive self, connecting with the true authentic self is possible as long as we can get past our own egos and preconceived notions. Many people don't believe they have the ability or the right to see, hear and feel the angels in their lives because they've been taught that connecting to the angelic realm isn't real, that they need to be more spiritual in order to do so, or that connecting is somehow not of God. Shelley says this couldn't be further from the truth. "It's the most holy thing ever."

Shelley's relationship with God has always been good and she has always trusted Him in every area of her life at all times. "I have always said He will get me this far and He will get me to where I need to go. So I have always believed that deep down inside."

Vicki O'Sullivan Feels Angels in Her Life Every Day

When she was about five years old, Vicki O'Sullivan recalls, she would see beings of light in her room. She is sure they were angels because they brought her feelings of warmth, peace and love.

"I had a warm, fuzzy feeling and they had a fuzzy outline and kind of a glow is what I can remember."

As she grew older these visions went away but angels showed up again in her life when she turned twenty-eight. At that time, she took a Reiki course which, she says, helped her to tap into her ability to see from what she calls her third eye, her intuitive self.

On Christmas Day 1999 she was travelling to Woodstock, New Brunswick, with her family to visit her father. Vicki is confident an angel intervened to keep them from a head-on collision with another vehicle.

"All of a sudden freezing rain and sleet came down. My husband was driving my truck. I said, 'Put it in four-wheel-drive.' He didn't for a second. The truck started to swerve all over the road and then we started spinning. I looked up and said, 'Oh my God!'"

They were on the wrong side of the road with a white car headed straight for them. Then, suddenly, the car seemed to vanish.

"It disappeared. It literally disappeared. My husband saw it, our girls saw it. It felt like a hand had picked us up and set us in the ditch."

Their truck was badly damaged but no one was injured. She has no idea what happened to the other car. All she knows is it left a deep impression on her and her husband.

"We were going so fast and we were spinning and we hit a deep ditch. But we landed very softly. It just kind of felt like we had been picked up and placed out of harm's way. My husband saw the white car and he said someone, something, somehow helped us out here."

While she doesn't see angels anymore, Vicki definitely feels them around her. It's mostly a knowing, the feeling of a presence that comes over her when it happens. Whenever she does energy healing work, such as Reiki, she will call the angels into her workspace to help her. Before each session she says, "All beings of light, angels and anyone for the highest purpose that wants to come and help this person on their journey and with this healing, I ask you to be in the room." Then she will feel warmth and a real sense that angels, guides and the ascended masters are with her.

Many of her clients have told her they feel more than just her hands on their body during a Reiki treatment. She believes these are angels here to help heal people in whatever way they need.

Angels need permission to intervene in people's lives. That's why she asks the angels to be in her life every day and to help her in her work. When she has a serious problem that she has no idea how to deal with, she will give it to the angels and no longer worry about it. It isn't long, she says, before she has found answers to problems. Within a few days things seem much better.

"All of a sudden I get an idea, an e-mail, a phone call or something that will solve or help the problem. Just because they are not coming and standing in front of you doesn't mean the angels aren't there. I just think they do things in subtle ways. I think they might guide someone who I need to talk to to call me. Or I might be in a certain place at a certain time. I have heard songs on the radio when I am really upset and it will feel like a message."

She sometimes will have thoughts that she describes as the whispers of angels come to mind that are answers to problems. And sometimes she will actually hear their voices. They come as an inner voice to tell her what she needs to know.

"I hear things. Sometimes it's my own voice. Sometimes it's a different voice. But always it's an inner voice."

When people talk about changes in the planet and what might happen in the future she gets excited. To her, the future is nothing to fear as some people do because they are sure a time of Armageddon is upon us. Changes are coming to this planet and to the way we live, of that she is sure, but she says it is nothing to fear.

"I think we could have made it easier on ourselves but we have chosen not to. We may go through a little bit of a rough period of adjustment. Our environment is going to be different; our whole money system and the way we work will be radically different. We are going to have to have another way of doing things. The old ways are going to be gone."

Vicki thinks the people who will have a difficult time with this shift are the ones who will have a hard time letting go of old ways and embracing these changes. There is much fear now. The angels are here, she says, to help take away this fear. They are here to tell us that yes, there are changes coming to this planet and to the people who live on it, but also to tell us we need to trust and embrace those changes.

As spiritual beings having an earthly experience, Vicki says people come to earth with their life path mapped out for them before they are born. We are on this planet to have experiences and learn lessons, in her opinion.

"I think we came here to be in love, to have fun, to experience things in the physical. I really think the angels want us to trust enough to let go. I think the people who are able to let go of the past and our old ways and accept what's coming and to be connected in our hearts and to the earth and open to other people will be fine."

She believes no matter what happens to the planet, we will continue to go on because we are spirits of energy living within the confines of physical bodies.

In her opinion angels are Divine beings who haven't crossed over to earth to experience what it is to love here as people do, while earth angels are people who do amazing things to help others. These are angels who have asked to come to earth to have a human experience. "I'm not sure they even realize they are earth angels."

She thinks we can come back to earth many times to learn lessons and to have various experiences. Her youngest daughter, now thirteen, was two years old when she told Vicki she chose her as her mother when she was still in Heaven planning her life experience here on earth.

"She said, 'Do you know I picked you to be my mom? I just knew that you were going to be the perfect mom for me.'"

When we choose our earthly life experience, Vicki says, we also choose the length of our stay here and when we will die. But if something gets in the way of that time and we call on divine intervention the angels will help keep us from dying before our time.

An Angel Saved Dianne L. From a Car Accident

Dianne L. says angels saved her life and the lives of her friends during a snow-storm. The visibility was poor the night she drove with two friends when the roads were very slippery.

"As I made a turn to go up a little hill there was a transport truck coming in the other direction. There were at least two other cars behind the transport. I lost control of my car."

She knew that nothing she did with the steering wheel would get them out of the terrible mess they were in.

"I swerved and started to go across the road directly in front of the transport. I thought, 'Oh my God. This is the end.'"

She is sure angels took control in that moment.

"I think they had their hands on that steering wheel or on the car. All of a sudden the car made a 360 turn and I ended up in the ditch on the same side of the road where I had come from."

She still isn't sure how the truck managed to avoid hitting her vehicle head-on because they were no more than thirty feet away from a collision.

Dianne's husband passed away in 2009, but the pain of his loss has been eased because she feels the comforting presence of her angels around her.

She attended an angel seminar recently and wanted a sign that her husband was there with her. She felt anxious. She wanted to feel her husband's presence. She closed her eyes and felt a tightness in her chest because of the emotions she was experiencing. As she waited for a sign that he was near she felt a big tear drop on her cheek. She knew she wasn't crying so she wondered whether her contact lens has come out.

"I opened my eyes and I blinked and could see clearly, so I knew my contact was in place. I brushed my cheek and there wasn't anything there. I looked on my clothes because I knew something fell but there was nothing."

She took this as a sign that the spirit of her husband or an angel was with her that night. She asks angels to protect her and she is sure they do.

"I know they are there protecting me. I can't tell you how I know but I just know somebody is there looking out for me."

While she doesn't call her angels to help her every day, she will ask for their help when she feels she needs some extra protection. Knowing angels are there to protect her in all things makes her unafraid. She doesn't feel lonely or depressed and gives some of the credit to her angels.

"I miss my husband a lot but I feel there is something, someone or even him helping me to get through this."

Dianne has felt the presence of an angel and says the sense of angels near her gives her great comfort. She wants to learn more about angels and make a greater connection with them. She hopes that by studying Reiki she will be able to raise her energy level so she can connect with angels in some way.

While she was raised Roman Catholic, she is now opening herself up to exploring other means of a deep connection to God.

"I don't believe in a hierarchy and all the things they say you must do and shouldn't do. I think you need to go with your heart and know what is right and what is wrong, and if it feels wrong to you then it is wrong."

Increasingly she tries to listen to her inner voice and to what her heart is saying to her. She agrees there are many things that divide us as human beings including language, culture and religion but the presence of angels in our lives is a unifying thing.

4

Earth Angels

I believe the biggest gift we are given as human beings is the capacity to be earth angels, but some people are born with a desperate, innate need to help others. Many are often compelled to help and heal family, friends and strangers – to the point of their own detriment. Does this describe your nature? If so, you could be an earth angel.

In her book *Realms of the Earth Angels*, Dr. Doreen Virtue describes earth angels: "Do you feel different from other people, as if you were dropped off on this planet and wonder when someone's coming to take you home? If so, then you may be an Earth Angel, which is another term for lightworker, Indigo, Crystal, or one of the other words used to describe a person who incarnated for the express purpose of helping the world be a better place. Every person is born with a personal mission to learn and grow. Each of us elects a theme for our life in which we'll work on a particular life lesson such as patience, forgiveness, or compassion. Yet Earth Angels also choose a global mission in addition to a personal mission … and this global mission is to provide a service to the world. If you have a passion and a talent for healing, teaching, or helping others, yet you yourself have substance-abuse problems, weight issues, relationship challenges, and the like, then you may be an Earth Angel. If you are highly sensitive and you abhor violence in any form, then you may very well be an Earth Angel."

Dr. Virtue goes on to say, "Again, the inside of everyone is the same: a beautiful, pristine spark of Divine light. However, as a lightworker, your spark of light may have spent time in Heavenly realms far from Earth. Those lifetimes that you've logged in the angelic realm, the elemental kingdom, or on other planets, have influenced who you are today. Although you inhabit a human body, your soul feels like a traveler in a foreign country – because that is, in essence, what you are."

All of my life I have felt compelled to help others. I have always felt the pain of others very deeply and have felt physically ill at the sight of violence. I have frequently struggled with weight issues and have suffered through many relationship issues. If what Dr. Virtue says is so, then perhaps I am an earth angel. I don't know whether that is true but what I truly believe, beyond all doubt, is that every human being has the capacity to act as an earth angel to others. That is, within us all we have the ability to choose to perform acts of kindness, to support or help others in any way we can. It can be as big as helping save someone's life or as small as giving a stranger a word of encouragement or even a smile.

Have you ever felt compelled to do something for someone you don't know? Perhaps you opened your wallet and handed money to someone ahead of you in the grocery store because you had a feeling they couldn't afford the few things they had placed on the checkout counter. In those times it is as though angels whispered in your ear to do something selfless for someone else. Or perhaps, indeed, you are an earth angel.

I have felt compelled in this way many times. While writing a newspaper article about the increase in the number of working parents being forced to turn to food banks for help, because their minimum wage incomes didn't meet all of the family's financial demands, I met a father of three.

Although I didn't know how I was going to pay for gas to put in my car and buy milk for the rest of the week, I listened to the voice that whispered in my ear to buy the family some food. I had a taxi driver deliver the groceries to the family's run-down apartment, with his promise he would not say where the food had come from.

I say this not to call attention to what I had done. Rather, I share this with you because that small act may have helped to relieve the stress that father was under. But believe me when I tell you I was the one who really benefited. It made me appreciate all that my family has been blessed with and I was filled with joy at the prospect of making someone else's life a little easier.

As for the worry over how I was to pay for gas for my car and buy milk – it was resolved the next day with an expense cheque I received through work. I believe when we listen to the still small voice inside of us that says "do some good for someone else" we will be rewarded by the warmth we feel in our hearts. Our fiscal and physical needs will be met too. My husband often reminds me there is no need to worry about things such as money because our needs are always provided for. It is true. For I have found that when I worry about a lack of money, what I receive is lots of anxiety. When I believe that all of my needs will be met they always are.

Suzanne Riley is confident her needs will be met. She is living proof that there is no need to worry about going without when you choose to help someone else, because God will always meet our needs.

"We need food, shelter and clothing," she says. "Beyond that, the rest is gravy. It doesn't mean you have to live the life of a pious monk and have nothing, but the ability to give up things and to share with others is what it means to be an earth angel."

She understands the importance of doing things to help others, whether they are family, friends or complete strangers. If the sharing of things and doing kind acts to help complete strangers is part of what it means to be an earth angel, then Suzanne is indeed one. It is typical for this woman to give all of the savings in her bank account to help people she doesn't know when she hears an inner voice that tells her it is the right thing to do.

"My husband came home one day and he noticed our savings account went from four thousand to two dollars. A woman who was struggling on her own as a single mother had found a job, but she couldn't take it because she didn't have a car. We went and bought her an old Dodge Dart. When I say 'we' I did it, but I told my husband 'we' had done it. There are times when I feel compelled to do these things and my husband agrees this is the right thing to do."

Her intentional and frequent acts of kindness are something her family has come to accept and also take on in their own right. Her son Jake learned early in life the importance of giving to others who are in need. "Do unto others as you'd have them do unto you," is this family's creed.

We all have free will and there are many people who will hoard their possessions. This miserly attitude doesn't bring them happiness. Likely, they are the ones who find themselves sad, unfulfilled and lonely. When you do good things and give of yourself to others it comes back to you in the end. Some people call it good karma, but Suzanne says this is the behaviour of earth angels and it is also God's will.

There are many stories we've heard about people who find themselves in the right place at the right time to help someone in distress or danger. Several New Brunswickers served as earth angels by taking action to help save the lives of strangers who were in trouble.

Dorothy Blanchard was able to help a group of teenagers who fell through river ice one winter afternoon. She was delivering a cake to the Jemseg Lions Club Hall when the door burst open and two teenage girls came in, soaked to the skin. The girls told her three boys had fallen through the ice on the Jemseg River. They had attempted to pull the boys out, but broke through the ice themselves. Dorothy called 911 and helped the girls warm up. Emergency crews quickly responded and pulled the three boys from the river. Because of her actions the teens survived.

Nicolas Andrieu received the Governor General's Certificate of Commendation for his selfless and brave actions. In January 2006 he saved a woman from a masked attacker in Fredericton. The Fredericton Police Force also presented him with a Certificate of Merit, the highest award they can bestow on a civilian. Police said he rescued the woman from a serious sexual assault by confronting her assailant. He later provided information to the police, which led to an arrest and conviction.

Jim and Andrea Blagden were visiting her brother's home in the north end of Saint John on a Sunday evening in June 2009 when they heard a baby crying. Although unsure where the persistent sound was coming from, they could tell that somewhere nearby a child was in distress. Then they noticed it was a youngster in a third storey apartment building window across the street. Jim Blagden and his brother-in-law ran as fast as they could to the building. While his brother-in-law ran to the third floor apartment, Jim stood beneath the window. Within seconds, two-year-old Jayden Olson fell out. Jim later told reporters that the time just before the little boy fell was a blur. He recalls he told the toddler to hang on but then the boy fell.

"I had my arm out and he hit my forearm and after he hit my body, he kind of bounced in the air and still went down. And at the last second I grabbed his ankles. It was odd because it's like he fell and then all of a sudden I was holding his ankles and it was like, how did this happen?"

The boy was frightened and had a bump on his head, but was otherwise fine. Many people have called Jim Blagden a hero but he doesn't consider himself one and says he was just glad he could help.

A volunteer firefighter in Harvey, New Brunswick, was called a hero and an earth angel for saving a mother and a baby from a submerged car in an icy water-filled ditch. Jerrad Swan was driving home on Highway 3 at about five p.m. in December 2008 during a snowstorm. High winds were causing whiteout conditions. He was following a transport truck when he saw approaching headlights spin in a circle. Stopping to investigate, he heard a baby crying and a woman screaming. He climbed down the bank and broke through thick ice into chest-deep freezing water, where he found Malory Montgomery and her baby boy Bowen Orser inside a car submerged in one and a half metres of icy water.

The boy's mother had managed to climb into the back seat to free the baby from his car seat and she passsed him to Jerrad. He clambered up the slope, left the baby with another motorist who had stopped, and then went back into the water for the mother. He threw her on his shoulders and carried her across to the bank. By this time a third driver stopped, so he had the help of two men who took the woman from him. They carried her up the embankment and put her in Jerrad's car. Next they returned and helped Jerrad, who was suffering from hypothermia, climb the steep incline.

About ten minutes later the ambulance and volunteer fire crew arrived. The ambulance took the mother and child to hospital in Fredericton, about fifty kilometres northeast of Harvey, while Jerrad's friends on the volunteer fire department tried to help him. By this time he was so cold he couldn't walk. The volunteer firefighters placed him in the back of the rescue van to try and raise his body temperature. Jerrad was taken to a hospital where he was treated for hypothermia, bruises, cuts and scrapes incurred when he smashed through the thick ice.

Many people have called him a hero. When receiving commendations for his bravery, Jerrad told reporters he wasn't a hero. He said real heroes are the soldiers in Afghanistan. Instead, he said, he was simply a firefighter who did what he was trained to do. But many people who read about this miraculous rescue disagree. They believe he is indeed a hero and an earth angel.

One of those people is Malory Montgomery's friend Kristal Hopkins. "She was coming back home and the roads were bad. A transport truck was on her side of the road and she went off the road. I think she was trying to avoid striking the transport. She went down into the ditch and into the water. She said the baby was in the back seat crying and she was trying to get him out. By the time she had the baby out of his car seat the firefighter came down and took the baby out."

Kristal Hopkins believes Swan is an earth angel. "I do. Yes I do. I really do think there are angels and I think he was put in the right spot at the right time. If he might not have been there the outcome would have been different. I've seen that a lot."

Malory Montgomery has told Kritstal that she and her son survived thanks to Jerrad. Kristal says Malory agrees that he is indeed an earth angel.

It seems earth angels run in the Swan family. Jerrad Swan's father, Levurn Swan, I believe, is an earth angel too. In November 1999, just at dusk, I was driving home after work. I was six months pregnant with my daughter Mary Louise. As I approached the swampy marshland on either side of the Hanwell Road in Fredericton, I was driving about eighty kilometres per hour. From the woods, out bounded a cow moose and her calf. I slammed on the brakes. I could hear the sound of screeching tires. I knew there was no way I was going to avoid striking the animals. I cried out, "God, help me. Help my baby."

Somehow I managed to avoid striking the massive animal that was in the lead. But the calf, unfortunately, struck my front bumper, rolled up on the hood and crushed the passenger side of the windshield before it rolled off and into the ditch. I pulled over to the side of the road and reached for my cell phone. The shattered glass cut my hand. With blood running down my hand I dialed 911. But the signal strength wasn't powerful enough to remain connected with the operator. I was unable to tell her where I was or what had happened.

I thought I was okay but was worried about my baby. I was also concerned about the safety of other drivers. The cow moose kept crossing back and forth across the road searching for her now dead calf. I flashed my car's lights to warn drivers of her presence. By now it was completely dark and there would be no way to see her until it was too late.

I was crying. Again I called out to God. "Lord, please protect these people as they drive on this road. Keep them from striking this animal. And please God help me get out of here."

Just then an SUV pulled over. A man got out. I recognized him. It was Levurn Swan.

"Are you okay?" he asked.

"I think so but I'm worried about my baby."

He looked down at my rounded belly and understood that I needed to get to the hospital. He put me in the back seat of his car. His wife was seated next to him and they assured me everything was going to be fine. As we drove, they dialed their cell phone until they connected with the 911 operator. The RCMP was dispatched to the scene to keep other motorists from having an accident with the moose. I was taken to the Dr. Everett Chalmers Regional Hospital emergency department.

When Levurn told the triage nurse I was six months pregnant and had just struck a moose with my car, they didn't waste any time. Immediately, I was taken to one of the examination rooms. A fetal heart monitor was attached to my abdomen and a doctor came in to make sure the baby and I were not hurt. I was fine and the baby I was carrying was unharmed too. I never did publicly thank Levurn Swan for his help that day. So thank you, Levurn, for coming to my rescue. I believe God kept me and my baby safe that evening, and I believe he put you in the right place at the right time to get me to the hospital and to get the police to the area to keep others from being hurt. You are an earth angel to me.

One hot August evening in 2004, my husband and I were entertaining company. The children were playing outside when suddenly we heard screams from the front yard. Our daughter, Mary Louise, then four years old, burst through the front door screaming, "Nicky's getting stung!" Our two-year-old son, Nicolas, had disturbed a nest of yellow jackets that had taken up residence under our deck. Everyone in the house ran for the door.

A cloud of angry, swarming insects were doing their best to defend their territory. Nine-year-old Bryan Michalak was there too. When stinging insects such as bees, wasps and hornets are swarming, it is best to get as far away as possible. This brave boy could have run for cover. He didn't.

"We were under the deck. I think Nicky stepped on the insects' nest. They were flying all around him. He kept saying there were bugs on him. I grabbed his hand and tried to pull him out from beneath the deck but he wouldn't come. Then he ran but he tripped and fell. I told Mary Lou to go get

you and Mr. Rob. I carried him to the stair landing. Then I started taking all
the hornets off him," Bryan explained, when asked to describe what happened.

As I listened to him recall the nightmarish scene, I became very
emotional. The thought of this youngster having the strength of character to
put my baby boy's safety above his own well-being really touched the deepest
part of who I am as a mother. Despite the fact that he too was getting stung,
Bryan did what he thought he should do to keep Nicky from receiving possibly
dozens of stings.

"I got stung either once or twice. I didn't want him to get stung. I
didn't know if he was allergic to stings or not. That's why I pulled all of them
off," he said.

Nicky was stung five times and Bryan several times too. We called the
provincial Tele-Care number to make sure we knew what to do to treat stings.
Nicky and Bryan, thank God, were fine. "I wasn't scared. I'd do it again,"
Bryan said.

This young man put his safety on the line to help a much younger
boy. At the time Bryan Michalak said he wasn't exactly sure what a hero was.
I told him he should take a close look in the mirror and he'd see one. Now
that I'm getting to know more about angels and how God uses people as earth
angels I can clearly see that Bryan is one of them too.

One summer afternoon, B.G. was on her way to a friend's home to pick up
keys to a cottage where she had been invited to stay. On the road to her friend's
home she noticed a car broken down on the side of the road with a dishevelled
man beside it. She was somehow reminded of her son. She wondered whether
she should stop. "I stopped as other cars were driving by and felt I was safe."
The man, who was delivering newspapers, told her his car needed a boost.
He was upset because the old car kept breaking down and he was worried
he wouldn't be able to get the newspapers delivered. She could have given
him a boost from her car; instead, she suggested he try the batteryoperated
booster pack she kept in her trunk. It worked. The man was thrilled. Then she
suggested he take the booster pack in case he experienced more trouble along
his route.

"He couldn't believe it. Told me I was an angel and had given him a
miracle that day. He wanted to hug me but offered his hand, which I accepted. What amazed me is he kept saying, 'It's a miracle. It's a miracle.' He kept
coming back to that, shaking his head as if he truly couldn't believe it." This

woman delights in helping others but she prefers to keep these good deeds to herself. For this reason she agreed to speak about it on the condition that her name wasn't revealed. "Angels never directly tell their good work, you know. It is secret work more or less."

Earth angels, it is said, have difficulty living in their physical body. B.G. says this makes sense to her. She has suffered from physical pain for about as long as she can remember. "Pamela Nadeau says because I am an earth angel I find it tough to be in my physical body. It's really been hard for me. I've had a lot of difficulty for most of my life with chronic pain. But I manage that through going to a higher place. I don't take much for pain medication."

She feels compelled to help others, she says, even complete strangers to the point where she sometimes creates problems for herself and others. While staying at a friend's cottage, she wanted to do something nice for her friend to thank her for her generosity. She noticed one of the cottage's screen doors was in need of paint so she got the materials and went to work. But rather than making the door look better she managed to make a complete mess of things. She confessed what she had done and offered to pay for someone to fix the mess that she had made. It ended up costing her a hundred dollars.

B.G. says she doesn't feel like an earth angel most of the time. "But I do insist on justice for people and always have. That's one of the roles I have taken." In her opinion we all have the capacity to be earth angels. Throughout her life, she has been put in other people's lives, she believes, to help them.

She now feels well enough physically to be able to help people when they need her. For two years she was unable to do so and had to reach out to others for help. "It was a black period for me. It was a dark period."

It feels natural for her to help others and, she says, that's when she thrives. "When I am in service to others I feel great." Whatever she does to help someone, she says it makes her joyful. "I think most of the time it's doing more for me than it's doing for them."

She hesitates to talk about what she has done for others because she doesn't want to be seen as being self-congratulatory. "What you give out to people, you receive so much more back in return. It's huge and it comes from the people and places you least expect."

B.G. has gone to angel channeller Pam Nadeau to find out why she feels compelled to help others, sometimes to her own detriment, and why she feels out of sorts in her body.

Pam said, "I am remembering that first session I had with her, in which I was told she was an angel who wished to incarnate. This is her first life as a human being. So I read it through those eyes and I thought, wow, she is crashing and burning and crashing and burning. Learning a lifetime's worth in one round, wow. I would not just call the screen door a lesson, I would call it the moment she realized that she was in fact a human. She is human now. I would say from her insights since then that she is seeing that an angel does not have to go out and save the world, but rather that her presence alone is a random act of kindness. I would say it was her angelic heart that caused her to give away her battery-powered device to the man in such clear need. This is heart stuff, not head stuff. So she, the angel, is moving from head to heart in short order over a very eventful lifetime."

Earth angels are very gentle people, yet they have a strength that defies their fragility. In her practice as a registered massage therapist she is known as Mavis Lamont. This is the name her parents gave her when she was born, but she prefers to be called Aria of Serenity. She believes she is an earth angel. She agrees that God can put people in the right place at the right time to save someone from death or injury. Sometimes there are divine interventions where God puts people in places to do certain things. These people appear just at the right time for the right experience. They can act as earth angels, but Aria of Serenity says she believes there are others who come to earth in human form who are indeed angelic beings.

"There are some of us here to do certain work, and we are here from the time we are born to the time we physically die – then we have our next job. To come to earth as a physical being is a beautiful gift and many angels are waiting to do that. Angels cannot lick ice cream. They cannot hold some-one or be held. They feel love always but they cannot understand what it is to physically hold someone in intimacy because they are not physical forms. So for those angelic beings who want to experience all these things, they want to come to earth as a physical being."

Walk-ins, she explains, are those beings who take the place of someone who decides it's their time to die. This can happen when someone has a near-death experience. Their soul leaves their body and goes to Heaven and another spirit takes their place in the body.

When she was a child, her parents went to church and sent her to Sunday school. They were hard-working people who had faith in a greater power but there was never any talk of angels. "Heavens no, my mother would be horrified." When she was a very young girl she thought about the pure, loving and beautiful place inside her. She always had a strong sense of the importance to be kind and benevolent to others. The first time she experienced angels was when she was taking a massage therapy course. She returned to school when she was nearly fifty. One of her girlfriends had attended a workshop on angels. It fascinated her and she wanted to learn more about them.

"Shortly after that I received word my father had terminal cancer." She knew she couldn't change the diagnosis, but she knew she could help make his journey into death a little more comfortable. She took a course in Reiki, therapeutic touch and cranial sacral therapy which is all energy work.

"They have nothing to do specifically with the angelic realm, but what they do have to do with is energy and angels are energetic beings." She remembers that first day she had a sense of real angelic energy during a class. "I can still see the vision. Out of the right hand side of my inner vision, a door opened and a brilliant light shone through. It was my visual experience of seeing for the first time."

She can hear, see and feel angels around her. "Not all the same and not all the time. My greatest gift is being clairsentient, which is feeling. You know like when the wind blows? It can be like that. I see angels sometimes. I don't get them as a physical form like you and I, but they just pop up in my mind's eye like a slideshow. Sometimes they will say who they are. I've seen Christ a couple of times. Sometimes I will specifically see one angel or another. Mother Mary comes to me often. Because I don't see all of the time, I have a collection of ways that they are brought to me. I generally have to ask who they are. When it is the right one, they will send shivers through me. I see through touch. It's a physical, palpable energy field. It can be a tingling thing. There are receptors in your hands and this is how I feel it when I am working with small energy fields. The big ones, I virtually bump into them. You never know at the time whether they are spirit guides or whether they are people's guardian angels."

Guardian angels come to you when you are born, to keep you from harm. "I had a client who stepped off a sidewalk in Toronto and a hand from behind him pulled him back quickly, but when he looked behind there was nobody there."

Aria of Serenity always asks for confirmation about whether the spirit she is encountering is an angelic being, to be sure she is dealing with an angel of light or a lower entity that's from a dark place. Aria says people must be careful when dealing with the spiritual world. Along with the angelic higher realm there is a low vibration energy that contains negative spirits – they can be very frightening, especially when you are unprepared to deal with them.

"We all have a vibration and if you are a negative thinker, you are one who sees the glass half empty as opposed to the glass being half full. If you are one who looks to the doom and gloom of every experience, you will draw that negative energy to you. Because my vibrations are very high I draw upon the purest of energies, because I refuse the others to be with me. When they are, I have a faith in the Divine in knowing that I only need to ask for protection and that it will be given to me. There are specific angels that do that. You don't have to know who they are, you just have to ask God for protection. We all are energetic beings. You carry within you an energy force and you actually have an incredible cell memory. From the time you are born, you bring with you certain experiences and knowledge from before."

She believes people have come to earth many times to experience many things. This is extremely difficult for many people to accept, and something the Christian faith has had difficulty accepting. "If you've ever had a past life experience through past life regression, you'll be taken to some of those places and they will resonate with you."

All cultures, all religions around the world believe in angels. Aria says, "We are all children of God and we are all part of the plan. You're given scenarios that will take you left, right, down the middle. You always will have a choice." In her experience angels are around us at all times. They don't make any decisions, they don't make any judgments. They are here to create joy and abundance. They do not ever intervene. They are like your breath. They are energy beings that exist solely to walk you through your life. "I'm an earth angel. I just know. I've been told many times. I've known for a long time. We are all angelic beings. Earth angels are here to do work – special work."

5

Angel Orbs and
Photographic Evidence of the Spiritual Realm

A Photo of the Night Sky Changed Judy Gaudreau's Life

In 2005 Judy Gaudreau had just acquired a new camera and wanted to capture a full moon image with it. She hadn't been sleeping well. Her husband was working a night shift and she was very disturbed by the problems they were experiencing with their twenty-three-year-old daughter.

"I would get up at three in the morning because I just couldn't sleep. I'm not a religious person. I don't normally pray, but someone gave me this Praying Parent book. I picked out ten prayers and I would say them every morning. I thought, we've tried everything and nothing is working."

At five a.m. on January 25, 2005, she was looking out the window and saw a night sky with a full moon and some clouds. It was the perfect opportunity to get the photo she wanted. "I stepped out on my front porch and zoomed in with my camera. When I zoomed in there was a face beside the moon. I yelled out 'Holy shit!' I hit burst mode, where you can get five shots really quickly. The hair went up on my arms and I thought no one's going to believe this. Absolutely no one will. I came back into the house and I downloaded the pictures onto my laptop and I looked at it and I thought, oh my."

People think it's a computer-generated image or that she has altered the photo in some way. Judy says she hasn't done anything to it – it's exactly what appeared in the sky in that early morning when she took the photo.

Before this, she didn't believe in angels. Another daughter, who has cerebral palsy, is a quadriplegic and non-verbal. Judy has gone through what she describes as "a life of hell." Often she questioned why her life was the way it was. She wondered why, if there was a God, her life was so difficult. Often she would wake early in the morning and say aloud, "You are not hearing my prayers."

She took the photo to spiritual medium Suzanne Riley, who told her the name of the photo was supposed to be Faith Is Not by Sight Alone. "Then I realized I needed a visual. I was asking for a sign of something. We are not our bodies. When you pass on, you know this is not the end."

At the time Judy took this photo she had no understanding of its significance or meaning. She now knows what it really is. "It's my sign of what some people call God. Is it an angel or God? I don't know." While she might not be sure exactly what it is, she does know for certain that this experience and this photo changed her life. It created in her a desire to learn as much as she could to make sense of the spiritual side of her life.

Now she says she has tapped into her psychic abilities. "We all have it but we are brainwashed as we grow up. I have turned off the ego and I understand that we are just a shell and that our minds control everything. Every thought, every word that comes out of you the universe hears and brings it back to you. It might not be the way you want. It depends on how you put it out there."

Judy believes angels are all around us. She's always looking for signs of them and those signs, she has discovered, are everywhere. "There are always signs everywhere you go. I am very in tune to all of that. I know the spirit world is around us all of the time. We are all Divine beings. We are all equal. We are all the same. We are spirits having a human experience."

She believes increasing numbers of people around the world are having spiritual experiences with angels because they desire something more in their lives. Many are becoming desperate because they are disconnected from their spiritual selves because of all of the technology currently available. Even though communication is now instantaneous, we've lost the ability to truly connect with one another on any deep, meaningful, spiritual level. She believes people are spiritually starved and desperately searching for something that fills the void within.

She also believes that in the next several years there will be a huge shift in the way people live their lives. Life as we know it will end and a new way of doing things will happen. She believes this will happen when technology will fail and force people back to face-to-face communications – like the time in the not-too-distant past when people spent more time together. People will end up moving back to the essence of who we are as human beings and to real, fulfilling relationships. "Everyone is getting sucked into that technology hole and that is not what our path is supposed to be."

Judy is no longer afraid of death as she once was, because she knows that her spirit goes on. Whether you call it your intuition, the voice of an angel, Divine being, spirit or energy, this is real and it exists in everyone's life if they are willing to allow it in. "If you don't want to believe in it, that's fine, but if you ask for help or if you need to have some guidance, it will be there. They know what we need and what's best for us."

She asks for help and guidance everyday. It can be very big things in life or very small things. As a photographer, she has dozens of photos with orbs. In her opinion, some are definitely the manifestations of angels and spirits. One, for example, was taken of her by her husband outside a chapel. She sent it to Suzanne Riley, who explained from what she could see and feel from the photo, the orb above her was that of an archangel. When Suzanne sees photos with orbs of light in them, sometimes she feels nothing, while at other times she'll feel a rush of excitement. Sometimes she will see an orb in a photo and she'll know with everything inside of her that this truly is the evidence of angelic presence as opposed to others, which are nothing more than dust or moisture in a camera.

"They look different. When it is moisture or dust, you have an orb. When it is spiritual you will see form, shape and intricacies inside the orb. For me it isn't so much what they look like but what I feel when I look at them. It's like a really warm rolling pin with mild, comfortable, 'feels good' energy running right up my back. I have seen and experienced this up to six times in my life. This is what I tell people. Take what you know to be true. We are allowed and able in this generation to do that."

Judy always gets orbs in photos she has taken of her grandchildren, who are very intuitive. "Usually on occasions such as birthdays or Christmas, I always end up getting large orbs with eyes. I don't try and look for it. It's unexpected. But to me it's happening on just about every occasion." Before she took that photo of the face in the sky beside the moon, she says she never got any photos with orbs in them. She believes it's because the angels and spirits want to manifest in front of her because she is becoming more open to this now.

Judy was inspired to write this poem after her encounter with that face in the night sky, which she believes was a visual sign of reassurance that God and the angels heard her prayers:

God Answers

As tears fell down my cheek,
I prayed the Lord would hear me speak.
Not knowing whether my words would be heard,
I asked for a sign to confirm.
Looking out at the heavens above,
There was a sign in the clouds of love.
I no longer questioned my faith in Christ,
As there was a clear sign in the night.
God will hear our prayers at home,
Faith is not by sight alone.

Joie Pirkey Has Seen Angel Orbs Since She Was a Child

As far back as she can remember, Joie Pirkey has been able to see what looked like bubbles of bright white light. Often, they would seem to pop into the room, float down and rest on people's heads. She asked her mother what they were. But as her mother couldn't see them and dismissed her questions, most of the time Joie ignored these bubbles of light. "If a large number came in at once I would watch to see what they'd do. I recall people asking me what I was looking at, but I'd change the subject because, if and when I tried to explain them, I almost always was dismissed. I would see them inside and outside, in any type of lighting."

When she became a teen she began to see them with her eyes closed, as if they were behind her eyelids. These orbs of light were almost always bright white, but a few times she saw them as blue. They seemed completely normal to her because they had been with her for as long as she could remember. "As time passed and I began to experience other supernatural things, I noticed that these 'light orbs' would increase when the other 'stuff' would happen. By other stuff I mean getting words of knowledge about people, knowing things about places that I had no way of knowing, seeing things others couldn't see or hear."

Joie committed her life to Jesus Christ in 1981, when she was in high school, because of the supernatural things she'd seen, and she knew she needed to devote her life to Christ. "I knew also that some of the things that were happening to me were from God. My mom was a Charismatic Catholic and I went often to the prayer meetings with her. I have always been very intrigued by the things of God. I began to search the Bible for some understanding, and found that experiences like mine were actually common in the Scriptures. I've wondered about the disconnect that I saw in the Church, but found deep solace in the fact that most of the people mentioned in the New Testament had similar things happen to them."

Not long after she committed her life to God, she spoke about her experience with the saving power of Jesus in front of hundreds of people at a number of Roman Catholic confirmation classes. She was initially scared to speak in front of so many people. Then, just as she began to speak, she saw about ten to fifteen light orbs drop into the room from the ceiling. "Their combined light made the back of the room glow." That experience helped bring peace to her. In time she was able to see thousands of the light orbs at once and also fully revealed angels. "These orbs looked as they always did. They varied in size and intensity. As they got close to me they would just sort of emerge into a full figure of a man with extremely large wings. These angels were dressed in bright white robes and their wingspan was as wide as they were tall. The wings, when down, stood up off their shoulders about a foot. They were magnificent!"

Joie asked what these light orbs were and, she says, the Holy Spirit told her they are angels. She will tell people when she sees a light orb and where it is. Then they will photograph the area and it will always appear in the photos exactly where she saw it.

Joie describes one of the first times she experienced angel orbs. "I was travelling to Eucha, Oklahoma, to speak at a three-day conference. Michelle Little and I had a plan. When I would see the angels come into the church, I would mention it and point. Michelle would snap the shot. We took nearly twenty-five pictures in twenty-four hours, and there were angels on every one. That night was the third angel orb vision. When the vision began, I asked what the orbs were. For the third time the Holy Spirit answered, 'Angel.' But then He added, 'When will you stop being ashamed of the signs and wonders?'

"I couldn't honestly say. I knew what people would think, and that still mattered to me more than it should. I asked the Holy Spirit if He would prove to me that these things were angels by not letting anyone on the Internet have a viable explanation. The following day we searched all morning. We found some very interesting hypotheses. I am not trying to develop a theology of angels here. I am simply telling my story and showing the evidence that exists. I do believe that these experiences align with Scripture and an orthodox theology of angels. Seeing the angels is a very small and insignificant part of my ministry and spiritual life. I believe that the photos are a sign and wonder. I believe that the foundation and substance of my ministry and spiritual life is Jesus. He has asked me to share the angel stories, and that alone is my motive for doing so."

Joie Pirkey is the founder and president of Shouts of Joy Ministries in Little Chute, Wisconsin. She has degrees in pastoral studies and behavioural science from North Central University and she has been in ministry for more than twenty years.

Jocelyn Clark Has Photos of Angel Orbs

While some people are able to see orbs of light, Jocelyn Clark has lots of photos of them. She took photos of her nephew who was driving a horse at the Fredericton Exhibition. Her nephew had hitched the horse to a cart, and she felt a little bit nervous because he'd just gotten the cart and wasn't used to driving the horse with it.

"I didn't want any harm to come to him. I just invoked the angels to protect him. When I took the photo of him it was amazing. He was surrounded by I don't know how many orbs."

Jocelyn enjoys photography and was taking photos of mushrooms one day. "If you read Doreen Virtue's books, she talks about fairies and the elementals being out in the grass. I took this photo and you can see these little orbs around the mushroom. I think they're fairies."

Recently, Jocelyn was going through some emotional healing from a childhood trauma. She went to a counsellor who told her she had sadness she needed to express. She encouraged her to go into the woods and find a place where she could be alone and scream.

"As children, a lot of us are taught not to scream and we repress stuff. So I thought, I need to do this. I felt it would help me. I walked into the woods. The angels aligned all of this. I was supposed to be working until the evening, but I thought if I could get four hours off work, I'd do it. They let me leave in the afternoon. My daughter was at the babysitter's and my husband was at work. I walked back into the woods and I found a place – the most peaceful place and I felt really surrounded by angels. I felt they were helping me through this part of my healing journey. I screamed. I can't tell you how it felt. It was an amazing experience. I felt like all of that got out of my body.

"I'd just gotten back to the house when my husband and daughter came home. It was like perfect timing. I wanted to show them the place I had gone to do that healing. I asked the angels to guide me to the right place. There was a trail through the woods and there were two pine trees. I call them the Hands of God. Right before those trees they guided me to the place. Three days later I went back with my camera because I wanted to remember. When I took the photo it was the most amazing orb I had ever seen and I had captured it on my camera."

Marjorie Jewett Believes She Has Photos of Ghosts and Angels

Marjorie Jewett has taken a couple of photos which she believes are evidence that we are not alone, that there are angels and the spirits of loved ones around us. A couple of years ago at Thanksgiving she took some photos she is sure are evidence of the presence of her deceased in-laws. When she downloaded it on her computer she could clearly see the image of someone standing behind her son-in-law. She showed it to someone who works at the University of New Brunswick's photography department.

"Two other people there examined the photograph with him. He came back and said, 'They are stumped. Can I see where the photo was taken and the camera just to make sure it wasn't double exposure?' He came here and looked and said, 'No way was it flashback.' He went back to the university; they find it extremely interesting but they have no idea what it is."

She showed it to a psychic medium who says the photo includes the spirits of Marjorie's in-laws who are around the family. Marjorie and her husband took many photos on a trip to Prince Edward Island. In those photos there are several purple colours and a couple of white orbs. When she showed them to psychic medium Claire McGee, Claire suggested it could be an angel.

6

Encounters with the Spiritual Realm

A Glimpse Into the Great Beyond

I originally wrote the following piece for the October 31, 2009, edition of *The Daily Gleaner*.

What happens after we die? Many people look for answers from spiritual mediums. Brett MacFarlane [who has since changed his name to Paleki Phaphapeuneua], Suzanne Riley and Claire McGee say our deceased loved ones are happy where they are and will often drop in on us to see how we are doing. Usually they will show up in times of celebration and can communicate with us in many ways.

A certain song will play on the radio that will remind you of them. When lights flicker, televisions, radios and computers turn on and off and when telephones ring but there is no one there, you can be sure your loved one has dropped in to say hi. They will communicate by other means too; a whiff of their favourite perfume or their favourite foods are signs. So are rainbows and soaring eagles, to let you know they are near, these mediums say.

"Materialization is one of the most complex ways for a spirit to communicate with us. It takes an incredible amount of effort on their part," says MacFarlane.

When the spirit of a loved one appears, MacFarlane says, it is very rare and happens because they have an urgent message for you. All of these mediums explain that everything in this world and in the afterlife is energy.

When we are in spirit form, we exist on a higher energy field than when we are incarnate. When a loved ones dies, it is a time of celebration in Heaven, they say, because they are being welcomed back home.

Sometimes people hesitate to make contact with their loved ones after they have passed because they think they have better things to do in Heaven. While they are busy having experiences there, they are still connected to us and want to connect with us.

"You cannot waste their time. They are always connected to you. They have an attachment to you. If they know you are talking to them they will come through," says MacFarlane.

In McGee's experience, the best way people can communicate with their deceased loved ones is to relax the body, clear the mind and visualize them or pose a question and wait for the response to come to mind.

"Some people will say, 'Can you show me a sign please?' And they will do that. When you feel a squeeze in your side, warmth in your chest or a cool breeze on your face it is actually them talking to you. It happens all the time," says McGee.

Riley says our thoughts, intentions and conversations are heard by those we love who are no longer here. When we think about them they know it and when we say hello it is heard and sometimes they will respond.

None of these mediums recommend séances. You could be opening yourself up to lower-energy vibrations and also it is forcing a spirit to come through who might not want to. When you want to contact a loved one that's passed, MacFarlane says, it is important not to do so when you are crying or feel depressed. "If we cry they will have a hard time coming across. If you are down, they have to drop their energies even lower to make contact." If their energy levels drop too low, they can become stuck here.

Sometimes when a person dies, they either do not know they are dead, or they are not ready to go and want to remain in this world. But as soon as a spirit realizes and accepts it is no longer alive, most are willing to go home. But when spirits don't know they are dead, MacFarlane and McGee say, they tend to hang around places where they were when they were alive.

"These are the ones that tend to haunt houses," says MacFarlane.

If unwanted or frightening things happen in a home, it is usually be-cause a spirit is being playful or having fun with the living. It is exciting for some earthbound spirits to scare the living and receive energy from that fear. But a spirit cannot remain where it is not wanted and when it is told to leave.

If you bless a space and make it holy, a lower level energy won't be able to come through.

Hauntings, McGee adds, happen when souls believe they cannot cross over or are earthbound by something or someone that keeps them here. McGee used to live in a home on Main Street in Fredericton. Often, she would entertain the spirit of a woman in the house, a woman who used to live there. Sometimes when spirits don't know they are dead they can become confused and afraid. Mediums and others who are sensitive will pick up on this fear. "The spirit isn't trying to scare them, but it is trying to make them feel their presence so they can understand the spirit's story."

Once their story has been heard, and the soul realizes it is dead, McGee says, in her experience, it is willing to go home. Occasionally, but not often, Riley says, souls will come back to look over where they have been. "It is like a visit. Their time is not like ours. For them time is not a concept. What could be a hundred years for us could be a finger snap for them."

But Riley says she doesn't believe there are such things as hauntings. Rather, like a fingerprint left behind on an object, people will leave energy imprints behind in places where they used to live. Usually when you see a ghost, it's because something traumatic happened to someone in death. The apparition that you see is the energy left behind from that traumatic time. "There is nothing to fear. When people talk about poltergeists, hauntings, negative things happening in a house, that is negative energy. That is normally human-manifested. It plays on our own fears and insecurities. There can be negative energies. When someone such as a murderer or a rapist dies, their frustrations and negative energy remain. It can make for some scary times until you know that all you need to do is cleanse the area, clear the space, put positive energy there and deflect it."

Riley will receive about five calls each month from people who are having trouble with negative energies in their homes. "I don't go and clear the house. I tell people how to do it. The most powerful way is through prayer; reclaim your space."

Some people will return to cemeteries to leave flowers at headstones to remember their loved ones, but cemeteries are what most mediums refer to as "dead zones" because the spirits of the dead are not there. When people die, their spirits cross over rather than hang around cemeteries, these mediums explain. However, if this is where you choose to communicate with your loved ones, they will return to you there during your visit.

What is our passing like and where do we go? All three of these spiritual mediums agree that when we are preparing to die and when we pass, the spirits of loved ones are there to help us make the journey. "In speaking to people, who have had near-death experiences, there was a warmth and calm, and then we are home. Typically when we pass, those we have loved who have passed already tend to come to greet us.

"This is a blessing that is given and we rejoin those souls that made imprints on our lives here on earth – those who were our family and friends," says Riley.

People who have had near-death experiences often describe a bright, white light, a tunnel or a hallway. "Others will describe it as a calm meadow with a bridge they cross." Riley says in her communication with spirits, she has been told that when someone dies, any pain or suffering they might have felt when they were alive is gone. Often, people who come to mediums ask whether their loved ones miss them. The mediums say they do not, because that connection of togetherness and love always stays with them and they know eventually we will join them. And, MacFarlane adds, when we die we do not miss this world because the place we go to is far better than this world.

McGee says our deceased loved ones are very content with where they are and with what they are doing. And, because time doesn't exist, and they know they will see us again soon, they don't grieve like we do.

All of these mediums say our loved ones will remind us they are around in subtle ways. They can and do come to us in our dreams and our thoughts. When we feel warmth, love, excitement, it is likely their way of telling us they are near and want us to be as happy and content as they are in the afterlife.

For more information about this subject, go to www.abreathofafrica. com, www.readingsbysuzanne.com or www.trainyourbrainforsuccess.ca.

My Encounters With The Dead

I have seen, heard and felt the spirits of the dead. In 1989, I lived in a historic Loyalist home in Saint John, New Brunswick. It was a beautiful old building. The descendants of the original owners were an elderly couple who occupied the basement and first floor. The second and third storey contained an apartment which they rented. The place was furnished with antiques, many of which were the belongings of the original homeowners. In one of the parlours, there were the portraits of those ancestors. I believe it was also filled with the spirits of those who'd lived there before.

Not long after I'd moved in with a couple of roommates, I had my first of several ghostly encounters. It happened on a Sunday morning. My room was on the first floor of the apartment and my roommates' bedrooms were on the next floor. We had planned to go to church that morning. I walked out of my bedroom, down the hallway and stood at the bottom of the stairs. Then I felt something behind me. When I turned, I saw what appeared to be a woman, arrayed in old-fashioned attire, including a long dress, bonnet, and gloves; she held a Bible.

She smiled at me, as if she was waiting to go with us. The home had been an Anglican Church parsonage. Was the spirit of the woman the wife or daughter of a church leader who had once lived here? One thing I am certain of: I did see this ghostly image. She was in no way frightening so I didn't feel threatened. I blinked, looked again, and she was gone.

At the time it happened I wasn't prepared to discuss what I had seen. I thought, "This is crazy. That never happened. I can't say anything or my roommates will think I'm mentally unstable." So I went upstairs and asked if they were ready to leave.

They both stared at me. Immediately, they started asking if I was okay and said I looked ill. They told me the colour had drained from my face, that I was white as a sheet. I told them what I'd seen. Both women seemed to be shocked by my story. One felt we should bless the apartment to eliminate any evil presence. So she prayed and told the spirit to leave. I am not sure if the spirit of the woman I saw did vacate the apartment, but I never saw the apparition again. But this isn't the end of the story. There were many strange things that happened in that house.

Eventually both of my roommates moved out so I lived alone in that big old place for a while. Frequently I would hear people having conversations when there was no one in the place but me. My things would disappear and then reappear. Lights would turn on and off. There would be sudden temperature changes. I would hear doors opening and closing.

In 1991 I had an encounter with what I believe was the negative energy of an earthbound spirit, who had not crossed over and was playing tricks to make me afraid and feed off that fear energy. It happened late one night several hours after I had attended a church service in Moncton, where I had clearly felt the presence of God. It was a wonderful, encouraging service that made me understand how much God loved me and everyone in the world. When I went to bed on that very warm July night, I wondered how I would sleep because it was so hot in my bedroom.

I opened the windows but there was no breeze. Neither did the fan help to cool the air. Eventually, I managed to fall asleep. Sometime in the early morning I awoke suddenly. The room was icy cold. Although I saw nothing, I felt I wasn't alone. Whatever it was, I had an overwhelming sense that the being meant to harm me in some way. I felt an indescribable fear, the likes of which I never felt before or since. The only thing I could think to do was to call out to God to take away the fear. I commanded the thing and the feeling to leave me in the name of Jesus Christ. Immediately the cold air warmed and I was able to close my eyes with the sense that someone was standing over my bed keeping me from all harm for the rest of the night. I do believe God sent one of His warrior angels to my rescue to protect me from those in the spirit world that wanted to do me harm.

But mostly living in that house wasn't so bad. I knew I wasn't alone and that was okay. I also knew there were spirits about when my cat would stare at nothing and hiss before it ran away. Mostly the spirits who dropped in from time to time were friendly, as was the case with the ghost lady. I truly believe that place was haunted. The ghostly encounters I had twenty years ago are as real to me now as if I had them yesterday.

Encounters Others Have Had With the Other Side

I am not alone in my belief that the spirits of the dead like to spend time among the living. Marjorie Jewett says her home is filled with the spirits of friends and family who have crossed over, but like to visit every once in a while. She was only four years old when her twin brother John died from influenza and dehydration. She has a clear memory of his body being taken from her family's home. All her life, she says, she has had a sense of his presence. "I feel sometimes that he tries to live through me. I have a sense that he's around."

And there are other spirits in her life around her. Marjorie isn't the only one who's seen, heard and felt these spirits. Youngsters in her home will stand and stare into mid-air and giggle. She knows they are seeing the spirits of friends and relatives who have died and crossed over.

"We have many in this house. You can tell by a fragrance. Once in a while I'll be sitting watching TV and, out of the corner of my eye, I will see David's dad go to the kitchen sink to wash his hands; you can smell cigar smoke so I know that's his father. There is no smoking in this house. It's his father Sandy Jewett. He lived and died here."

Her mother-in-law also died in this home. Often Marjorie says she knows her mother-in-law Maude is there. She can smell her scent, a flowery perfume she wore in life. Once, while waiting for her husband to come home, Marjorie was alone on a cool, fall day. All of the windows were closed, but a curtain started to move back and forth. She knew it was her mother-in-law looking out the window for her son to come home. "I'm just in the habit of saying, 'Hi Maude.' She is looking out the window for David to come home and drive her to bingo."

The scents and sights in this house aren't the only telltale signs that spirits of loved ones are near. Frequently she will hear footsteps climbing the stairs. Sometimes there will be the sound of music playing from the former master bedroom where her in-laws slept.

"Once we heard music coming from the corner of the room. I said to David, 'Listen to this. I never knew your father was a romantic.' If I asked for the music to be played a little louder, it would come a little louder."

The Signs That Life Continues After Death

Others have had reassurances from deceased loved ones after they've passed. They want to communicate they are fine in the afterlife and send messages to their loved ones that they're happy and thinking of them. Madonna Bennett was always close to one of her uncles, who developed terminal cancer. Just before Christmas they had a wonderful visit but she knew it would be the last time she saw him.

When he died she travelled to Ontario for the funeral. The weather was very unsettled with thunderstorms when she visited her aunt at their lakeside home the day before the service. Her grandmother told her there likely would be a rainbow. She went outside and saw "the most amazing rainbow I'd ever seen in my life right over the water. I took pictures of it. I felt like it was him."

A few months later Madonna visited a spiritual medium so she could connect with her uncle. "I asked my uncle whether he sent me a gift after he passed away. The medium said, 'He's saying yes and he's showing me water and colours over water, or something colorful and bright over water.' I just started to cry and I said it's a rainbow. She said, 'He's saying yes, yes!'"

An Angel Comforted Rennetta Smith

Rennetta Smith grew up in a French Acadian Roman Catholic home. She has been aware of angels since her early childhood. When she was three months old, doctors told her parents she would not likely live any more than six months. They'd misdiagnosed her with leukemia, giving her chemotherapy which she didn't need. She was in the hospital for much of the first three years of her life, coming close to death several times. "They almost killed me more than once with treatment."

What the doctors thought was leukemia was in fact a bleeding disorder called Von Willebrand disease, which was finally properly diagnosed when she was seventeen, just before her mother passed away. The near-death experiences she had as a baby have resulted in a very intuitive nature.

Rennetta has had many encounters with the dead since she was a very young child. Often she would tell her mother she had been playing with children and speaking to adults, and her mother would say they were already dead. The first time she saw a spirit she recognized, it was her grandfather on Christmas Eve. "He was just standing there with a big smile. He didn't say anything. Honestly, it scared the hell out of me. He was dead. I was twelve. I ran down the stairs like a bat out of hell. Having that experience as a twelve-year-old freaked me out."

She believes her near-death experiences, coupled with extensive time in hospitals where there is so much death, helped her to become more intuitive and able to see spirits and know when people are about to die. This has continued throughout her entire life. The departed come to her because she is open to communicating with them. She has seen her mother, grandmother, grandfather and father.

"I've hugged my mother, and my mother has been gone almost seventeen years. I took her death very hard. I was with her in a dream and she came to say goodbye to me, but it wasn't a dream. I woke up and could smell her perfume on my clothes. My mother smoked and I could also smell her cigarette smoke. My mother, I know, is in Heaven but I also know she is around. We are not separated. We are sharing the same space; it's just that when we transition from the human to the other form, we just don't see it. That's why sometimes we feel somebody behind us or we feel somebody touch our shoulder or we feel goosebumps. They're not gone; they just exist in a different energy."

Rennetta's able to tune into that higher energy level on which the deceased operate. She can't call deceased loved ones to come to her, but if she is in a place of great need they will come. She is also able to see negative energies. She has no idea why these energies are fear-based rather than love-based. She isn't sure whether it's because of the kind of death the person had, or how they lived when they were in human form, but she is very sure there are negative, fear-based energies. "I don't talk to them. I don't like them. I can always tell by their eyes."

"If we as a society of people who live on this earth are living a fear-based existence, then that is the energy that we are putting out there. If we are loved-based then that too is the energy we are putting out there."

Her father passed away in June 2009 after a battle with cancer. She spent the week with him before he died. It was an amazing time of love and caring and sharing. She prepared all of his favourite foods. They laughed together. She helped him write his obituary and to say everything he wanted to say about his life. The last week of his life, she saw her mother's spirit there watching everyone and waiting to help his spirit leave his body when it was his time to go. "She was standing in the corner of the kitchen looking at us. I told him, 'Dad, Mom's here.'" He died in his own bed at home.

The night of her father's wake, her boyfriend told her he was leaving her to marry an old girlfriend. She was very distraught. When she returned to her father's home she decided to sleep in his bedroom where he died. That night she felt as though someone was in the bed with her, cuddling her. She felt warm and comforted. "I felt feathers and giant wings. I felt cocooned. I could feel the feathers tickling my nose as I breathed. I felt it was Archangel Michael because that's who I call on. I wasn't alone."

Before he died, often her father talked about what he would do on the other side. He asked her who the head angel was in Heaven. She told him it was Archangel Michael. "He said, 'That's the job I want.' You have to understand that Dad was very involved in the church. Everybody called him God as a joke because he was at church so much."

Rennetta has seen her father's spirit only once since his passing. He doesn't come to her because he knows she is fine and doesn't need him to be around her as much as her sisters do. Often the spirits of our loved ones are around us because we aren't willing to let them go, she explains.

Where does she believe her father is now? "He's fighting with Michael over Michael's job. Two days after Dad died there were the craziest thunderstorms. I looked at Patsy, my stepmother, and said, 'Do you think that's Dad and Michael?'

"We just went to Prince Edward Island and the first night we were there, there was a crazy, crazy, huge thunderstorm. It was reaching an uncomfortable place of being and I said, 'Okay Dad, leave Michael alone long enough for me to get home from PEI.' And it stopped, literally it stopped that quickly."

Angels are very important to her. She is starting to have a sense of them in her life and calls on Archangel Michael daily and other angels and saints such as Mother Mary. She speaks to them as she would speak to anyone. She asks Michael to assist her with everything from money issues to her children. Angels, she says, want people to know they are here and that they are present in our lives and available to help us if we only ask for their help. "Just ask for anything you want that fits into the big picture of your life and it will be yours that easily."

Laverne Stewart

Rennetta believes more people are encountering angels now because we are at a point where there is a huge spiritual shift. "I didn't think the battle would happen in my lifetime, but the shift is happening so quickly that I am not so sure now. We are going from a technological, masculine age into a spiritual, feminine age. We are going into a spiritual phase. It isn't necessarily a religious phase, even though the world's religions have a place. It will all change. I think it's time for Wicca to come back. I think it's time for the feminine to come back, for natural healing to come back."

She dismisses doomsday scenarios as nothing more than certain people trying to generate fear in others. She believes giant corporations and governments are using fear to control the masses. In her opinion, people are being kept in fear so the powers that be can remain in control. She does acknowledge Armageddon but, she says, it is coming in the form of a change in the way people think and how they behave. "I think you will see us living more naturally and more communally. We are going to go back to getting jobs where the jobs work around our lives instead of life working around our jobs. Those things are all going to change. There is going to be an Armageddon, but it will come as a huge shift. We will start exchanging goods. There will be less cash exchanging. We have to go back to that or we are going to destroy the planet. The shift has to happen and it has to happen quickly because we are killing ourselves and we are killing our children and we are killing our planet."

What role do angels play in this shift? They are here to help people who become aware of the shift to make this transition. She has let go of many of her material things because she realizes they are not important in her life. She is moving forward in her life and into the future without fear. She has no fear of negative energies because she doesn't allow it in her life. "I think angels and spirits will come to you in the least fearful way."

Angels exist in Smith's life and help her when she needs them most. She recalls a time she had to take her son to the hospital with an ear infection. It was cold and her car's battery was dead. In the parking lot a man offered to boost the battery. As he did, she put her young son in the car and buckled him in. "Justin turned around and said, 'Where did the man go?' He was gone. He didn't have enough time to run into the hospital. He was gone. Justin said, 'Did you see that God sent us an angel to boost the car? Wasn't that cool?' I said, 'Well, you are right.' I turned my head and I looked and there was nobody there. That's a guardian angel."

As a single mother money has been very scarce at times. Rennetta's experienced occasions when she didn't have the money to buy milk for her children, and then found money that literally appeared as if it was Heaven sent.

"You're a single mom and you don't have money for milk and you put on a coat that you haven't worn in two weeks and there's a twenty-dollar bill in the pocket. Now, when you're a single mom and you have kids and money is tight, you do not misplace twenty dollars. You never misplace any money when you are a single mom going to university. How did it get there? The angels put it there. That's what I tell my kids."

Afterword

This book has taught me so much. One of the greatest things I have learned from it is that even though we might question our lives, God and the angels have everything well in hand.

When we agree to follow our true path our lives go forward, smoothly and effortlessly. When I agreed to take this on and asked the Almighty to help me with this book, I had no idea what was to come but He did. It was already in motion. God and the angels had everything in order right from the beginning. Doors opened that I didn't even know existed. People came into my life to share their stories which have blessed me deeply and I hope they have blessed you too.

I know this for sure. God is real. Angels exist and are all around us to help us to live our best possible lives. Our life in this world is only a fraction of who we truly are. We are spirits having an earthly experience. While we are here we can live full, joyous lives. The wonders and possibilities of everything in body and spirit are available to us if we open our hearts and minds to it.

We can see if we open our eyes. We can hear if we choose to listen. We can feel if we allow God and the angels to draw near.

What I also know beyond any doubt is that those we love who are no longer with us in body are still nearby in spirit. The spirits of those we love are as close as a thought or the whisper of their names. They are with us in times of celebration. They see us as we continue in this world from where they are. They come to us in many ways – a rainbow, a soaring eagle, even floating butterflies are all signs they want us to take notice of and are their way of showing us how close they really are.

Our loved ones now in heaven are saying, "We are here. We love you. We never leave you. We watch over you. We will be together again."

Bibliography and Online Sources

Barnes, Deana. Stories of Angelic Encounters. http://newinepouring.wordpress.com

Finnamore, Alice. *The Glory of Being: A Biblical Journey Into Abundance*. Lulu.com, 2006.

Forrest, Karen. *Angels Of The Maritimes By Your Side*. Lawrencetown Beach, Nova Scotia: Pottersfield Press, 2008.

Forrest, Karen. *Canadian Angels By Your Side*. Lawrencetown Beach, Nova Scotia: Pottersfield Press, 2009.

Gaudreau, Judy. Faith Is Not By Sight Alone. (poem and photo) 2005.

Gill, Barbara. *Soul Gifts: The World's Self-Help Book*. "My Father Flies Like an Eagle." Events Planning Associates Ltd., 2006.

Gill, Barbara. Tis From There We Flew. (self-published).

Jacquart, Joanne. *The Caper: The Monty Lewis Story*. 1992 http://www.martyangelo.com/caper_monty_lewis.htm

Kehler, Katherine. Angelic Encounter Story of Her Father. www.thoughtsaboutGod.com

Virtue, Doreen. *Angel Numbers 101*. Carlsbad, California: Hay House Inc., 2008.

Virtue, Doreen. *Realms of the Earth Angels*. Carlsbad, California: Hay House Inc., 2007.

Pirkey, Joie. Shouts of Joy Ministries. Photos and personal document. Little Chute, Wisconsin.

www.islamawareness.net

www.worldofchristians.net

www.beliefnet.com

www.angelfocus.com

For more information about the psychics, spiritual mediums and others
interviewed in this book, please see:

www.healerofhearts.ca

www.readingbysuzanne.com

www.askyourguides.com

www.abreathofafrica.com

www.trainyourbrainforsuccess.com

www.dreambringersstudio.com

www.yourhealingjourney.ca

www.intrinsicmotion.com

www.karenforrest.com

www.shoutsofjoyministries.com

www.bridgesofcanada.com

www.newinepouring.wordpress.com

www.thoughtsaboutgod.com

www.shandarahsplace.com

www.onangelwings.ca

www.quantumangel.com

About the Author

Laverne Stewart has been putting thoughts to paper as long as she has been able to hold a pencil. She knew in high school that a writing career was her life's ambition. After a year in radio, she made the move to television news, spending eleven years with CTV in Halifax, Saint John and Fredericton. She made the leap to print media in 1999, when she accepted a position as a news reporter with *The Daily Gleaner*. Now she is happily covering good-news stories as a feature writer at that newspaper. When she isn't writing at work, she does so at her home near Harvey Station, New Brunswick.

Her life is full and happy, thanks to the people who are in it. She is married to her soon-to-be-sainted husband Robert Burtt, for lovingly accepting her for whom she is for the past eighteen years. She is mother to Mary Louise and Nicolas, whom she describes as her little angels with crooked halos. Also included in her family is Tess, a Labrador retriever, and tabby cat Stripes. When she is not writing about angels and spirit guides, she is listening carefully to hear them whispering to her.